THE EUROPEANISATION OF LAW

The United Kingdom Comparative Law Series is produced by the United Kingdom National Committee of Comparative Law in association with The British Institute of International and Comparative Law

UNITED KINGDOM COMPARATIVE LAW SERIES
VOLUME 18

THE EUROPEANISATION OF LAW

Edited by

THOMAS G. WATKIN
Senior Lecturer in Law
University of Wales, Cardiff

UKNCCL
1998

Published by
The United Kingdom National Committee of Comparative Law

British Library Cataloguing in Publication Data. A catalogue record for this book is available from the British Library

ISBN 0 904281 13 2

Printed in Great Britain by Alden Press, Oxford

Distributed by
The British Institute of International and Comparative Law
Charles Clore House, 17 Russell Square, London WC1B 5DR

Visit the UKNCCL Website at http://www.iel.bham.ac.uk/ukinccl/

TABLE OF CONTENTS

NOTES ON CONTRIBUTORS

Hans-Jörg Albrecht is the Director of the Max-Planck Institute for Foreign and International Criminal Law in Freiburg, Germany. He also teaches criminology, criminal justice and criminal law at the University of Freiburg.

John Bell is Professor of Public and Comparative Law at the University of Leeds. His publications include *French Comparative Law* (1992), *Principles of French Law* (with S. Boyron and S. Whittaker, 1998) and *French Administrative Law* (with L.N. Brown, 5th edn., 1998).

Alberto Cadoppi is *professore associato* of Criminal Law and Comparative Criminal Law at the University of Parma, Italy. He also teaches Comparative Criminal Law at the University of Trento.

Rudolf Carpanini is Professor of English Language at the Faculty of Political Science, University of Pavia and was formerly the Director of the Institute of Modern Languages at the same University.

Hanns Engelhardt is Dr. iur, and Judge at the Bundesgerichtshof, Karlsruhe, Germany.

John Gibson MA (Oxon) is a Lecturer in Law at the Cardiff Law School, University of Wales, where he specialises in research and teaching in Environmental Law.

William M. Gordon is Douglas Professor of Civil Law at the University of Glasgow. One of his particular interests is Roman Law and the influence of its ideas on modern legal systems.

Nicholas Grief is Head of the School of Finance and Law and Professor of the Law of International Organisations at Bournemouth University. Formerly he was Reader in International Organisations Law at the University of Exeter.

Jean-Claude Helin is Professor at the Faculty of Law, University of Nantes, France.

David J. Ibbetson is Fellow and Tutor in Law at Magdalen College, Oxford.

Augur Pearce is currently engaged in doctoral research at Cambridge where his area is the confessional obligations imposed upon the clergy of the national churches of England and Prussia since 1800. He was formerly visiting Lecturer in English Law at the Europa-Universität, Frankfurt-an-der-Oder.

Reiner Schulze is Professor of German and European Private Law at the Westfälische Wilhelms-University of Münster and Director of the Institute of German and European Legal History. He was formerly Professor of Civil Law and German and European Legal History at the University of Trier.

Thomas Glyn Watkin is Senior Lecturer in Law and Director of the Centre for Contemporary Civil Law Studies at the University of Wales, Cardiff.

Reinhard Zimmermann is Professor of Private Law, Roman Law and Comparative Legal History at the University of Regensburg, Germany.

TABLE OF CASES

Court of Justice of the European Communities (alphabetical)

Court of Justice of the European Communities (chronological)

European Court of Human Rights

English and Welsh Courts

French Courts

German Courts

Scottish Courts

TABLE OF LEGISLATION

EUROPE

AUSTRIA

FRANCE

GERMANY

HUNGARY

ITALY

SPAIN

UK

MULTILATERAL CONVENTIONS

PREFACE

Thomas Glyn Watkin

In September 1995, Cardiff Law School was host both to the annual conference of the Society of Public Teachers of Law and to the annual colloquium of the United Kingdom National Committee for Comparative Law. The theme of the Colloquium was 'The Europeanisation of Law' and the essays presented in this volume are a record of the colloquium's proceedings.

The theme of the Europeanisation of Law was particularly appropriate for the Cardiff Colloquium for several reasons. Cardiff Law School was among the first United Kingdom law schools to introduce degree schemes which integrated rather than just combined the study of law and modern languages. These commenced with degrees with Italian and Spanish, which were at that time unique in the United Kingdom, and later expanded to embrace French, German and Japanese, the last of which was also unique at the time of its inception. The degrees are described as integrated rather than as joint or combined honours schemes inasmuch as they seek to bridge the disciplines involved. Their aim is not merely to produce graduates in English Law who are fluent in reading, writing and speaking the other modern language concerned, but also who have a sound basic knowledge of the law and general culture of the other country. To this end, all of the schemes involve the teaching of the legal system of the other country to the students while they are at Cardiff in preparation for a year's study at a Law faculty in the other country. It was a particular pleasure to receive at the Colloquium delegates from Cardiff's partner institutions in Europe, several of whom contributed papers and all of whom contributed greatly to the discussions and to the European nature of the event. Our thanks are due to all those who came to Cardiff whether from home or abroad and who by their support made the Colloquium such a happy as well as an intellectually stimulating occasion.

During 1995, it had been decided that the expertise which Cardiff had developed in this field should be consolidated by the establishment of a Centre for Contemporary Civil Law Studies within the Law School. The Centre was inaugurated at the start of the Colloquium. The Centre's work focuses in the main upon the study of the laws and legal systems of modern civilian jurisdictions rather than upon comparative law. The theme chosen for the colloquium was intended to reflect this. The colloquium opened with a keynote address from Professor Reinhard Zimmermann, a paper which forms a part of his signal contribution to the development of a European legal consciousness in our generation. There then followed a series of sessions devoted to particular aspects of the Europeanisation of law, beginning with the place of legal history and language training in the process, followed by examinations of developments in private international law, constitutional law, ecclesiastical law, administrative law and criminal law. Some of the speakers at these sessions came from Cardiff's partner institutions in Italy, Germany and France - Pavia, Trier, Nantes, and the universities of Berne, Konstanz, Trento, Parma and Oviedo were also represented. I am most grateful to my colleagues at the Centre and in the Law School generally who arranged for their colleagues in partner institutions to attend. I wish particularly to thank Stewart Field, Nigel Foster, Andrew West and James Young for their assistance and for chairing sessions of the colloquium. Two papers given at the colloquium do not unfortunately appear here: they are Professor Von Hoffman's examination of 'The Europeanisation of Private International Law' and Professor Hans-Heiner Kühne's contribution on 'The Europeanisation of Criminal Law'. Two of the papers contained in the volume were not actually part of the colloquium but rather of the proceedings of the SPTL Conference which followed. These are the paper by Professor Schulze, which was given at the Legal History section of the SPTL, and the paper by Professor Cadoppi, which formed part of the deliberations of the Criminal Justice section. I am grateful to them both for allowing their papers to appear in this volume, and to the convenors of the respective subject sections, Professor David Sugarman of the University of Lancaster and Peter Alldridge and Professor Celia Wells of the Cardiff Law School, who arranged these talks and chaired sessions.

Thanks are also due to the Council of the UKNCCL for its support both during the organisation of the colloquium, during the meeting and since then in supporting this publication. I also wish to record my thanks to the British Institute of International and Comparative Law for agreeing to publish the colloquium proceedings in its series, and especially to the director, Mr. Piers Gardner and the publications manager, Mr. Joe Macdonald Hill, for their help. During the course of the colloquium I was ably assisted both by my colleagues mentioned above and by two students of the Law School, both now graduates, Rachel Fenton and Marianna Patanè. On the administrative and financial side, thanks are also due to Mr. Andrew Hopkins, then departmental administrator of the Law School, for the considerable assistance he afforded and for his support and good humour throughout. Professor John Wylie, then Head of Cardiff Law School, was always forthcoming with enthusiastic encouragement and practical support for which I am indebted.

I am grateful to the contributors for the prompt submission of their papers for this volume in the format requested, which has made my task as editor that much easier. My secretary, Linda Mackleworth, has assisted greatly in the arrangements for gathering in the papers and co-operating with the contributors. The Indexes, Bibliography and Tables were meticulously prepared by Emma White, then a student, now a graduate of the Law School, whom the Law School generously provided as a research assistant to perform an arduous but necessary task. I am also indebted, as always, to my wife, Jane, for assisting me in checking the final drafts of the manuscript.

As will be apparent from the above, the colloquium and this volume are the result of a team effort on behalf of the staff and students who are, at the end of the day, the Centre for Contemporary Civil Law Studies. It has fallen to my lot to edit the papers, but the credit belongs to all who have contributed and helped. We all hope that the effort put into the work has been worth while and that it will prove the first of many such joint endeavours to emerge from the Cardiff Centre.

1

SAVIGNY'S LEGACY

Legal history, comparative law, and the emergence of a European legal science*

Reinhard Zimmermann, Regensburg

I

1) In September 1814 the Congress of Vienna was inaugurated. It had been convened in order to determine the parameters of a new constitutional dispensation for Europe. The old system of government had collapsed under the impact of the French Revolution and the subsequent Napoleonic Wars. More particularly, the 'Holy Roman Empire of the German Nation' had ceased to exist. During the one and a half centuries following the Peace of Westphalia, it had managed to provide an institutional framework for peaceful coexistence and dispute regulation[1]. Yet, it had widely been regarded as an inefficient anachronism, bogged down by elaborate procedures and laborious protocol. The famous natural lawyer Samuel Pufendorf had even

---

* This is the (somewhat extended) text of an address first delivered at the opening of the Colloquium of the United Kingdom National Committee of Comparative Law in Cardiff on 11.9.95 and has also been published in (1996) 112 *Law Quarterly Review* 576 ff.

1 This has been emphasised, very pointedly, by Michael Stolleis in a newspaper article programmatically entitled '*Vom Monstrum lernen*' (Lessons from the Monster), *Frankfurter Allgemeine Zeitung* of 24 August 1992.

referred to it as a constitutional monstrosity[2]. Somewhat less monstrous, but still rather complex, was the *Deutscher Bund*, a federation of forty-one formally independent 'German' States, which was to be established by the Congress of Vienna: a fairly unsatisfatory compromise solution considering the wave of patriotism that had swept the German states in the course of the Wars of Liberation[3].

But it was not only the old system of government that lay in ruins. Nearly all of Europe possessed the same institutions and these institutions collapsed everywhere: this is how Alexis de Tocqueville described the situation in retrospect[4]. One of these institutions was the system of private law that had prevailed in central and western Europe since the days of the 'Reception': the Roman-Canon *ius commune*. It had provided the cornerstone for the emergence of an essentially unified, European legal culture[5]. With the rise of rationalism and under the impact of the emerging nationalism, however, it had started to disintegrate[6]. Even before the French Revolution, the enlightened rulers of the two most influential States within the 'Roman' Empire had set the wheels in motion to enchant their subjects with a codification, both rational and comprehensive, that would enable them to know their rights and duties within society[7]. The French *code civil*, the most famous and

---

2 *De Statu Imperii Germanici* (1667; most recent ed. by Horst Denzer, 1976). Cf. also, most recently, Klaus-Peter Schroeder, '*Der Dreißigjährige Krieg, das Alte Reich und Samuel von Pufendorf (1632 - 1694)*', (1995) *Juristische Schulung* 959 sqq.

3 For a well-balanced exposition of the constitutional history of Germany, see Otto Kimminich, *Deutsche Verfassungsgeschichte* (2nd ed., 1987).

4 Cf. the discussion by Hans Hattenhauer, *Europäische Rechtsgeschichte* (1992), pp. 517 sqq.

5 For details, see Helmut Coing, *Europäisches Privatrecht*, vol. I (1985), pp. 7 sqq.; Reinhard Zimmermann, '*Das römisch-kanonische ius commune als Grundlage europäischer Rechtseinheit*', (1992) *Juristenzeitung* 10 sqq.; *idem*, 'Civil Code and Civil Law: The "Europeanization" of Private Law within the European Community and the Re-emergence of a European Legal Science', (1994/95) 1 Columbia Journal of European Law 82 sqq.; Harold J. Berman, Charles Reid, '*Römisches Recht in Europa und das ius commune*', (1995) 3 *Zeitschrift für Europäisches Privatrecht* 3 sqq.; Manlio Bellomo, *The Common Legal Past of Europe 1000 - 1800* (1995), pp. 55 sqq.

6 For a general discussion, see Helmut Coing, *Europäisches Privatrecht*, vol. II (1989).

7 For a modern evaluation of the Prussian *Allgemeines Landrecht* of 1794, see Andreas Schwennicke, *Die Entstehung der Einleitung des Preußischen Allgemeinen Landrechts von 1794* (1993) and Gerhard Dilcher, '*Die janusköpfige Kodifikation - das preußische Allgemeine Landrecht (1794) und die europäische Rechtsgeschichte*', (1994) 2 *Zeitschrift für Europäisches Privatrecht* 446 sqq.; on the Austrian *Allgemeines Bürgerliches Gesetzbuch*, see Walter Selb, Herbert Hofmeister (eds.), *Forschungsband Franz v. Zeiller (1751-1828)* (1980); Werner Ogris, '*Zur Geschichte und Bedeutung des österreichischen Allgemeinen bürgerlichen Gesetzbuches (ABGB)*', in: *Liber Memorialis*

also historically most fertile of the 'natural law codifications' was rooted in the same intellectual soil[8]. At the same time, however, it became a potent symbol of the one and undivided nation that had emerged from the revolutionary upheavals following the storming of the Bastille. The idea of a European common law, based on the Roman legal sources, appeared to be as dead as the Holy Roman Empire with which it was traditionally associated.

2) 1814 was also the year when a well-known professor of Roman law at the University of Heidelberg, A.F.J. Thibaut, published a programmatic booklet under the title *Über die Notwendigkeit eines allgemeinen bürgerlichen Rechts für Deutschland* (On the Necessity of a General Civil Law for Germany)[9]. He clearly recognised that he was living in a period of transition that was full of potential. He argued that a General German Civil Code, modelled on the French *code civil*, would facilitate the emergence of an undivided German nation. It would also provide a bulwark against the forces of political reaction. And it would render the law easily accessible, transforming what used to be a maze of arcane subtleties and disputes into a 'vital possession' of the entire nation.

Yet, in spite of all its brilliance and patriotic fervour, Thibaut's proposal did not carry the day. By the end of the 1810s it was clear that, at least for the foreseeable future, Germany was not to have a general code of private law. And indeed, until the end of the century, its legal landscape remained a patch-work quilt. Austria, to be pushed out of the *Deutscher Bund* after the battle of Königgrätz, had its *Allgemeines Bürgerliches Gesetzbuch*. The Prussian territories, including Westphalia, Bayreuth and Ansbach, were governed by the *Preußisches Allgemeines Landrecht*. In the Rhine-Province, in Alsace and Lorraine the *code civil* applied. The Grand Dutchy of Baden had adopted the *Badisches*

François Laurent (1989), pp. 376 sqq. For a succinct account in English, see Konrad Zweigert, Hein Kötz, *An Introduction to Comparative Law* (2nd ed., reprint 1992, transl. Tony Weir), pp. 141 sqq., 165 sqq. On the history and significance of the codification movement in general, see Reinhard Zimmermann, 'Codification: history and present significance of an idea', (1995) 3 *European Review of Private Law* 95 sqq. For other recent assessments of codification in Europe, see Pierre Legrand, 'Strange Power of Words: Codification Situated', (1994) 9 *Tulane European and Civil Law Forum* 1 sqq.; Bellomo, see n. 5, *supra*, 1 sqq. ('National Codifications: Triumph and Crisis').

8 Cf. Franz Wieacker, *A History of Private Law in Europe*, transl. Tony Weir (1995), pp. 269 sqq.; James Gordley, 'Myths of the French Civil Code', (1994) 21 *American Journal of Comparative Law* 459 sqq.

9 For a modern edition, see Hans Hattenhauer (ed.), *Thibaut und Savigny: Ihre programmatischen Schriften* (1973), pp. 61 sqq.

Landrecht which was based on a translation of the *code civil*. Some places in Bavaria lived according to Austrian law, while in parts of Schleswig-Holstein Danish law prevailed. Most of the remaining German territories still administered justice according to the *ius commune*. Yet the *ius commune* was only applicable *in subsidio*, and countless more specific territorial or local laws could therefore govern a particular dispute[10].

This was not, of course, a very convenient state of affairs, at least not for the burgeoning commercial community. Thus it is hardly surprising that we find pressure for legal unification arising, first and foremost, in the trade-related fields of law. A first significant step in this direction was the establishment of a German Customs Union (*Deutscher Zollverein*) in 1833. In 1848, the law of negotiable instruments was unified[11], and between 1861 and 1866 nearly all the states of the *Deutscher Bund* adopted the draft of a General German Commercial Code (*Allgemeines Deutsches Handelsgesetzbuch*) that had been completed in 1861[12]. A draft law of obligations (*Dresdener Entwurf*) was published in 1865. Although it was never adopted, it was to have great influence for the further development of the law of obligations in Germany[13].

In the meantime, however, another, intellectually much more powerful, legal link between the various German states had been established: a common legal science based on a common set of sources and inspired by the same methodological convictions. The basic propositions dominating nineteenth century legal science in Germany had first been outlined by Friedrich Carl von Savigny, most influentially, perhaps, in his famous essay *Vom Beruf unserer Zeit für Gesetzgebung und Rechtswissenschaft* (Of the Vocation of our Time for Legislation and Legal Science) which had been published in 1814 in

10 Cf., e.g., Wolfgang Wiegand, '*Die privatrechtlichen Quellen des Usus modernus*', in: Dieter Simon (ed.), *Akten des 26. Deutschen Rechtshistorikertages* (1987), pp. 237 sqq.; Bellomo, see n. 5, *supra, passim*.

11 See Ulrich Huber, '*Das Reichsgesetz über die Einführung einer allgemeinen Wechselordnung für Deutschland vom 26. November 1848*', (1978) *Juristenzeitung* 785 sqq.

12 See Christoph Bergfeld, '*Preußen und das Allgemeine Deutsche Handelsgesetzbuch*', (1987) 14 *Ius Commune* 101 sqq. See also Karsten Schmidt, *Das HGB und die Gegenwartsaufgaben des Handelsrechts* (1983).

13 For all details concerning the history of codification in 19th century Germany, see Barbara Dölemeyer, in: Helmut Coing (ed.), *Handbuch der Quellen und Literatur der neueren europäischen Privatrechtsgeschichte*, vol. III/2 (1982), pp. 1421 sqq.; and see Michael John, *Politics and Law in Late Nineteenth-Century Germany* (1989).

order to refute Thibaut's ideas[14]. Unlike Thibaut, Savigny did not admire the French civil code, and he regarded the *Preußisches Allgemeines Landrecht* as a slapdash piece of work. More generally, he argued that codification was 'inorganic', unscientific, arbitrary and hostile to tradition. At best, it was unnecessary, at worst it would distort and stifle 'organic' legal development. This did not, of course, mean that the German legal landscape should remain as patchy as it was. 'As to what we aim at, we are in agreement', he wrote in reply to Thibaut, '[for] we want a national community whose scientific endeavours focus upon one and the same object'. But, he added, the right way towards that goal was not a piece of legislation but rather an 'organically progressive legal science which may be common to the whole nation'[15]. Savigny himself laid the foundations for the kind of legal science required in a number of celebrated books and articles, among them in particular *Das Recht des Besitzes* (The Law of Possession, 1803), *Geschichte des römischen Rechts im Mittelalter* (History of Roman Law in the Middle Ages, 1815-1831), *System des heutigen Römischen Rechts* (System of Contemporary Roman Law, 1840-1849) and *Das Obligationenrecht* (The Law of Obligations, 1851/53). The law within a given period, he argued, cannot be understood in isolation, for the present is tied, indissolubly, to the past from which it has emerged. Legal science therefore has to be of an historical nature - its main task is the intellectual penetration, adaptation and rejuvenation of the legal material as it has come down to us[16].

Savigny's legal historicism stimulated the emergence of a national community of scholars, of German unification on a scholarly level. Roman law, obviously, provided the historical foundation for the *ius commune*, as it had prevailed in Germany and still prevailed in parts

---

14 Easily accessible today in Hattenhauer, see n. 9, *supra*, 95 sqq.

15 Savigny, *Beruf*, 192.

16 Cf., in particular, '*Ueber den Zweck dieser Zeitschrift*', (1815) 1 *Zeitschrift für geschichtliche Rechtswissenschaft* 1 sqq. There is a vast literature on Savigny, the central figure in 19th century German (probably even European) legal history. Cf., e.g., the articles published on the occasion of his 200th anniversary in (1979) 8 *Ius Commune* 9 sqq. and (1980) 9 *Quaderni Fiorentini* 1 sqq.; cf. also the contributions in (1989) 37 *American Journal of Comparative Law* 1 sqq.; Joachim Rückert, '*Savigny's Konzeption von Jurisprudenz und Recht, ihre Folgen und ihre Bedeutung bis heute*', (1993) 61 *Tijdschrift voor rechtsgeschiedenis* 65 sqq.; Gerd Kleinheyer, Jan Schröder, *Deutsche Juristen aus fünf Jahrhunderten* (3rd ed., 1989) 239 sqq. (with an extensive bibliography). The three most important recent monographs are Joachim Rückert, *Idealismus, Jurisprudenz und Politik bei Friedrich Carl von Savigny* (1984); Horst Heinrich Jakobs, *Die Begründung der geschichtlichen Rechtswissenschaft* (1992) and Dieter Nörr, *Savignys philosophische Lehrjahre: Ein Versuch* (1994). The present article predominantly draws on Savigny's programmatic articles.

of it. Equally obviously, therefore, it constituted the starting point for any serious attempt to comprehend, and further refine, contemporary private law. The new approach came to be dubbed 'pandectist' because it used the most important body of the Roman legal sources (the Digest, or Pandects) to strive towards an internally consistent and logical system of concepts, rules and principles[17]. The pandectist school of legal science secured the leading place for Germany in the world of nineteenth century legal scholarship; it was much admired by lawyers all over Europe and exercised a significant influence on the legal development in countries like France, Italy and Austria[18]. When a German Civil Code (*BGB*) was eventually enacted, 86 years after Thibaut had advocated and Savigny opposed its preparation, it owed its maturity to the conceptual foundations laid by pandectist legal science[19].

II

1) Our situation in Europe today is similar to that in early nineteenth century Germany in many respects. For, once again, we are

---

17 For details, see Wieacker/Weir, see n. 8, *supra*, 279 sqq.; Wolfgang Wilhelm, *Zur juristischen Methodenlehre im 19. Jahrhundert* (1958); Mathias Reimann, 'Nineteenth Century German Legal Science', (1990) 13 *Boston College Law Review* 837 sqq. On the rise of the Roman law professoriate in early 19th century Germany, see James Q. Whitman, *The Legacy of Roman Law in the German Romantic Era* (1990).

18 For France, cf. Alfons Bürge, *Das französische Privatrecht im 19. Jahrhundert* (1991), pp. 150 sqq.; for Austria: Werner Ogris, *Der Entwicklungsgang der österreichischen Privatrechtswissenschaft im 19. Jahrhundert* (1968); for Italy: Reiner Schulze (ed.), *Deutsche Rechtswissenschaft und Staatslehre im Spiegel italienischer Rechtskultur während der zweiten Hälfte des 19. Jahrhunderts* (1990); for Switzerland: Pio Caroni, '*Die Schweizer Romanistik im 19. Jahrhundert*', (1994) 16 *Zeitschrift für Neuere Rechtsgeschichte* 243 sqq.; for the Netherlands: J.H.A. Lokin, '*Het NBW en de pandektistiek*', in: *Historisch vooruitzicht, BW-Krant jaarboek 1994*, pp. 125 sqq.; for Sweden: Jan-Olof Sundell, 'German Influence on Swedish Private Law Doctrine 1870-1914', (1991) *Scandinavian Studies in Law* 237 sqq.; for England: Peter Stein, 'Legal Theory and the Reform of Legal Education in Mid-Nineteenth Century England', in: *idem, The Character and Influence of the Roman Civil Law* (1988), pp. 238 sqq.; for Scotland: Alan Rodger, 'Scottish Advocates in the Nineteenth Century: The German Connection', (1994) 110 *Law Quarterly Review* 563 sqq.; John W. Cairns, 'The Influence of the German Historical School in Early Nineteenth Century Edinburgh', (1994) 20 *Syracuse Journal of International Law and Commerce* 191 sqq.; for the United States: Mathias Reimann, *Historische Schule und Common Law* (1993); *idem*, 'A Career in Itself - The German Professoriate as a Model for American Legal Academia', in: *idem, The Reception of Continental Ideas in the Common Law World 1820 - 1920* (1993), pp. 165 sqq.

19 For a general evaluation, see Wieacker/Weir, see n. 8, *supra*, 371 sqq.

living in a period of transition. Contrary to nearly all the other disciplines taught at a modern university, legal science in Europe has, at least for the last hundred years, been predominantly national in substance, outlook, and approach. Since the continental legal systems have been codified, there have been, in principle, as many legal systems as there are national states. This is reflected in our law curricula and examination requirements[20], in the conditions for the appointment of law teachers, in the approach adopted by our courts in their decisions, and in the topics dealt with in our legal literature. French professors at French universities have started to write textbooks on French law to be read by French students, German professors at German universities to write textbooks on German law to be read by German students. Thus, in Germany, scores of legal writers continue their stern and unrelenting endeavours to penetrate the mysteries of *Fremdbesitzerexzeß* within the so-called *Eigentümer-Besitzer-Verhältnis*[21] and to draw ever finer distinctions between that consequential loss which is closely related to defective work and that which is not[22]. Exquisite as these specimens of German legal science may appear to be to a German lawyer, they are not of great concern to the international community of scholars. To an English lawyer, presumably, they look as confusing and exotic as the abracadabra of conditions, warranties and intermediate terms, or the niceties of the so-called doctrine of consideration, appear to his German colleague.

This national isolation of legal science is as anachronistic today as the particularism of legal sources in early nineteenth century Germany. After the devastations of the Second World War, the era of political nationalism was widely perceived to have come to an end. The (three) European Communities were designed, in the second half of the 1950s, as a springboard towards the eventual achievement of European unity[23]. The preamble to the EEC Treaty of 1957 asserted a

---

20 For criticism, see Hein Kötz, '*Europäische Juristenausbildung*', (1993) 1 *Zeitschrift für Europäisches Privatrecht* 268 sqq.; Bernhard Großfeld, '*Europäisches Recht und Rechtsstudium*', (1993) *Juristische Schulung* 710 sqq.; Gerard René de Groot, 'European Legal Education in the 21st Century', in: Bruno Witte, Caroline Forder (eds.), *The Common Law of Europe and the Future of Legal Education* (1992), pp. 7 sqq, Axel Flessmer, '*Deutsche Juristenausbildung*' (1996) *Juristenzeitung* 689 sqq.

21 Cf. (1994/95) 1 *Columbia Journal of European Law* 63 sqq.

22 For details, see Reinhard Zimmermann, 'Extinctive Prescription in German Law', in: Erik Jayme (ed.), *German National Reports in Civil Law Matters for the XVIth Congress of Comparative Law* (1994), pp. 164 sqq.

23 For an historical account, see Thomas Oppermann, *Europarecht* (1991), pp. 12 sqq.; Stephen Weatherill, Paul Beaumont, *EC Law* (1993), pp. 1 sqq.

determination 'to lay the foundations of an ever closer union among the peoples of Europe'. The actual progress towards this aim has turned out to be slower than originally envisaged: first and foremost, the EC has remained an economic community. However, the (Maastricht) Treaty on European Union, which was signed in February 1992, not only details the steps toward economic and monetary union but appends additional fields of activity (such as culture) and envisages common policies in matters such as foreign affairs, security and justice. Obviously, therefore, the political will exists to advance the process of European integration on an economic, political and cultural level. This process would be greatly facilitated by the removal of the legal nationalism still prevailing in Europe today[24]. Article 3(h) of the EC Treaty therefore specifically envisages the 'approximation' of the laws of the Member States 'to the extent required for the proper functioning of the common market' to be a task of the Community.

2) In recent years, we have indeed experienced a significant process of legal harmonisation in areas as diverse as unfair competition law, antitrust law, intellectual property law, labour law and company law. Contract law and liability law have been affected, mainly, by the Product Liability, Consumer Credit and Doorstep Selling Directives[25]. Yet, in spite of all these efforts, the present state of European legal unification is not at all reassuring[26]; for we are dealing with no more than fragments of - more or less - uniform law, inserted rather unorganically and in a somewhat higgledy-piggledy fashion into the respective national legal systems. Rather than having gained in coherence, rationality and predictability, the law has tended to become

---

24 Cf. already Walter Hallstein, '*Angleichung des Privat- und Prozeßrechts in der Europäischen Wirtschaftsgemeinschaft*', (1964) 28 *RabelsZ* 228 sqq.

25 For details, see (1994/95) 1 *Columbia Journal of European Law* 68 sqq. (with comprehensive references to the relevant literature). On the important EC Council Directive on Unfair Terms in Consumer Contracts of 1993 see, for England, most recently Hugh Beale, 'Legislative Control of Fairness: The Directive on Unfair Terms in Consumer Contracts', in: Jack Beatson, Daniel Friedman (eds.), *Good Faith and Fault in Contract Law* (1995), pp. 231 sqq. Concerning Germany, see Oliver Remien, '*AGB-Gesetz und Richtlinie über mißbräuchliche Verbrauchervertragsklauseln in ihrem europäischen Umfeld*' (1994) 2 *Zeitschrift für Europäisches Privatrecht* 34 sqq.; for France, cf. Claude Witz, Gerhard Wolter, '*Die Umsetzung der EG-Richtlinie über mißbräuchliche Klauseln in Verbraucherverträgen*', (1995) 3 *Zeitschrift für Europäisches Privatrecht* 885 sqq.

26 I have tried to substantiate this statement in (1994/95) 1 *Columbia Journal of European Law* 73 sqq.

disjointed. Its application has not been streamlined but has, instead, acquired a new dimension of complexity.

It may be possible to iron out these difficulties by way of codifying European private law. In two resolutions dating from May 1989 and May 1994 the European Parliament has, indeed, called for such a step to be taken[27]. This is the path mapped out, in 1814, by A.F.J. Thibaut. But, as in 1814, it is highly questionable whether the enactment of a *Code Civil Européen* would, at the present time, be practicable, or even desirable. Moreover, we have come together today as 'public teachers' - and, I presume, researchers - of law. Our own domain is legal scholarship rather than legislation and the specific challenge with which we are faced today is the creation of a legal science 'which may be common to the whole of Europe' and which may thus inspire and sustain a European private law. This automatically raises the question of the relevance of Savigny's programme in our present situation.

III

That situation is characterised by a significant change of paradigm: the gradual emergence of a European (as opposed to merely national) private law. At the same time, however, our mental frame of mind is still largely moulded by those national legal systems. This rather unfortunate discrepancy has only comparatively recently been recognised[28]. The introduction of joint degrees in law and languages with an obligatory year spent at a law school in another country constitutes an attempt to

---

27 See the discussion by Winfried Tilmann, '*Eine Privatrechtskodifikation für die Europäische Gemeinschaft*', in: Peter Christian Müller-Graff (ed.), *Gemeinsames Privarecht in der Europäischen Gemeinschaft* (1993), pp. 485 sqq.; *idem*, '*Zweiter Kodifikationbeschluß des Europäischen Parlaments*', (1995) 3 *Zeitschrift für Europäisches Privatrecht* 534 sqq. Cf. also the contributions in A.S. Hartkamp, M.W. Hesselink *et al.* (eds.), *Towards a European Civil Code* (1994) and Jürgen Basedow, *Europäisches Vertrehsrecht für europäische Märkte* (1996).

28 Cf., e.g., as far as Germany is concerned, Peter Ulmer, '*Vom deutschen zum europäischen Privatrecht?*', (1992) *Juristenzeitung* 1 sqq.; Peter Hommelhoff, '*Zivilrecht unter dem Einfluß europäischer Rechtsangleichung*', (1992) 192 *Archiv für die civilistische Praxis* 71 sqq.; Peter-Christian Müller-Graff (ed*.), Gemeinsames Privatrecht in der Europäischen Gemeinschaft* (1993); Uwe Blaurock, '*Europäisches Privatrecht*', (1994) *Juristenzeitung* 270 sqq.; Fritz Rittner, '*Das Gemeinschaftsprivatrecht und die europäische Integration*', (1995) *Juristenzeitung* 849 sqq. And see the editorial of (1993) 1 *Zeitschrift für Europäisches Privatrecht* 1 sqq., the first journal created with the intention to provide a forum for the emergence of a European private law.

come to grips with it[29]. Our present situation is, however, not only characterised by a national particularisation of legal science. Ever since the rise of public law in the early modern era[30] we have seen the emergence of new and specialised disciplines. The disciplinary divides appear to be deeply entrenched today; they have significantly contributed to the law having become disjointed. Each new subject has been transformed into a microcosm of its own, without much interrelationship with the others or with the general legal system. European Community law itself has, for a long time, been regarded as a specialised field of study which has commonly been treated as a branch of public law. Moreover, the regulations and directives emanating from Brussels have tended to reinforce the centrifugal forces that have characterised the development of private law over the past few decades. At the same time, since they are supposed to have some bearing on the proper functioning of the common market, these Community enactments often reflect a certain policy bias. Yet, the institutions of private law do not derive their significance only from their contribution to the creation or maintenance of free markets[31]. Company law and contract law are more than mere appendages of the free movement of goods, persons, services and capital. Thus, there is the obvious danger that neither the systematic wholeness of our legal systems nor the other fundamental values informing them are borne in mind sufficiently[32].

---

29 In Germany, unfortunately, the pecularities of the legal training system, particularly its rigid regulation by the State and the system of state examinations (for details, see Reinhard Zimmermann, 'An Introduction to German Legal Culture', in: Werner Ebke, Matthew W. Finkin (eds.), *Introduction to German Law* (1996), pp. 27 sqq.) are impeding the necessary transition to educating European, as opposed to German lawyers. At least, however, a basic knowledge of European law (though only insofar as there is a relationship with German private, criminal or public law) has been added to the canon of obligatory subjects by the German Law on the Judiciary (*Deutsches Richtergesetz*); for a discussion, see Heino Schöbel, '*Privatrecht und Europarecht in der Ersten Juristischen Staatsprüfung*', (1995) 3 *Zeitschrift für Europäisches Privatrecht* 139 sqq. Generally on the influence of legal training on legal harmonisation in Europe, and on the concept of a European law school, see Axel Flessner, '*Rechtsvereinheitlichung durch Rechtswissenschaft und Juristenausbildung*', (1992) 56 *RabelsZ* 243 sqq.; Roy Goode, 'The European Law School', (1993) 13 *Legal Studies* 1 sqq.; and the contributions referred to above, n. 20.

30 Magnificently described by Michael Stolleis, *Geschichte des öffentlichen Rechts in Deutschland,* vol. I (1988), vol. II (1992).

31 (1993) 1 *Zeitschrift für Europäisches Privatrecht* 2.

32 Cf., concerning early 19th century legal scholarship, Friedrich Carl von Savigny, *System des heutigen Römischen Rechts*, vol. I (1840), p. XXIII. He points out that the one-sided appreciation of everything that is new has led many to revel in individual and incoherent ideas and opinions and to abandon, in view of such disintegration, the possession of the intellectual wholeness of legal scholarship *('... und*

This disintegration may well lead to a pervasive cynicism about law. If we look at law in national isolation, if we no longer recognise its internal coherence, and if we proceed from the assumption that every epoch produces its own existence, and with it its own legal rules, law will appear to be an entirely arbitrary artifact. The faith in law as an autonomous discipline will be shaken. This is indeed what has happened at many of the elite institutions in the United States, where comparative law and legal history have been marginalised and where doctrinal scholarship is looked upon with a certain degree of unconcealed disdain[33]. The law reviews are full of articles on new or different voices[34], on law and storytelling[35], on the unalienated relatedness immanent within our alienated situation[36], or on property law as a phallic metaphor[37]. Young academics have to engage in the business of paradigm shifting in order to secure tenure[38]. They often do not even aim at establishing an intellectual link with legal practice[39]. There is a growing disjunction between legal science and what is commonly referred to as the legal profession[40]. As a result there is the grave danger that legal scholarship, as pursued at the law schools, is turned into a

---

über dieser Zersplitterung den zusammenhängenden Besitz des Ganzen unserer Wissenschaft zu versäumen').

33 Cf., e.g., Harry T. Edwards, 'The Growing Disjunction Between Legal Education and the Legal Profession', (1992) 91 *Michigan Law Review* 34 sqq.; Richard A. Posner, 'The Deprofessionalization of Legal Teaching and Scholarship', (1993) 91 *Michigan Law Review* 1923 sqq.; A.W.B. Simpson, 'The Rise and Fall of the Legal Treatise: Legal Principles and the Form of Legal Literature', (1981) 48 *University of Chicago Law Review* 677 sqq.; Paul D. Carrington, 'Of Law and the River', (1984) 34 *Journal of Legal Education* 222 sqq.

34 Alex M. Johnson, Jr., 'The New Voice of Color', (1991) 100 *Yale Law Journal* 2007 sqq.

35 'Symposium Legal Storytelling', (1989) 87 *Michigan Law Review* 2073 sqq.

36 Peter Gabel, Duncan Kennedy, 'Roll Over Beethoven', (1984) 36 *Stanford Law Review* 1.

37 Jeanne L. Schroeder, 'Chix Nix Bundle-O-Stix: A Feminist Critique of the Disaggregation of Property', (1994) 93 *Michigan Law Review* 239 sqq.

38 Cf. the analysis by James Gordley, 'Mere Brilliance: The Recruitment of Law Professors in the United States', (1993) 41 *American Journal of Comparative Law* 367 sqq.

39 Cf., e.g., Sanford Levinson, 'Judge Edwards' Indictment of "Impractical" Scholars: The Need for a Bill of Particulars', (1993) 91 *Michigan Law Review* 2010 sqq.

40 Cf., in particular, Edwards, (1992) 91 *Michigan Law Review* 34 sqq. For an attempt to assess 'American Law Review scholarship', see Reinhard Zimmermann, 'Law Reviews - *Ein Streifzug durch eine fremde Welt*', in: *idem, Amerikanische Rechtskultur und europäisches Privatrecht* (1995), pp. 87 sqq. Cf. also, concerning his own time, Savigny, *System* (n. 32) XXV (disjunction between theory and praxis 'the main evil of our legal condition').

mere intellectual game, whereas legal practice sinks to the level of a common craft. It was exactly this danger that Savigny intended to combat when he set out to write his *System des heutigen Römischen Rechts* [41]. And it is today, I believe, one of the central features distinguishing legal scholarship in the United States from that in England (and continental Europe). The briefest comparative glance at the *Law Quarterly Review* reveals that in approach, outlook and focus it is much closer to the *Juristenzeitung* than to the *Harvard Law Review*. For, to 'a lawyer, its articles and comments may be indispensable professional tools. To a judge, whose decisions provide grist for the law review mill, the review may be both a severe critic and a helpful guide'[42]. Legal scholarship in England, in other words, still has a distinctly European flavour.

IV

1) A legal practice informed and sustained by legal scholarship, and an approach to legal scholarship that is always mindful of the fact that, ultimately, law serves an eminently practical function: that is what Savigny was aiming for. Unless we want to succumb to a mood of fashionable cynicism and are prepared to abandon an essential part of our cultural heritage, we wil' have to do the same. For law is both a constituent feature and a characteristic emanation of European culture[43]. Not surprisingly, therefore, it exhibits a number of attributes which distinguishes ıt from dispute regulation ın other cultures[44]. It is administered by a body of professional experts who have received a specialised training for their task. The central institution providing such training is typically a university. As a university subject, law is submitted to methodical reflection and analysis: it is the object of a 'legal science' (in the sense of *Rechtswissenschaft*). European legal

---

41 *System* (n. 32) XX ('*Wo ... die Trennung zwischen Theorie und Praxis eine absolute wird, da entsteht unvermeidlich die Gefahr, daß die Theorie zu einem leeren Spiel, die Praxis zu einem bloßen Handwerk wird*').

42 This is what Earl Warren once said about the American law reviews: (1953) 1 *UCLA Law Review* 1.

43 The following two paragraphs draw on my Foreword to Tony Weir's translation of Franz Wieacker's magisterial *Privatrechtsgeschichte der Neuzeit,* see n. 8 *supra*, pp. V sqq.

44 For a succinct summary, see Harold J. Berman, *Law and Revolution: The Formation of the Western Legal Mind* (1983), pp. 7 sqq.; Franz Wieacker, 'Foundations of European Legal Culture', (1990) 38 *American Journal of Comparative Law* 1 sqq.; Peter Häberle, '*Europäische Rechtskultur*', in: *idem*, *Europäische Rechtskultur* (1994), pp. 9 sqq.

science, in turn, is based on the belief that the legal material does not constitute an indigestible and arbitrary mass of individual rules and cases, but can be reduced to a rational and organised system. It aims at presenting law as a logically consistent whole. And it attempts to demonstrate how individual rules and the decisions of individual cases can be derived from general propositions, and how they can be understood and related to each other. A determined effort is made to rationalise the application of the law.

Such rationality significantly contributes to the attainment of justice. Sadly, however, experience has shown that perfect justice can never be procured in our world. Every generation of lawyers is therefore called upon to search for as good an approximation as possible, given the challenges and requirements of their own time. Law thus acquires an inherently dynamic character. It is always developing[45]. But it is developing within an established framework of sources and methods, of concepts, rules and arguments. It constitutes a tradition which is constantly evolving. We are today the heirs of that tradition. It is an infinitely rich traditon that has significantly contributed to the level of sophistication of modern Europe. But it is important for us always intellectually to reacquire that heritage, if we wish to preserve it and to contribute to its organic evolution. It is as impossible for us today to fashion our own existence (including our own legal rules) as it was in 1814: as in every other epoch within the history of European law our law develops '*in unauflöslicher Gemeinschaft mit der ganzen Vergangenheit*'[46]. Even a supposedly new subject such as insurance law[47] requires the existence of a general law of contract and has started to develop within the doctrinal parameters thus established. We cannot hope to understand our law in isolation from the past and thus it is as necessary today as it was in 1814 to define the type of approach required as an historical one. Indeed, we can still say, as Savigny once did, that the most fundamental distinction between the various approaches to law imaginable is that between an historical and an a-historical type of legal

45 See Berman, see n. 44, *supra*, 9.

46 Savigny, (1815) 1 *Zeitschrift für geschichtliche Rechtswissenschaft* 3. And see, today, James Gordley, 'Comparative Legal Research: its Function in the Development of Hamonised Law' (1995) 43 *American Journal of Comparative Law* 555 sqq..

47 On the history of which, see Coing see n. 6, *supra*, 561 sqq.; J.P. van Niekerk, 'Sources of Insurance Law', in: Robert Feenstra, Reinhard Zimmermann (eds.), *Das römisch-holländische Recht: Fortschritte des Zivilrechts im 17. und 18. Jahrhundert* (1992), pp. 305 sqq.

scholarship[48]. In a way, I suppose, it is easier for a common lawyer to grasp the importance, or perhaps even necessity, of an historical approach to law[49]. For in the countries of continental Europe we have, for a long time, been blindfolded by an attitude Franz Wieacker has referred to as textual positivism: the legal solutions to the cases coming before the courts have to be found by an exegesis of the code[50]. And even if Josef Esser[51] (and many others) have revealed this crude form of positivism as a myth, codification still continues to have a significant impact on the ideology of private lawyers: they hardly ever venture beyond a study of the code, the court decisions based on its provisions, and the textbooks, commentaries, monographs and articles devoted to what generally tends to be accepted as French or German private law.

2) Yet, it is important to realise that codification has not brought about an entirely new era within the history of European law[52]. The Prussian Code apart, all European codifications are characterised by a considerable built-in flexibility which have, by and large, made them stand the test of time. Their draftsmen took to heart Portalis' famous observation that the task of legislation is to establish general principles, rich in implications, rather than to descend into the details of every question which might possibly arise[53]. Thus, the scene was set for an

---

48 Savigny, (1815) 1 *Zeitschrift für geschichtliche Rechtswissenschaft* 1 sqq. (‘*Wer die mannichfaltigen Ansichten und Methoden, die von jeher unter den deutschen Juristen herrschend gewesen sind, genau betrachtet, wird finden, daß sie sich auf zwey Hauptclassen, die Juristen selbst also auf zwey Schulen, zurückführen lassen, zwischen welchen allein eine Grundverschiedenheit angenommen werden kann . ... Die eine dieser Schulen ist durch den Namen der geschichtlichen hinreichend bezeichnet: für die andere dagegen ist ein positiver Name kaum zu finden möglich. ... Wir wollen sie daher in Ermangelung eines anderen Ausdrucks die ungeschichtliche Schule nennen*’).

49 This explains the impact of the ideas of Savigny's Historical School on 19th century English and American legal thinking; see Reimann, *Historische Schule und Common Law* (n. 18) *passim*, esp. pp. 246 sqq. The relevance of legal history is also emphasised by Goode, (1993) 13 *Legal Studies* 3 sq.

50 Wieacker/Weir see n. 8, *supra*, 363 sqq. Cf. also Bellomo see n. 5, *supra*, 11 sqq.

51 Josef Esser, *Grundsatz und Norm in der richterlichen Fortbildung des Privatrechts* (2nd ed., 1964); *idem*, *Vorverständnis und Methodenwahl in der Rechtsfindung: Rationalitätsgarantien der richterlichen Entscheidungsfindung* (1970).

52 See the discussion in (1995) 3 *European Review of Private Law* 42 sqq. and, as far as German law is concerned, ‘German Legal Culture’ see n. 29 *supra*, pp. 10 sqq.

53 See Zweigert/Kötz/Weir see n. 7, *supra*, 92. For comment see, most recently, Shael Herman, ‘*Schicksal und Zukunft der Kodifikationsidee in Amerika*’, in: Reinhard Zimmermann (ed.), *Amerikanische Rechtskultur und europäisches Privatrecht* (1995), pp. 52 sqq.

alliance, not for confrontation, between legislation and legal science; and, as a result, it appears to be generally recognised today that a code has to be brought to life by active and imaginative judicial interpretation and doctrinal elaboration[54]. In spite of the codes, the European legal tradition is still evolving. But, as has been pointed out above, it is evolving within an established conceptual, systematic and doctrinal framework which has originated long before the codes[55]. When a contract has come into existence, under which circumstances breach of contract may lead to a right of termination, by means of which criterion the amount of damages recoverable has to be limited, which types of error prevent a contract from coming into operation (or provide the basis for a right of rescission): these and a whole range of other questions have been discussed for many centuries, and the search for the most appropriate answer should not be (and is in fact not always) deflected by an odd quirk in the wording of a code. Any critical evaluation of the solution suggested by the code - its quirkyness or otherwise - presupposes comparison with other solutions, both past and present. Codification, in other words, does not present an obstacle for an historical legal science. Nor is our situation altogether different, in that respect, to that which Savigny encountered: after all, he was confronted by the three great codifications of natural law prevailing in different parts of Germany.

V

1) As far as I can see, there are two objections that may be raised against comparing the task of creating a common European legal science with that of establishing the historicial school of jurisprudence in the early nineteenth century. The one concerns the position of the English common law. '"What have we here? Who is that savage?" a foreign jurist would ask, with no small wonder, if the writings of Sir Edward

---

54 For further discussion see, e.g., Karsten Schmidt, *Die Zukunft der Kodifikationsidee: Rechtsprechung, Wissenschaft und Gesetzgebung vor den Gesetzeswerken des geltenden Rechts* (1985), pp. 67 sqq.

55 In a paper entitled 'The Civil Law in European Codes' I have tried to show that the modern civil codes all carry an unmistakably civilian imprint, and that the common tradition thus provides the background for an evaluation of their differences and similarities: D.L. Carey Miller, Reinhard Zimmermann (eds.), *The Civilian Tradition and Scots Law:Aberdeen Quincentenary Essays*, to be published in 1997. For a detailed analysis of the extent to which the German Civil Code (and the process of its application) are embedded in an ongoing (civilian) tradition, see (1994/95) 1 *Columbia Journal of European Law* 89 sqq. Cf. also the comments by Savigny, *System* (n. 32) XXVIII concerning the codifications he was faced with.

Coke, for example, were laid before him. "Whence comes this wild man; naked, tattooed, painted ..., with rings and fantastic toys in his ears and nostrils, - from what island of the South Sea, or from what trackless forest? It cannot be that he was the Attorney-General of the King of England in an age of refinement - the contemporary of Cujacius..."'[56]. This is how many continental lawyers essentially still think today, when they are confronted with the casuistic nature of the English law, with its bizarre traditionality, or with its peculiar interlocking of common law and equity. Indeed, the English themselves like to cultivate the notion of their law as flourishing in 'noble isolation'[57] from Europe.

Of course, it is true that England has never experienced a reception of Roman law *in complexu*. But it would be a gross oversimplification, were we to imagine that all continental legal systems have received Roman law to the same extent and in the same manner. Not without reason do many textbooks of comparative law distinguish between the Germanic and the Romanistic legal families[58]. If we look at individual legal problems, we find a considerable diversity of solutions adopted by the various codes. According to the German Civil Code, the vendor is liable if he does not transfer ownership in the object sold; according to the French *code civil*, the vendor's liability is based on eviction[59]. German law distinguishes between different types of breach of contract, French law proceeds from the broad concept of *inexécution*[60]. French law recognises vicarious liability *stricto sensu*, German law does not[61]. French law allows ownership to pass upon conclusion of the sale, German law subscribes to the 'abstract' system of transfer of ownership[62]. French law, unlike German law, does not

---

56 Thomas J. Hogg, 'An Introductory Lecture on the Study of the Civil Law' (1831), as reprinted in Michael H. Hoeflich, *The Gladsome Light of Jurisprudence* (1988), pp. 96 sqq. (99 sq.).

57 J.H. Baker, *An Introduction to English Legal History* (3rd ed., 1990), p. 35.

58 Cf., for example, Zweigert/Kötz/Weir see n. 7 *supra*, 63 sqq.

59 Reinhard Zimmermann, *The Law of Obligations: Roman Foundations of the Civilian Tradition* (1990, reprint 1993), pp. 293 sqq.; Wolfgang Ernst, *Rechtsmängelhaftung* (1995).

60 *Law of Obligations* see n. 59 *supra*, 783 sqq.; Zweigert/Kötz/Weir see n. 7 *supra*, 523 sqq.

61 *Law of Obligations* see n. 59 *supra*, 1120 sqq.; Hans Hermann Seiler, '*Die deliktische Gehilfenhaftung in historischer Sicht*', (1967) *Juristenzeitung* 525 sqq.

62 *Law of Obligations* see n. 59 *supra*, 271 sqq.; Franco Ferrari, '*Vom Abstraktionsprinzip und Konsensualprinzip zum Traditionsprinzip - Zu den Möglichkeiten der Rechtsangleichung im Mobiliarsachenrecht*', (1993) 1 *Zeitschrift für Europäisches Privatrecht* 52 sqq.

recognise a specific legal institution called *mora creditoris*.[63] According to the *code civil*, set-off operates *ipso iure*, according to the *BGB* it requires a specific declaration[64]. Many more examples could be mentioned. Yet, given some insight into historical background and comparative context, it is not difficult for a modern private lawyer from one jurisdiction to understand the rules contained in other civil codes, to recognise similarities and to evaluate differences, and to identify the common foundations underlying all of them[65].

2) It is my contention that matters are not, in principle, much different, as far as the supposedly deeply entrenched civil law/common law dichotomy is concerned. Since the days of the Norman conquest, England was never entirely cut off from continental legal culture[66]. The agents for this process of reception were legal writers from Bracton to Blackstone and Birks and judges like Sir Matthew Hale, Lord Holt and Lord Mansfield, Lord Chancellors and Civilians, institutions like Oxford and Cambridge, Doctors' Commons and the Court of Admiralty, Church and merchants. Modern English contract law was shaped by massive borrowings from authorities like Pothier and Domat, Grotius, Pufendorf, Burlamaqui and Thibaut[67]. In many cases, of ccurse, civilian inspiration led to results that do not conform to modern continental civil law. Thus, for instance, we read in the most famous of the so-called 'coronation cases'[68]: 'The real question in this case is the extent of the application in English law of the principle of the Roman law which has been adopted and acted on in many English decisions'. This principle, which provided the point of departure, is the civilian rule *debitor speciei liberatur casuali interitu rei*[69]: the debtor is relieved of his duty to deliver the

---

63 *Law of Obligations* see n. 59 *supra*, 817 sqq.; Uwe Hüffer, *Leistungsstörungen durch Gläubigerhandeln* (1976), pp. 61 sqq., 87 sqq.

64 *Law of Obligations* see n. 59 *supra*, 760 sqq.

65 This point is elaborated in the article 'The Civil Law in European Codes', as quoted above, n. 55. Cf. also Bellomo, see n. 5, *supra*, XIII ('Plurality was thus part of the "system"').

66 See, for further elaboration, Reinhard Zimmermann, '*Der europäische Charakter des englischen Rechts: Historische Verbindungen zwischen civil law und common law*', (1993) 1 *Zeitschrift für Europäisches Privatrecht* 4 sqq.

67 A.W.B. Simpson, 'Innovation in Nineteenth Century Contract Law', (1975) 91 *Law Quarterly Review* 247 sqq.; James Gordley, *The Philosophical Origins of Modern Contract Doctrine* (1991), pp. 134 sqq.; Zimmermann, (1993) 1 *Zeitschrift für Europäisches Privatrecht* 43 sqq.

68 *Krell* v. *Henry*, [1903] 2 KB 740 (CA) at 747 sq.

69 Cf., e.g., Hermann Dilcher, *Die Theorie der Leistungsstörungen bei Glossatoren, Kommentatoren und Kanonisten* (1960), pp. 185 sqq.

object if it has been destroyed through no fault of his own. In about the middle of the nineteenth century, English judges began to read this rule into the parties' agreement[70]. For this purpose they availed themselves of a construction which also originated in Roman law: the introduction of a (tacit) resolutive condition. The doctrine of 'frustration of contract' which eventually emerged corresponds functionally to the civilian *clausula rebus sic stantibus*.[71] That doctrine, too, had been constructed of Roman building blocks, although as such it had also been unknown to Roman law[72].

As long as one does not focus on specific solutions found in the Roman sources but takes account of the inherent flexibility of the civilian tradition, its potential for growth and productive assimilation, one may easily conceive of the English common law as a specific emanation of a European, or Western, legal tradition. Over the centuries, of course, it has developed a number of pecularities. So have the continental legal systems. But it is obvious today that these pecularities and jagged edges, on both sides of the Channel, are in the process of being worn away. Basil Markesinis refers to a 'gradual convergence'[73], James Gordley to a 'vanishing distinction' between common law and civil law[74]. This applies both to the substance of the law and to its institutional and methodological framework. The German *BGB*, to mention but one example, is today enveloped by thick layers of case law which anybody who wishes to apply the law has to be thoroughly familiar with. In many important fields a typical case law approach prevails: the recognition of 'leading cases' as starting points for new developments and principles, distinguishing, and arguing from case to

---

70 *Taylor* v. *Caldwell*, (1863) 3 B & S 826 sqq.; see, e.g., Max Rheinstein, *Die Struktur des vertraglichen Schuldverhältnisses im anglo-amerikanischen Recht* (1932), pp. 173 sqq.; G.H. Treitel, *Unmöglichkeit, 'Impracticability' und 'Frustration' im anglo-amerikanischen Recht* (1991).

71 *Law of Obligations* see n. 59 *supra*, 579 sqq.; Klaus Luig, '*Dogmengeschichte des Privatrechts als rechtswissenschaftliche Grundlagenforschung*', (1993) 20 *Ius Commune* 193 sqq.

72 For a detailed exposition on the use of tacit conditions within the history of European contract law, see Reinhard Zimmermann, '"Heard melodies are sweet, but those unheard are sweeter ...": *Conditio tacita, implied condition und die Fortbildung des europäischen Vertragsrechts*', (1993) 193 *Archiv für die civilistische Praxis* 121 sqq.

73 *The Gradual Convergence: Foreign Ideas, Foreign Influences and English Law on the Eve of the 21st Century* (1994). Cf. also B.S. Markesinis, 'Judge, Jurist and the Study and Use of Foreign Law', (1993) 109 *Law Quarterly Review* 622 sqq.

74 '*Common law und civil law: eine überholte Unterscheidung*', (1993) 1 *Zeitschrift für Europäisches Privatrecht* 498 sqq.

case[75]. English lawyers, on the other hand, have learnt to re-evaluate the role of legal writers. Gone are the days when an English judge could express his regret that textbooks are more and more quoted in Court[76]. Today, the 'jurist' is rather regarded as a fellow pilgrim 'on the endless road to unattainable perfection' and it is acknowledged, on the authority of Geoffrey Chaucer, that 'conversations among pilgrims can be most rewarding'[77]. These are just two examples illustrating the growing convergence. Many more could be provided. In their entirety they appear to be leading to a change of perspective which, significantly, is not confined to the academic community. Thus, Sir Thomas Bingham (as he then was) in his F.A. Mann lecture entitled 'There is a World Elsewhere' has suggested that the 1990s may be remembered as the decade 'when England - and I emphasise England - ceased to be a legal island, bounded in the north by the Tweed, and joined, or more accurately rejoined, the mainstream of European legal tradition'[78]. And Lord Goff, under whose guidance the House of Lords has recently revolutionised the English law of unjustified enrichment, has remarked, *à propos* a meeting with German judges, that he found hardly any difference between English and German law, as far as application and development of the law by the judiciary are concerned[79]. There is no way back into 'This Other Eden', as it was once inimitably conjured up by Lord Denning[80]. Both in the continental legal systems and in England the law is shaped by Parliament, the courts and the academic fraternity[81]. The balance of power and authority may differ but the need for co-operation is appreciated everywhere.

---

75 For details, see 'German Legal Culture' see n. 29 *supra*, pp. 16 sqq..

76 *Union Bank* v. *Munster*, (1887) 37 ChD 51, at 54 (per Kekewich J).

77 *Spiliada Maritime Corporation* v. *Consulex Ltd.*, [1987] 1 AC 460 (HL) 488 (per Lord Goff of Chieveley). Cf. also Peter Birks, 'Adjudication and Interpretation in the Common Law: a century of change', (1994) 14 *Legal Studies* 156 sqq. (emphasising, *inter alia*, the importance of Lord Goff's Maccabean Lecture of 1983).

78 (1992) 41 *International and Comparative Law Quarterly* 514.

79 (1994) 58 *RabelsZ* 443 sqq.; and see the report by Hans-Peter Kirchhof, (1994) 2 *Zeitschrift für Europäisches Privatrecht* 352 sqq.

80 Dennis R. Klinck, '"This Other Eden": Lord Denning's Pastoral Vision', (1994) 14 *Oxford Journal of Legal Studies* 25 sqq.

81 On judges, legislators and professors as the protagonists responsible for the development of European law, see R.C. van Caenegem, *Judges, Legislators and Professors* (1987); *idem*, *An Historical Introduction to Private Law* (1988), pp. 170 sqq.

VI

Common law and civil law are no strangers[82]. On the level of substantive law, this has been borne out, most recently, by the drafting of 'Principles of European Contract Law' that has been undertaken by a 'Commission on European Contract Law', sponsored by the Commission of the European Communities[83]. Of course, there are a number of significant differences: contrary to the continental legal systems English law does not recognise contracts in favour of third parties, it rejects penalty clauses and it regards 'specific performance' as an exceptional remedy[84]. A continental lawyer may be disinclined to admire the position adopted by the common law, but it is not difficult for him to understand it. After all, contracts in favour of third parties had also been alien to the Roman way of thinking and they only managed to establish themselves after centuries of fierce struggle against the principle of *alteri stipulari nemo potest* and the Roman concept of privity of contract[85]. The path towards recognition of specific performance, too, had for many centuries been obstructed by the Roman maxim of *omnis condemnatio pecuniaria*: whatever performance the defendant owed, he was invariably condemned into a sum of money. The French *code civil* still preserves this position with regard to

---

82 R.H. Helmholz, 'Continental Law and Common Law: Historical Strangers or Companions?', 1990 *Duke Law Journal* 1207 sqq. For a different evaluation see, most recently, Geoffrey Samuel, '*System und Systemdenken - Zu den Unterschieden zwischen kontinentaleuropäischem Recht und Common Law*', (1995) 3 *Zeitschrift für Europäisches Privatrecht* 375 sqq; Pierre Legrand 'Legal Traditions in Western Europe: The Limits of Commonality' in R. Jactenberg, E. Örücü, S. J. de Roo, *Transfrontier Mobility of Law* (1995), pp. 63 sqq.

83 Ole Lando/Hugh Beale (eds.), *Principles of European Contract Law*, Part I (1995); for an evaluation from an historical and comparative point of view, see Reinhard Zimmermann, '*Konturen eines Europäischen Vertragsrechts*', (1995) *Juristenzeitung* 477 sqq; Hugh Beale, 'The "Europeanisation" of Contract Law', in: R. Halson (ed.) *Exploring the Boundaries of Contract* (1996), pp. 23 sqq. Cf. also the *Principles of International Commercial Contracts*, edited by UNIDROIT, International Institute for the Unification of Private Law (1994); on which, see the contributions in (1992) 40 *American Journal of Comparative Law* 617 sqq.; Michael Joachim Bonell, '*Das UNIDROIT-Projekt für die Ausarbeitung von Regeln für Internationale Handelsverträge*', (1992) 56 *RabelsZ* 274 sqq.; Klaus Peter Berger, '*Die UNIDROIT-Prinzipien für Internationale Handelsverträge*', (1995) 94 *Zeitschrift für Vergleichende Rechtswissenschaft* 217 sqq.; and the contributions by Michael Joachim Bonell, Alejandro M. Garro, Hernany Veytia, Luiz Olano Baptista and Franco Ferrari in (1995) 69 *Tulane Law Review* 1121 sqq.

84 *Law of Obligations* see n. 59 *supra*, 45, 107 sq., 776 sqq.

85 *Law of Obligations* see n. 59 *supra*, 34 sqq.; Hein Kötz, 'Rights of Third Parties: Third Party Beneficiaries and Assignment', in: *International Encyclopedia of Comparative Law*, vol. VII, ch. 13 (1992), nn. 4 sqq.

obligationes ad faciendum; in Germany, the last vestiges of *omnis condemnatio pecuniaria* were only overcome in the course of the nineteenth century[86]. Yet, it is widely recognised among modern comparative lawyers that in the actual practice of German law the claim to specific performance does not have anything like the significance attached to it in theory[87]. At the same time, the traditional common law view seems to be losing some of its force in both the United States and in England[88]. In any event it is obvious that that view is explicable only on historical grounds. Article 4.102 of the Principles of European Contract Law is therefore based on a viable compromise between what appears to be right in principle and what is regarded as convenient in practice.

Concerning contracts in favour of third parties, the continental approach has prevailed. This is hardly surprising in view of the fact that even in England the common law is widely regarded as being 'clearly out of step both with modern practice and good sense'[89]. This is obvious not only in comparison with continental legal systems but also with Scotland[90] and the United States[91] and even with members of the Commonwealth like New Zealand and Australia[92]. Even historically, the

---

86 *Law of Obligations* see n. 59 *supra*, 770 sqq.; Karin Nehlsen-von Stryk, '*Grenzen des Rechtszwangs: Zur Geschichte der Naturalvollstreckung*', (1993) 193 *Archiv für die civilistische Praxis* 529 sqq.

87 Zweigert/Kötz/Weir, see n. 7, *supra*, 505 sqq.

88 Zweigert/Kötz/Weir see n. 7, *supra*, 519. Cf. also G.H. Treitel, *Remedies for Breach of Contract: A Comparative Account* (1988), pp. 43 sqq. South African law, a mixed legal system that has been, for some time, under the spell of English law, has now shed the limitations of specific performance derived from English practice: see *Benson* v. *S.A. Mutual Life Assurance Society*, 1986 (1) SA 776 (A); G.F. Lubbe, Christina Murray, *Farlam and Hathaway, Contract: Cases, Materials and Commentary* (1988), pp. 530 sqq. Scots law recognises the principle of 'specific implement': see W.W. McBryde, *The Law of Contract in Scotland* (1987), pp. 509 sqq.

89 Harvey McGregor, *Contract Code - Drawn up on behalf of the English Law Commission* (1993), p. 286.

90 Cf. T.B. Smith, '*Jus Quaesitum Tertio*: Remedies of the "*Tertius*" in Scottish Law', in: *idem, Studies Critical and Comparative* (1962), pp. 183 sqq.; McBryde, see n. 88, *supra*, 408 sqq.

91 Kötz, see n. 85, *supra*, n. 17.

92 Cf. the overview provided by Kötz, see n. 85, *supra*, n. 16. Of particular significance for Australian law is *Trident General Insurance Co. Ltd.* v. *McNiece Bros. Pty. Ltd.*, (1988) 165 CLR 107. As far as England is concerned, see now the Consultation Paper No. 121 of the English Law Commission: *Privity of Contract: Contracts for the Benefit of Third Parties* (1991); on which, see Jack Beatson, 'Reforming the Law of Contracts for the Benefit of Third Parties', (1992) 45 (2) *Current Legal Problems* 1 sqq.; Hugh Beale, 'Privity of Contract: Judicial and Legislative Reform', (1995) 9 *Journal of Contract Law* 103 sqq; and now Law Com. No. 242 with the same title (1996).

privity of contract doctrine appears to be less deeply entrenched than is commonly assumed. It has recently been argued that until the second half of the seventeenth century the common law courts were quite prepared to grant protection to third parties. The change of opinion appears to have been partly attributable to a selective reception of the continental will-theory as propounded by Domat and Pothier[93].

Conventional penalties, unlike contracts in favour of third parties and specific performance, were never, in principle, rejected in the course of the development of the civilian tradition. They fulfilled important functions. In particular, they could be used to exercise pressure upon a promisor to render a performance that he did not want to, or was not able to, promise directly[94]. In medieval English law, so-called 'penal bonds' were at least as popular and at least as important[95]. They fulfilled a very similar function. Both English law and Roman law also realised that conventional penalties are dangerous. The Roman lawyers developed ways and means to assist the debtor against his creditor claiming the penalty[96]. They carefully analysed the requirements for forfeiture and they also allowed the debtor unilaterally to purge forfeiture of the penalty. In the long run, however, this was not regarded as sufficient. Medieval canon lawyers therefore allowed the courts to reduce excessive penalty clauses *ad bonum et aequum*[97]. This very exceptional right to interfere with a contractual term has been endorsed by a variety of modern codifications, among them the *BGB*[98]. The common law courts adopted a more radical approach: they rejected penalty clauses altogether. This step gave rise, however, to a cumbersome and unsatisfactory distinction between penalties in a narrow sense and liquidated damages clauses[99]. This distinction (which, strangely, has also crept into German law[100]) has been severely

---

93 Vernon V. Palmer, *The Paths to Privity: The History of Third Party Beneficiary Contracts in English Law* (1992).

94 *Law of Obligations* see n. 59 *supra*, pp. 38 sq., 97.

95 See A.W.B. Simpson, *A History of the Common Law of Contract* (1987), pp. 113 sqq., 118 sqq., 123 sqq.

96 See *Law of Obligations* see n. 59 *supra*, 110 sqq.

97 *Law of Obligations* see n. 59 *supra*, 106 sqq.; Treitel, see n. 88, *supra*, 223 sqq.; and see now, for all details, Ralf-Peter Sossna, *Die Geschichte der Begrenzung von Vertragsstrafen* (1993).

98 § 343 *BGB*. Cf. also, most recently, Art. 6:94 (Dutch) *BW*.

99 Cf., e.g., Treitel, see n. 88, *supra*, 208 sqq.

100 Helmut Heinrichs, in: Palandt, *Bürgerliches Gesetzbuch* (54th ed., 1995), § 276, n. 54.

criticised[101] and it is not surprising that Professor McGregor's Contract Code, drafted in the late 1960s but only published in 1993, places both types of clauses on the same footing[102]. Quite understandably, therefore, the Principles of European Contract Law have followed the continental approach[103].

VII

There is, however, also a range of problems where it is not the English common law but one of the continental legal systems that turns out, in an historico-comparative perspective, to be the European outsider. Concerning breach of contract this is true of German law. Here we find a body of rules that has been developed around a highly artificial concept of (supervening) impossibility devised by Friedrich Mommsen, and inspired, largely, by the Roman regime applicable to *certam rem dare* obligations[104]. This is particularly odd in view of the fact that our modern general law of contract derives from the consensual contracts of Roman law, not from the law of stipulations entailing *certam rem dare*[105]. With regard to the former, liability had to be assessed according to the standard of good faith (*ex fide bona*), and there was thus no need for the strict categorisation of specific types of breach of contract characteristic of the modern German approach[106]. Of central importance was the question whether, and under which circumstances, the failure to perform, or to perform properly, was attributable to the debtor, before he could be made liable for *quod interest*; and this was indeed the very

101 Treitel, see n. 88, *supra*, 233 ('The common law rules ... manage to get the worst of both worlds').

102 McGregor, see n. 89, *supra*, 132 sqq.

103 Art. 4.508 Principles of European Contract Law.

104 Friedrich Mommsen, *Die Unmöglichkeit der Leistung in ihrem Einfluß auf obligatorische Verhältnisse* (1853). For a discussion, see Christian Wollschläger, *Die Entstehung der Unmöglichkeitslehre: Zur Dogmengeschichte des Rechts der Leistungsstörungen* (1970), pp. 123 sqq.; Susanne Würthwein, *Zur Schadensersatzpflicht wegen Vertragsverletzungen im Gemeinen Recht des 19. Jahrhunderts: Grundsätze des Leistungsstörungsrechts im Gemeinen Recht in ihrer Bedeutung für das BGB* (1990); *Law of Obligations* see n. 59 *supra*, 783 sqq., 809 sqq.

105 Cf. Klaus-Peter Nanz, *Die Entstehung des allgemeinen Vertragsbegriffes im 16. Jahrhundert* (1985); John Barton (ed.), *Towards a General Law of Contract* (1990); *Law of Obligations* see n. 59 *supra*, 537 sqq.; Reinhard Zimmermann, 'Roman-Dutch Jurisprudence and its Contribution to European Private Law', (1992) 66 *Tulane Law Review* 1689 sqq.; Robert Feenstra, '*Die Klagbarkeit der pacta nuda*', in: Robert Feenstra, Reinhard Zimmermann (eds.), *Das römisch-holländische Recht: Fortschritte des Zivilrechts im 17. und 18. Jahrhundert* (1992), pp. 123 sqq.

106 *Law of Obligations* see n. 59 *supra*, 788 sqq., 807 sqq.

question that preoccupied the authors of the older *ius commune* (as opposed to Mommsen, Windscheid and the draftsmen of the *BGB*). Following this pattern of the *ius commune* is the French *code civil*[107]. Its Article 1147 refers to *inexécution*, a broad concept which covers all forms of breach of contract (that is, those cases where one of the parties '*ne satisfera point ... son engagement*'). A similarly streamlined set of rules, centred around a uniform concept of breach of contract, has been developed in English law[108]. The Vienna Convention on the International Sale of Goods, the German commission charged with the reform of the law of obligations, the Unidroit Principles of International Commercial Contracts and the Principles of European Contract Law all follow the latter approach[109].

Mora creditoris (delay in accepting performance) presents another significant discrepancy between German law on the one hand and French and English law on the other, for neither of the latter two legal systems recognise it as a specific institution in its own right[110]. It is not easy to determine, in this instance, which of the two regimes is preferable.

Determination of price, on the other hand, is a problem area where French law appears to be out of step with modern developments. Article 1108 *code civil* requires every contract to have '*un objet certain*'. '*Objet*' in terms of this rule and in terms of Article 1129 *code* civil is also, for instance, the counterperformance to be given for the performance of services, the transfer of an object, etc. As far as the contract of sale is concerned, Article 1591 *code civil* specifically determines that the price has to be '*déterminé et désigné par les parties*'. These rules are based, unmistakably, on Roman law. Article 1591 is the codified version of the *certum pretium* requirement for the Roman contract of sale[111]. The more general rule of Article 1108, in turn, appears to represent an intermediate stage within the grand development from the fragmented Roman law of contracts (which focused on individual types of contract, the constituent elements of which, as a matter of course, had to be the object of the agreement of the parties)

---

107 Cf., e.g., Zweigert/Kötz/Weir, see n. 7, *supra*, 532 sqq.

108 Cf., e.g., Zweigert/Kötz/Weir, see n. 7, *supra*, 539 sqq.; *Law of Obligations* n. 59 *supra*, 814 sqq.

109 Cf., e.g., Peter Schlechtriem, '*Rechtsvereinheitlichung in Europa und Schuldrechtsreform in Deutschland*', (1993) 1 *Zeitschrift für Europäisches Privatrecht* 217 sqq.; Zimmermann, (1995) *Juristenzeitung* 480 sqq.

110 Cf. (1995) *Juristenzeitung* 489 sq.

111 It is discussed in a number of interesting fragments; see *Law of Obligations* see n. 59 *supra*, 253 sqq.

towards the modern, general concept of contract (which emphasises the freedom of the parties to design their own contract)[112]. Thus, according to the modern point of view, it only has to be ascertained whether the parties had intended to be bound[113]. This is, indeed the approach adopted by the *BGB*[114]. So, in particular, determination of the price may be left to one of the contracting parties, be it that he has to decide 'in an equitable manner' or even in his free discretion[115]. This obviously represents a deviation from Roman law. It is based on pandectist doctrine[116] which had managed to venture, in Jhering's famous words, beyond Roman law by means of Roman law. In the meantime, incidentally, the *Assemblée Plènière* of the *Cour de Cassation*, in a spectacular reversal of its previous interpretation of Article 1129 *code civil*, has adopted a much more liberal approach to certainty of price in long term supply agreements[117].

Another problem with regard to which French law adopts a very rigid attitude (more rigid, especially, than English and German law) is the effect of change of circumstances on the duty to perform contractual obligations. The French approach reflects the attitude adopted in Roman law. Both English and German law are more sympathetic towards the debtor (as was, incidentally, the *ius commune*)[118].

---

112 Cf. Barry Nicholas, *The French Law of Contract* (2nd ed., 1992), pp. 115 sq.

113 Cf. Wolfgang Witz, *Der unbestimmte Kaufpreis* (1989), pp. 89 sqq., 155 sqq., and the comparative discussion by Barry Nicholas, 'Certainty of Price' in: *Comparative and Private International Law; Essays in Honor of J.H.* Merryman (199), pp. 247 sqq; A.T. van Mehren, 'The Formation of Contract', in: *International Encyclopedia of Comparative Law*, vol. VII, ch. 9 (1992), nn. 50 sqq; Lando/Beale, see n. 83 *supra* p. 69 sqq.

114 §§ 315 sqq. *BGB*.

115 § 315 I *BGB*.

116 For details, see Hans-Joachim Winter, *Die Bestimmung der Leistung durch den Vertragspartner oder Dritte (§ 315 bis 319 BGB) unter besonderer Berücksichtigung der Rechtsprechung und Lehre des 19. Jahrhunderts* (unpublished Dr. iur. thesis, Frankfurt, 1979).

117 Dalloz 1996, 13 (with note by L. Aymès; cf. the analysis by Claude Witz, Gerhard Wolter, '*Das Ende der Problematik des unbistimmten Preises in Frankreich*', (1996) 4 *Zeitschrift für Europäisches Privatrecht* 648 sqq.

118 Cf. Lando/Beale, see n. 83, *supra*, 112 sqq.; Zimmermann, (1995) *Juristenzeitung* 486 sq.

VIII

If, therefore, the English common law does not appear to render impossible the Europeanisation of private law legal doctrine, another serious obstacle may lie in the diversity of languages prevailing in Europe today. In Western Europe, writes Tony Weir[119], there are several languages and several legal systems. Nobody denies that they are different, the French and German languages, the Greek and Danish legal systems. Languages and law tally with each other. Nobody speaks European. How can we then have European law? But it has to be remembered that there is a very close interrelationship between the Nordic legal systems[120] even though, for instance, the Swedish and Finnish languages are remarkably different; that we can speak of a Swiss law but not of a Swiss language; that Savigny's historical school mangaged to create a German legal science in spite of the fact that close to twenty per cent of the German population were governed by French law; or that, the other way round, the English and US-American legal cultures appear to be worlds apart in spite of being based on a common language[121]. These are not merely insignificant exceptions. Moreover, it is certainly true that the emergence of the national States in the eighteenth and nineteenth centuries has not only led to the nationalisation of law and legal science mentioned above, but also to an entrenchment of the position of the national languages. This entrenchment has occurred at the expense of regional and other minority languages. Today, however, we see a reversal of the trend. All over Europe, minority languages are in the process of gaining back lost territory; in many cases, they have even found official recognition. The diversity of languages appears to be no longer regarded as a misfortune, but as an expression of a people's cultural identity. Umberto Eco has recently observed that we are dealing here with a process that is probably irreversible[122]. If, however, the process of European unification appears to be accompanied by a multiplication of languages,

---

[119] *'Die Sprachen des europäischen Rechts: Eine skeptische Betrachtung'*, (1995) 3 *Zeitschrift für Europäisches Privatrecht* 368 sqq.

[120] Cf., e.g., Gebhard Carsten, *'Europäische Integration und nordische Zusammenarbeit auf dem Gebiet des Zivilrechts'*, (1993) 1 *Zeitschrift für Europäisches Privatrecht* 335 sqq.

[121] Scotland, too, has managed to retain its own legal system in spite of the fact that English is spoken in both England and Scotland. For an overview, see Reinhard Zimmermann, Johann A. Dieckmann, *'Das schottische Privatrecht im Spiegel seiner Literatur'*, (1995) 3 *Zeitschrift für Europäisches Privatrecht* 898 sqq.

[122] Umberto Eco, *Die Suche nach der vollkommenen Sprache* (1994), p. 339.

the only practically feasible solution lies in the whole-hearted adoption of a background language for international communication[123]. This is the scenario envisaged by one of the leading scholars in the field of languages, and it is hard to see (especially if one subscribes to the idea that law and language tally with each other) why it should not be possible to devise a set of systematic, conceptual and doctrinal tools, of rules and principles facilitating international communication.

IX

The type of scholarship envisaged both here and elsewhere[124] would neither necessarily lead to nor require uniformity of legal rules and results. This used to be true in the days before the great codifications when Europe had a *ius commune*[125]. Whether an error of law excludes the possibility of reclaiming what has been delivered without legal ground was answered differently by different lawyers at different times and in different parts of Europe[126]. Yet, all over Europe, the same legal 'grammar' was employed: the dichotomy, in our example, between

---

123 Eco, see n. 122, *supra*, 339.

124 (1993) 193 *Archiv für die civilistische Praxis* 121 sqq., 169 sqq.; (1994/95) 1 *Columbia Journal of European Law* 63 sqq.; cf. also 'Roman Law and European Legal Unity', in: A.S. Hartkamp, M.W. Hesselink *et al.* (eds.), *Towards a European Civil Code* (1994), pp. 65 sqq.; the contributions of Eugen Bucher and Bruno Schmidlin, in: Bruno Schmidlin (ed.), *Vers un droit privé Européen commun? - Skizzen zum gemeineuropäischen Privatrecht* 7 sqq., 33 sqq.; Carlo Augusto Cannata, '*Usus hodiernus pandectarum, common law, diritto romano olandese e diritto comune europeo*', (1991) 57 *Studia et documenta historiae et iuris* 383 sqq.; Reiner Schulze, '*Allgemeine Rechtsgrundsätze und europäisches Privatrecht*', (1993) 1 *Zeitschrift für Europäisches Privatrecht* 442 sqq.; Bellomo, see n. 5, *supra*, *passim*; Jürgen Basedow, '*Rechtssicherheit im europäischen Wirtschaftsrecht*', (1996) 4 *Zeitschrift für Europäisches Privatrecht* 570 sqq. refers to 'postpositivistic' legal scholarship. For criticism, see Pierra Legrand 'European Legal Systems are not Converging', (1996) 45 *International and Comparative Law Quarterly* 52 sqq.; Geoffrey Samuel, Jac Rinkes, *Law of Obligations and Legal Remedies* (1996), pp. 339 sqq.

125 This is the main theme of Bellomo's book, see n. 5, *supra*. The norms of the *iura propria* (i.e. the legal systems in European kingdoms, principalities, cities, and corporations) 'found in the *ius commune* usable concepts, principles, rules, and technical terminology ... . This was true even when the *ius proprium* reacted against or diverged from the *ius commune*; when this occurred, by choice or out of ignorance, it created a problem of comparison with, hence of relation to, the *ius commune*. Thus for the keenest intellects and the greatest jurists in Europe of the Middle Ages, the *ius commune* turned out to be a formidable unifying force. It lay at the center of the law and was the symbol of its unity' (p. XIII).

126 For details, see *Law of Obligations* see n. 59 *supra*, 849 sqq., 868 sqq.

error iuris and *error facti*; the fragmented system of the Roman *condictiones* which, over the centuries, formed the basis for discussion of contested issues in enrichment law; and the prerequisites, generally agreed upon in principle, for the application of that most central of these enrichment actions, the *condictio indebiti*. The same legal grammar can still be usefully employed in order to comprehend the similarities and differences among the remedies for unjustified enrichment provided in the modern civil codes[127]. For their draftsmen invariably laid down rules concerning the restitution of benefits conferred by transfer and, in doing so, they were invariably inspired by the *condictio indebiti*. Of course, they took their cue not from the *condictio indebiti* of classical Roman law but as it was applied and interpreted in the practice of their time. Historical analysis can demonstrate why a particular code opted for a wide or narrow version of that remedy and it thus provides essential information for critically assessing that solution. Moreover, it enables us to see that the modern version of the *condictio indebiti* has abandoned, step by step, certain idiosyncracies of its Roman ancestor. It is this gradual development that is reflected in the different codes, from the *code civil* of 1804 to the Dutch *Burgerlijk Wetboek* of 1992[128].

The present example demonstrates the importance of Roman law for the development of what may be called the civilian tradition[129]. Obviously, Roman law is not its only ingredient and it would therefore be quite wrong to study the development of Roman law in isolation. It would be equally fatal to idealise the purity and truth of classical Roman law, to attribute to it some sort of eternal validity and to try to press the present into the strait-jacket of an heroic past. When we are faced today with a specific problem, a solution cannot be regarded as right merely by virtue of the fact that it has once been advocated by Ulpian or Publius Iuventius Celsus. Ulpian and Celsus, of course, were excellent lawyers and their views may therefore be persuasive. But they have to be evaluated in the institutional, ideological, social and economic context within which they were expressed; and this context may be completely different today. Once again, we may refer to Savigny's views on historical scholarship. The historical approach to legal science, he

---

127 Reinhard Zimmermann, 'Unjustified Enrichment: The Modern Civilian Approach', (1995) 15 *Oxford Journal of Legal Studies* 403 sqq.

128 For details, see (1995) 15 *Oxford Journal of Legal Studies* 408 sqq. For an analysis of the law of unjustified enrichment in historical perspective, cf. also the contributions in Eltjo J.H. Schrage (ed.), *Unjustified Enrichment: The Comparative Legal History of the Law of Restitution* (1995).

129 Cf. also, more generally, Rolf Knütel, '*Rechtseinheit in Europa und römisches Recht*', (1994) 2 *Zeitschrift für Europäisches Privatrecht* 244 sqq.

wrote[130], is completely misunderstood and distorted, if it is often presumed that the legal entities emanating from the past are posited as something which is in the highest degree exemplary and which has to retain its rule, in an unchanged form, over both the present time and the future. On the contrary, the essence of the historical approach consists in the dispassionate recognition of the value and individuality of every age[131]. What is emphatically insisted upon, however, is a comprehension of the vital connection that ties the past to the present. For without such comprehension we will only be able to observe the outward form of our legal condition, not to grasp its inner substance.

X

1) The implementation of this kind of approach today requires a change of perspective, as far as legal history is concerned[132]. Legal scholarship, in the course of this century, has largely ceased to be an historical science. At the same time, legal history, particularly in Germany, has increasingly emancipated itself from law. It has tended to become a matter for specialists who might equally well be accommodated in faculties of arts rather than law[133]. A neo-humanistic approach to legal history has superseded the historical approach to legal science. It has, for instance, led Roman law scholars to focus on the development of Roman law in antiquity. This type of scholarship has certainly been carried to an unparalleled level of sophistication. But our colleagues in modern private law, I fear, will hardly regard what is published in the *Zeitschrift der Savigny-Stiftung für Rechtsgeschichte* (i.e., in the name of the patron saint of an historical legal science!) as providing 'helpful guidance'[134] or intellectual stimulation for their own endeavours. More often than not they will even fail to see the point of many of these disquisitions, i.e. their relevance for the discipline of law.

---

130 Savigny, *System* see n. 32 *supra*, XIV sqq.

131 Thus, Savigny set out, in his *System des heutigen Römischen Rechts*, to dispute the applicability of Roman law even in a variety of areas where it had generally been taken for granted: *System* see n. 32 *supra*, XV sqq. To what extent he (and his successors) in fact carried out this programme, is another matter.

132 For a more detailed elaboration of this point, see Reinhard Zimmermann 'Roman and Comparative Law: The European Perspective', (1995) 16 *Journal of Legal History* 21 sqq.

133 The dangers inherent in, and resulting from, exclusive preoccupation with Roman law as a purely historical phenomenon have been perceived, at a very early stage, by Paul Koschaker, *Europa und das Römische Recht* (4th ed., 1966), pp. 341 sqq.

134 Cf. *supra*, n. 42.

Generally speaking, therefore, I think that we will have to re-establish the intellectual contact between legal history and modern legal scholarship. This requires, first of all, that we focus our attention on the many centuries dividing classical Roman law from our own time. Hitherto, just about every textbook of Roman law ends with the Justinianic compilation. Wieacker has provided the authoritative account of the second life of Roman law, i.e. the centuries between the revival of Roman legal scholarship in Bologna and its absorption into the modern codes. But his work deals with the legal science of private law as such, with the way in which private lawyers conceived of their subject and how these scientific thought patterns have changed over the centuries. Wieacker does not provide a history of the institutions of private law. That is why Wolfgang Kunkel remarked that the 'real core' of a history of private law was missing in Wieacker's book[135].

Only comparatively recently has the first sustained attempt been made, within the parameters set by Wieacker, to sketch the development of private law legal doctrine[136]. Much remains to be done to fill in the details of this picture. Some periods have, so far, remained largely uncharted or have only very recently started to receive their due attention. What do we make of the surprising complexity and diversity of legal sources already extant in the early Middle Ages[137]? What was the role of medieval canon law[138]? What did the *mos gallicus*[139], the late scholastics in Spain[140], their successors in the Southern Netherlands[141],

---

135 (1954) 71 *Zeitschrift der Savigny-Stiftung für Rechtsgeschichte (Romanistische Abteilung)* 511.

136 Helmut Coing, *Europäisches Privatrecht*, vol. I (1985) and vol. II (1989). For trenchant criticism of Coing's approach, see Wilhelm Brauneder, '*Europäisches Privatrecht - aber was ist es?*', (1993) 15 *Zeitschrift für Neuere Rechtsgeschichte* 225 sqq.

137 See Harald Siems, *Handel und Wucher im Spiegel frühmittelalterlicher Rechtsquellen* (1992); Maurizio Lupoi, *Alle radici del mondo giuridico europeo* (1994).

138 Cf., in particular, Udo Wolter, *Ius canonicum in iure civili* (1975); Berman, see n. 44, *supra*, 85 sqq.; Peter Landau, '*Der Einfluß des kanonischen Rechts auf die europäische Rechtskultur*', in: Reiner Schulze (ed.), *Europäische Rechts- und Verfassungsgeschichte: Ergebnisse und Perspektiven der Forschung* (1991), pp. 39 sqq.; Richard H. Helmholz (ed.), *Canon Law in Protestant Lands* (1992); James A. Brundage, *Medieval Canon Law* (1995); concerning England, see Richard H. Helmholz, *Canon Law and the Law of England* (1987); *idem*, *Roman Canon Law in Reformation England* (1990).

139 See the re-assessment by Klaus Luig, '*Humanismus und Privatrecht*', in: *Vestigia Iuris Romani: Festschrift für Gunter Wesener* (1992), pp. 285 sqq.

140 James Gordley, *The Philosphical Origins of Modern Contract Doctrine* (1991).

or the Dutch school of jurisprudence[142] contribute to the development of European private law? What about protestant legal science in sixteenth century Germany[143]? What did the *ius commune* in the last truly European phase of its development - the so-called *usus modernus pandectarum* - look like[144]? How far did the influence of the *ius commune* extend? Which Eastern European States form part of the civilian tradition[145]? And what about England[146]? What can we learn from the experience of so-called mixed legal systems[147]? What we also need are detailed studies of the development of individual legal doctrines, making up in their entirety a comprehensive history of legal institutions.

It can hardly be disputed that these kinds of studies fall into the proper domain of the legal historian. Yet, Savigny did not, I think, primarily aim at providing an agenda for legal historians. His main concern was legal science rather than legal history[148]. He emphasised the 'vital connection'[149] between past and present. And he saw that the development of the law is doomed to lose direction if the awareness of its historicity, or historical relativity, is lost. A legal system cut off from

---

141 Philippe Godding, *Le droit privé dans les Pays-Bas méridionaux du 12e au 18e siècle* (1987).

142 Robert Feenstra, Reinhard Zimmermann (eds.), *Das römisch-holländische Recht: Fortschritte des Zivilrechts im 17. und 18. Jahrhundert* (1992); cf. also (1992) 66 *Tulane Law Review* 1685 sqq.

143 Berman/Reid, (1995) 3 *Zeitschrift für Europäisches Privatrecht* 3 sqq.

144 Cf. the contributions in Dieter Simon (ed.), *Akten des 26. Deutschen Rechtshistorikertages* (1987), pp. 237 sqq.

145 Cf., e.g., Radim Seltenreich, '*Das römische Recht in Böhmen*', (1993) 110 *Zeitschrift der Savigny-Stiftung für Rechtsgeschichte (Germanistische Abteilung)* 496 sqq.; János Zlinszky, '*Das Recht, erhalten und neu belebt durch römisches Recht: Ungarns Verhältnis zum römischen Recht in der Vergangenheit und in der Gegenwart*', (1994) 62 *Tijdschrift voor rechtsgeschiedenis* 61 sqq.

146 Cf. *supra*, sub V. And see the various volumes that have appeared as part of the *Comparative Studies in Continental and Anglo-American Legal History* (Helmut Coing and Knut Wolfgang Nörr eds.).

147 Cf., e.g., the contributions in Robin Evans-Jones (ed.), *The Civil Law Tradition in Scotland* (1995); Reinhard Zimmermann, Daniel Visser (eds.), *Southern Cross: Civil Law and Common Law in South Africa* (1996).

148 Cf. also Wieacker/Weir, see n. 8, *supra*, 330 ('The historical school renewed the study of law by seeing it - in its own way - as "historical". It was not so much interested in historical research for its own sake as in producing a new kind of legal doctrine ...'.)

149 Savigny, *System* see n. 32 *supra*, XV ('*der lebendige Zusammenhang...*').

its historical moorings is bound to drift. It may believe itself to be proceeding in the light of pure reason; but that is a delusion[150].

2) What does this mean within the context of European private law? A European legal culture, centred around a common legal science and informed by the same sources, did once exist[151]. This 'old' European law is known as the Roman-Canon *ius commune*, and it was based on the reception of Roman law in medieval Europe. It would thus appear to be the most obvious, and natural, point of departure for what Savigny referred to as an 'organically progressive' legal science[152]. Unlike Savigny, of course, we cannot directly pick up the thread of the *ius commune*. After all, neither Samuel Stryk's *Specimen usus moderni pandectarum*[153] nor Bernhard Windscheid's textbook of pandectist legal science[154] represent the law as it is in force today. But we can ask whether, in spite of the nationalisation of law and legal science, common systematic, conceptual, institutional and ideological foundations have been preserved beneath the bewildering diversity and specificity of our modern legal rules. We may thus be able to find a common core of European law or, as Koschaker once put it, a 'European natural law'[155] - natural law not, of course, in the sense of a set of rules of axiomatic validity, but of certain doctrinal features which the European legal systems, as a result of their common historical development, happen to

---

150 W.A. Wilson, 'The Importance of Analysis', in: *Comparative and Historical Essays in Scots Law: A Tribute to Professor Sir Thomas Smith QC* (1992), p. 171. For a programmatic statement on the relevance of historical experiences for the modern lawyer, see David Johnston, 'The Renewal of the Old' (Inaugural Lecture, Cambridge, 1996).

151 See the references *supra*, n. 5.

152 Savigny, *Beruf* see n. 14 *supra*, 192 ('*organisch fortschreitende Rechtswissenschaft*') and at many other places. On the place of Roman law, within this context, see Savigny, *System* see n. 32 *supra*, XV, emphasizing the necessity to trace, within the entire body of German law, what is in fact of Roman origin in order not to be unconsciously dominated by it ('*damit wir nicht bewußtlos davon beherrscht werden*'); and he continues: '... *dann aber strebt [unsere Ansicht], in dem Umkreis dieser Römischen Elemente unseres Rechtsbewußtseyns dasjenige auszuscheiden, was davon in der That abgestorben ist, und nur durch unser Mißverständnis ein störendes Scheinleben fortführt* ...' (but then our approach aims at eliminating, within the environs of these Roman elements of our legal consciousness, whatever has in fact withered away, and merely continues to lead a troublesome shadow life, as a result of our misunderstanding); along the same lines p. XXXIII.

153 On Stryk see, most recently, Klaus Luig, '*Samuel Stryk (1640-1710) und der "usus modernus pandectarum"*', in: *Die Bedeutung der Wörter: Festschrift für Sten Gagnér* (1991), pp. 219 sqq.

154 On Windscheid, see Ulrich Falk, *Ein Gelehrter wie Windscheid* (1989).

155 Koschaker, see n. 133, *supra*, 343 sqq. (346).

have in common[156]. The *condictio indebiti*, for instance, is a doctrinal feature of this kind. We can also try to explain, and thus understand, in which respects, how far, and why the paths of the modern legal systems have diverged. We can enquire whether these divergences are of a fundamental or of a more ephemeral nature, whether they are based on ideological difference or misunderstandings, on time-specific eccentricities of a code or the idiosyncratic interpretation of authoritative texts. Only when we take account of all the aspects of the historical development will we be in a position to draw the lines that will enable us to see where we stand, where our European neighbours stand and where we stand in relation to each other.

3) As far as the continental legal systems are concerned, we may, incidentally, take account of at least three important factors counterbalancing the trend towards nationalistic isolation. In the first place, all modern codifications are, and have remained, emanations of one and the same tradition. Neither the French *code civil* nor the Austrian *ABGB* were intended to be codes of national, specifically French or Austrian law. They were universalistic in spirit, approach and outlook[157]. The same is true of the German *BGB*, even if it was caught up in a surge of nationalistic sentiment. Secondly, the common tradition underlying the modern codifications also contributed to the continued existence of a network of intellectual contacts between the legal systems. The *code civil*, in particular, was able to maintain its dominant position in large parts of Europe even after Napoleon had been defeated[158]. Pandectist legal learning of German origin, on the other

---

156 '*... ein Naturrecht, das nicht spekulativ aus der Vernunft, sondern streng historisch aus der Vergleichung derjenigen Privatrechtssysteme gewonnen wird, die zum rechtlichen Aufbau Europas und darüber hinaus der ganzen Kulturwelt beigetragen haben, an der Spitze das römische Recht, das die Verbindung zwischen diesen Rechtssystemen herstellt*': Koschaker, see n. 133, *supra*, 346.

157 Cf. Wilhelm Brauneder, '*Vernünftiges Recht als überregionales Recht: Die Rechtsvereinheitlichung der österreichischen Zivilrechtskodifikationen 1786 - 1797 - 1811*', in: Reiner Schulze (ed.), *Europäische Rechts- und Verfassungsgeschichte* (1991), pp. 121 sqq.; Reiner Schulze, *Französisches Recht und Europäische Rechtsgeschichte im 19. Jahrhundert*, in: *idem* (ed.), *Französisches Zivilrecht in Europa während des 19.Jahrhunderts* (1994), pp. 12 sqq. For the French code civil, cf. also Gordley, (1994) 21 *American Journal of Comparative Law* 459 sqq.

158 Cf. Hans-Jürgen Becker, '*Das Rheinische Recht und seine Bedeutung für die Rechtsentwicklung in Deutschland im 19.Jahrhundert*', (1985) *Juristische Schulung* 338 sqq.; Elmar Wadle, '*Französisches Recht und deutsche Gesetzgebung im 19.Jahrhundert*', in: Reiner Schulze (ed.), *Europäische Rechts- und Verfassungsgeschichte* (1991), pp. 201 sqq.; and see the contributions to Reiner Schulze (ed.), *Französisches Zivilrecht in Europa während des 19. Jahrhunderts* (1994).

hand, was influential all over Europe, from Sweden to Italy, and including France and Austria[159]. Similarly important was, thirdly, the rise of comparative law as a new and independent branch of legal science in the course of the nineteenth century[160]. Comparative research provided a rich source of inspiration for the draftsmen of nineteenth- and twentieth-century legislation[161].

XI

The latter point gives rise to two further observations. It will have become obvious that a modern historical school of jurisprudence cannot exclusively be based on historical scholarship in the traditional sense. Since European law consists of several legal systems, and since direct reference back to the old, genuinely European *ius commune* would entail a short-circuit, we will have to combine historical and comparative legal scholarship. This requires us to overcome yet another disciplinary divide that is as strange as it is, apparently, deeply entrenched. The legal historian will have to tell his story up to the very point where the comparative lawyer can take over - as long, of course, as neither of them is able to produce works that leave it open where legal history ends and comparative law commences[162].

A combination of comparative and historical scholarship (and this is the second point) also appears to be the most appropriate way of grasping the relationship between common law and civil law and of advancing the process of mutual understanding and harmonisation. It does not need to be emphasised that historical investigation provides the key to a proper comprehension of the common law. Such historical investigation will often reveal that specific features of English law,

---

159 Cf. *supra*, n. 18.

160 Cf. Zweigert/Kötz/Weir, see n. 7, *supra*, 47 sqq.; Max Rheinstein, *Einführung in die Rechtsvergleichung* (2nd ed., 1987), pp. 37 sqq.

161 Cf., in particular, Helmut Coing, '*Rechtsvergleichung als Grundlage von Gesetzgebung im 19. Jahrhundert*', (1978) 7 *Ius Commune* 168 sqq.

162 Cf. also, along similar lines, Hein Kötz, '*Was erwartet die Rechtsvergleichung von der Rechtsgeschichte?*', (1992) *Juristenzeitung* 20 sqq.; Gordley, (1992) 40 *American Journal of Comparative Law* 1002 sqq.; Abbo Junker, '*Rechtsvergleichung als Grundlagenfach*', (1994) *Juristenzeitung* 921 sqq. On the potential inherent in 'retrospective comparison of laws' cf. also Heinz Hübner, '*Sinn und Möglichkeit retrospektiver Rechtsvergleichung*', in: *Festschrift für Gerhard Kegel* (1987), pp. 235 sqq. Generally on the necessity of adopting a comparative approach, Markesinis, (1993) 109 *Law Quarterly Review* 622 sqq.

particularly of English contract law[163], were inspired, moulded or influenced by the ideas and concepts, the rules and institutions as well as the general intellectual undercurrents of the European *ius commune*[164]. This is hardly surprising in view of the fact that law is a particularly characteristic emanation of European culture and that England, after all, was part of that European culture[165]. Thus, we often have a common point of reference enabling us to appreciate existing differences and to trace the further development. We find these points of contact on all imaginable levels: terminology (debtor, creditor, obligation, contract, restitution, etc.), system, policy, theory, argument and manner of reasoning, principle and individual rule. But even where we do not find such point of contact, comparison with other legal systems makes us aware of the idiosyncrasies of our own. It enables us to consider how else a legal problem may be solved. It therefore paves the way towards critical evaluation and rational choice. This applies in all those cases where common law and civil law had to address the same questions: Is the law of contract based on the notion of promise or consensus? Is the validity of a contract dependent on equality of exchange? When is a mistake sufficiently serious to affect the validity of the contract? At which moment does a contract come into existence? What are the requirements and the consequences of breach of contract? In which way does contributory negligence on the part of the injured party influence his claim for damages? Or, to return to the example discussed above: how does the law deal with the restitution of unjustified enrichment?

Unless it is prepared to disregard basic precepts of *iustitia commutativa*, every legal system has to provide a restitutionary remedy. This holds true of the common law as much as of the continental legal systems. Continental law and common law traditionally draw a fundamental distinction (*summa divisio*) between contract and delict (or tort). In civilian parlance: obligations arise either from contract or delict[166]. The obligation to render restitution of a benefit received, however, is based neither on contract nor delict (though it was, on both sides of the Channel, for a long time thought to be of a 'quasi-

---

163 But not exclusively. Cf., e.g., concerning trust law, Patrick Glenn, '*Le trust et le jus commune*', in: Pierre Legrand Jr. (ed.), *Common law d'un siècle l'autre* (no year), pp. 87 sqq.

164 Cf. *supra*, n. 66.

165 For details, see the recent study by Jeremy Black, *Convergence or Divergence? Britain and the Continent* (1994).

166 Gai. III, 88; cf. *Law of Obligations* see n. 59 *supra*, 10 sqq.

contractual' nature)[167]. The general enrichment principle has now been recognised by the House of Lords[168]. This raises the question as to how best to organise an area of the law which has been bedevilled by historical accident and legalistic fiction. It appears to be widely recognised that one group of cases can be brought home under the general notion of 'restitution for wrongs'[169]. It does not substantially differ from the continental pattern of enrichment liability based on encroachment. Concerning enrichment by transfer (or, to use the classification adopted by Goff and Jones, 'Where the Defendant has Acquired a Benefit from or by the Act of the Plaintiff')[170] English courts have developed a variety of 'unjust factors'[171]. Failure of consideration is one of them; it is the English equivalent of the civilian *condictio causa data causa non secuta*[172]. Of central importance, however, has always been, and still is, mistake. For a long time, only liability mistakes were recognised. Enrichment based on liability mistake corresponds to the civilian *condictio indebiti*[173]: there has been no legal ground for the transfer and the plaintiff has been unaware of this lack of legal ground. 'Without legal ground' and 'error' are thus inseparably related to each other.

From here on, the paths have diverged. Continental legal systems have come to regard the claim for restitution as being based on the fact that a transfer was rendered without legal ground[174]. Of course, a plaintiff cannot be allowed to rely on the absence of a legal ground, if

---

167 See Peter Birks, 'English and Roman Learning in *Moses* v. *Macferlan*', (1984) 37 *Current Legal Problems* 11 sqq.; Peter Birks, Grant McLeod, 'The Implied Contract Theory of Quasi-Contract: Civilian Opinion in the Century Before Blackstone', (1986) 6 *Oxford Journal of Legal Studies* 46 sqq.

168 On *Lipkin Gorman* v. *Karpnale Ltd.* [1991] 2 AC 548, the decision that brought the breakthrough, cf. Peter Birks, 'The English Recognition of Unjust Enrichment', (1991) *Lloyd's Maritime and Commercial Law Quarterly* 473 sqq.; Sonja Meier, '*Bereicherungsanspruch, Dreipersonenverhältnis und Wegfall der Bereicherung im englischen Recht*', (1993) 1 *Zeitschrift für Europäisches Privatrecht* 365 sqq. See also Lord Goff of Chieveley, Gareth Jones, *The Law of Restitution* (4th ed., 1993), pp. 12 sqq

169 Cf., e.g., Peter Birks, *An Introduction to the Law of Restitution* (1985, reprint 1989), pp. 313 sqq.; Goff/Jones, see n. 168, *supra*, 641 sqq.

170 Goff/Jones, see n. 168, *supra*, 105.

171 For a comprehensive discussion of these 'unjust factors' cf. chapters 3 to 13 of Andrew Burrows, *The Law of Restitution* (1993).

172 Peter Birks, '*Konkurrierende Strategien und Interessen: Das Irrtumserfordernis im Bereicherungsrecht des common law*', (1993) 1 *Zeitschrift für Europäisches Privatrecht* 556 sq.

173 Cf. Birks, see n. 169, *supra*, 152 sq.

174 For details, see (1995) 15 *Oxford Journal of Legal Studies* 403 sqq.

he had first appeared to acknowledge that a legal ground existed. But it is quite unnecessary for a legal system to elevate 'error' to the status of an independent requirement for the claim for restitution. Restitution is refused wherever the transferor, at the time of rendering performance, knew about the absence of the legal ground. In England, on the other hand, 'error' was disattached from the notion 'without legal ground' and thus acquired the status of an independent 'unjust ground'. This may have been due to the fact that, *inter alia*, transactions which are unenforceable for lack of consideration could not be regarded as constituting a legal ground[175]. This created difficulties in cases where someone had erroneously paid in excess of the sum agreed upon. If he was to be allowed to recover the excess payment, his claim could not be based on a liability mistake, for the notion of lack of legal ground did not appear to make sense in these kinds of cases. Arguably, however, agreements without consideration may be taken to be effective insofar as they provide a legal ground even though they may be unenforceable (*Rechtsgrundabreden*). This argument would open up, once again, the possibility of evaluating the relationship between 'error' and 'without legal ground'[176]. That very issue has been canvassed in the civilian tradition for many centuries and the experiences gathered in the process may benefit the discussion in England. Such discussion will be facilitated by the fact that recent years have brought about a rapprochement of patterns of liability in other respects. Thus, the common law is in the process of abolishing the traditional (both as far as common law and civil law are concerned!) distinction between *error iuris* and *error facti*[177]. It was made possible by the simultaneous recognition of the defence of change of position[178]. For the further the legal system is prepared to take the principle against unjust enrichment, the more anxious it has to be to protect the reasonable reliance of those

---

175 Cf. *Larmer v. L.C.C.* [1949] 2 K.B. 683. This argument will be developed and substantiated in a forthcoming thesis by Sonja Meier.

176 Interestingly, the decision in *Westdeutsche Landesbank Girozentrale* v. *Islington London BC* (1994) 1 WLR 938 (CA) appears to point in the direction that a claim for restitution may be based on the absence of a legal ground.

177 For details, see Birks, (1993) 1 *Zeitschrift für Europäisches Privatrecht* 554 sqq.

178 *Lipkin Gorman* v. *Karpnale Ltd.* [1991] 2 AC 548; and see D.P. Visser, 'Responsibility to Return Lost Enrichment', (1992) *Acta Juridica* 175 sqq.; Meier, (1993) 1 *Zeitschrift für Europäisches Privatrecht* 377 sqq.; Goff/Jones, see n. 168, *supra*, 739 sqq.

who have disposed of what they have received. It is exactly this argument that explains § 818 III *BGB*[179].

XII

Jean Domat's *Les loix civiles dans leur ordre naturel*, Robert Joseph Pothier's *Traité des obligations* and the works of many others paved the way towards modern French law, and the German Civil Code would be inconceivable without Friedrich Carl von Savigny's *System des heutigen römischen Rechts*, Bernhard Windscheid's *Lehrbuch des Pandektenrechts* and a vast body of literature besides. The lesson is obvious. The essential prerequisite for the development of a European private law would appear to be the emergence of an 'organically progressive' legal science, which would have to transcend national boundaries and disciplinary divides and which would revitalise a common tradition. It would, at the very least, enable us to understand and determine the relative positions of our national legal systems *vis-à-vis* each other. It would supply a common legal 'grammar' for discussing general legal questions and evaluating possible solutions. It would provide us with a stock of systematic and conceptual tools, of rules and principles, which would reduce the existing legal systems to national variations of a common theme[180]. This change of perception would, in turn, be reflected in the way in which the national legal systems are interpreted and developed; and it would engender a new approach to legal education and to legal writing. It would reconstitute Savigny's Historical School of Jurisprudence on a European level.

---

179 *Law of Obligations* see n. 59 *supra*, 895 sqq., 900 sq.

180 Cf., e.g., the programme sketched by Kötz, (1993) 1 *Zeitschrift für Europäisches Privatrecht* 276 sqq. and implemented in Hein Kötz, *Europäisches Privatrecht* (1996).

2

EUROPEAN PRIVATE LAW AND LEGAL HISTORY

Regarding the discussion in Germany

Reiner Schulze

Recently, many legal experts from Germany and other countries have demanded a 'Europeanisation' of the science of private law[1] and a scientific view of 'the common principles of European private law'[2], especially concerning the law of contracts[3]. By turning to these

---

1 Helmut Coing, '*Europäisierung der Rechtswissenschaft*', (1990) *Neue Juristische Wochenschrift* (*NJW*), p. 937.

2 Bruno Schmidlin, Préface, in: Bruno Schmidlin (ed.), *Vers un drolt privé européen commun? - Skizzen zum gemeineuropäischen Privatrecht,* (Basel 1994), p. 5; A.S. Hartkamp/M.W. Hesselink/E.A. Hondius (ed.), *Towards a European Civil Code*, (Nijmwegen 1994); Bruno Oppetit, '*Droit commun et droit européen'*, in: *L'internationalisation du droit, Mélanges en I'honneur de Yvon Loussouarn*, (Paris 1994), p. 318.

3 Ole Lando, *European Contract Law*, (1983) 31 *American JCL*, p. 653; Lando, 'Principles of European Contract Law', (1992) 56 *Rabels Zeitschrift für ausländisches und internationales Privatrecht* (*RabelsZ*), p. 261, also published in (1992) 40 *American JCL*, p. 573; Lando/Beale (ed.), *Principles of European Contract Law, Part 1*, (Dordrecht 1995); Hein Kötz, '*Gemeineuropäisches Zivilrecht'*, in: Herbert Bernstein/Ulrich Drobnlig/Hein Kötz, *Festschrift für Konrad Zweigert*, (Tübingen 1981), p. 486 *et seq.*; Kötz, '*Rechtsvereinheitlichung Nutzen, Kosten, Methoden, Ziele'*, (1986) 50 *RabelsZ*, p. 3.

questions, jurisprudence not only reacts to economic and political developments (above all, the European common market), but already in this day and age the legal profession itself demands international comparison and a European alignment of the science of private law in many ways.

Three examples should suffice to demonstrate this:

(1) When applying European community law the European Court of Justice has to consider the common legal principles of the Member States as a basis for its decisions on the legal principles of community law - not only when dealing with damages according to Article 215 of the EC Convention (where the common legal principles are mentioned expressly) but also in many other cases. Therefore the European Community's jurisdiction largely depends on a comparative analysis of national private laws focusing on the common principles for certain matters[4].

(2) This is similarly true for regulations deriving from international agreements between European States even if they are not part of the community's law, for instance concerning the term 'civil and commercial matters' and many other terms in the Brussels Judgement Convention of 1968[5].

(3) The president of the German Federal Supreme Court has recently argued in favour of a comparative and harmonising interpretation of national private law from a European perspective[6]. In addition to the usual methods of interpretation in Germany - grammatical, historical, systematical and

---

4 Cf. Walter Hallstein, '*Angleichung des Privat- und Prozeßrechts in der Europäischen Wirtschaftsgemeinschaft*', (1964) 28 *RabelsZ*, p. 211; Winfried Tilmann, '*Zur Entwicklung eines europäischen Zivilrechts*', in: Walter Jagenburg/Georg Maier-Reimer/Thomas Verhoeven (ed.), *Festschrift für Walter Oppenhoff*, (Munich 1985), p. 495 *et seq*.; Peter-Christian Müller-Graff, '*Gemeinsames Privatrecht in der Europäischen Gemeinschaft: Ebenen und Gemeinschaftsprivatrechtliche Grundfragen*', in: Jürgen F. Baur/Peter-Christian Müller-Graff/Manfred Zuleeg (ed.), *Europarecht Energierecht Wirtschaftsrecht, Festschrift für Bodo Börner*, (Cologne 1992), p. 303 *et seq*.; Müller-Graff, '*Europäisches Gemeinschaftsrecht und Privatrecht*', (1993) *NJW*, p. 13; Reiner Schulze, '*Allgemeine Rechtsgrundsätze und europäisches Privatrecht*', (1993) *Zeitschrift für Europäisches Privatrecht* (*ZEuP*), p. 454 *et seq*.

5 Cf. Case 29/76 *LTU* v. *Eurocontrol* [1976] E.C.R. p. 1541 at p. 1551.

6 Walter Odersky, '*Harmonisierende Auslegung und europäische Rechtskultur*', (1994) *ZEuP*, p. 1.

> teleological - judges should use comparison with other European private laws to achieve an approximation regarding the solution of similar legal problems in different European countries. And what was said about the task of a comparative and harmonising interpretation of codified law must definitely be valid for a jurisdiction developing national law beyond that as uncodified 'judge-made law'. It may be a challenge for Anglo-Saxon law, and also for the newer practice of some continental European countries, where private law - with a growing temporal distance from the large private law codifications - is more and more becoming a 'mixed law'[7] composed of codification, statutes and judge made law.

Therefore, the attention of legal science and legal practice with regard to European community law and national private law is turned toward a comparative, Europe-orientated scientific analysis of private law.

Often, legal history is embodied in this interest: The European Court of Justice, for example, refers to traditions[8], to common law principles[9] and sometimes even to Roman law[10] in order to find contemporary general legal principles for the European community.

The question arising from the point of view of practice and science conclusively is that of legal history's contribution to modern European private law. For legal historians this means: 'Can their discipline make a contribution to a European science of private law and the contemporary development of common private law in Europe ?'

The legal historians in German-speaking areas differ in their opinion: Some assert that this is possible and attempt to achieve it. Hence, a Max-Planck-Institute was founded a few decades ago with this objective in mind and publications and periodicals with this objective came into being[11]. Other legal historians insist upon European legal

---

7 Gerhard Dilcher, '*Vom Beitrag der Rechtsgeschichte zu einer zeitgemäßen Zivilrechtswissenschaft*', (1984) 184 *Archiv für die civilistische Praxis* (*AcP*), p. 255 *et seq*. and 286 *et seq*.

8 Case 5/88 *Wachauf* v. *Bundesamt für Ernährung und Forstwirtschaft* [1989] E.C.R. p. 2609 at p. 2610; Case 265/87 *Schräder* v. *Hauptzollamt Gronau* [1989] E.C.R. p. 2237 at p. 2238 *et seq*.; Case 136/79 *National Panasonic* v. *Commission* [1980] E.C.R. p. 2033 at p. 2057; Case 44/79 *Liselotte Hauer* v. *Land Rheinland Pfalz* [1979] E.C.R. p. 3727 at p. 3745; Case 4/73 *Nold* v. *Commission* [19741 E.C.R. p. 491 at p. 507.

9 Cf. the lecture of Maximilian Herberger at the 30th Conference of German Legal Historians (*Deutscher Rechtshistorikertag*) in Bern 1994, not published yet.

10 Case 23/68 *Klomp* v. *Inspektie der Belastingen* [1969] E.C.R. p. 43.

11 See in particular Helmut Coing (ed.), *Handbuch der Quellen und Literatur der Neueren Europäischen Privatrechtsgeschichte, 1973-1988; Ius Commune* (vols. 1- 9 edited by Helmut Coing, vols. 10 -13 by Dieter Simon and Walter Wilhelm, and from

history's abstention from contemporary juridical tasks, warn against a 'shipwreck of historicity'[12] and against a 'blend of categories'[13] and only speak of '*ius commune*' when referring to the common law of the past. They fear the self-sacrifice of legal history through its participation in the science of European private law, perceive an unbridgeable gap between juridical and legal historical work and fulfill their own scientific assignment - as far as they also deal with valid private law - so to speak at two separate desks: sitting at one desk they think of themselves as jurists, sitting at the other as legal historians; and with this constant change of places they feel as if they must constantly adopt a new being.

The following fifteen points should encourage us to rethink this question. They should draw your attention particularly to three problems discussed controversially:

> May the legal historian use 'modern' terms like European legal history, European private law and so on? (points 1 - 5)
>
> Should he be engaged in the developing - or 'reconstruction' - of a European common law today? (points 6 - 10)
>
> And finally: Should legal history acquire a similar role for the European private law of our time as - in the nineteenth century - the famous '*Historische Rechtsschule*' (the historical law school of Friedrich Carl von Savigny) acquired for German private law? (points 11 - 15).

I should start by giving an explanation. In the nineteenth century, the historical law school constructed a common German private law on the basis of common legal traditions, although Germany was divided into different States with their own jurisdictions and legislation. Primarily it was an academic law, a law in the textbooks; but these textbooks were used for the education of law students at the law faculties in all the different German States; and they were used by the judges to interpret the different statutes in these States as far as possible in a common spirit.

---

vol. 14 (1987), as *Zeitschrift für Europäische Rechtsgeschichte* by Dieter Simon) and special issues of *Ius Commune*.

12 Pio Caroni, '*Der Schiffbruch der Geschichtlichkeit - Anmerkungen zum Neo-Pandektismus*', (1994) 16 *Zeitschrift für Neuere Rechtsgeschichte* (*ZNR*), p. 85.

13 Tomasz Giaro, *Europäische Privatrechtsgeschichte: Werkzeug der Rechtsvereinheitlichung und Produkt der Kategorienvermengung*, *Ius Commune*, Vol. XXI (1994), p. 1.

Those textbooks supplied the want created by the lack of codification for the whole of Germany. So the academic common German law of the historical law school prepared for the unification of law from 1815 - a long time before the political unification of the different German States into the German Empire was realised in 1871.

Later on, the textbooks of the historical law school became the doctrinal basis for the codification of private law in the whole of Germany in 1900. Therefore, the code of 1900, the German '*Bürgerliches Gesetzbuch*', Civil Code (which is still valid) can be regarded as a result of the historical law school. But on the other hand, because of the codification, most German lawyers limited themselves to looking into this modern law book, and historical research lost its importance for the German law of today. German legal historians are now discussing whether their discipline could re-establish its former importance for living law under a European perspective[14].

I MODERN TERMS IN LEGAL HISTORY

(1) In Germany, 'European' legal history has only become a field of research in the last decades, especially through the works of Franz Wieacker and Helmut Coing. Since then, the conception of legal history as a part of national history has yielded more and more to engagement with the European dimensions of legal development. Legal history is understood as a part of the history of European culture. It is no coincidence - and scientifically legitimate that this change from a national to a European perspective commenced in the nineteen-fifties literally coinciding with the genesis of the European communities and their new common law for Europe.

No historical research can isolate itself from the dependence of its questions and results from contemporary problems. There is hardly anyone working in history today who seriously claims that historical discoveries can be 'purely objective', independent of the situation of the researcher. Therefore there is no 'pure' history for the legal historian. The choice of the topic 'European legal history', the designation of

---

14 Cf. Franz Wieacker, *'Der gegenwärtige Stand der Disziplin der neueren Privatrechtsgeschichte'*, in: *Eranion Maridakis 1*, (Athens 1963), p. 339; Wieacker, *Privatrechtsgeschichte der Neuzeit*, 2. ed., (Göttingen 1967), p. 14, esp. note 12, 14; summarising the discussion in Germany: Heinrich Honsell, *'Das rechtshistorische Argument in der modernen Zivilrechtsdogmatik'*, in: Dieter Simon (ed.), *Akten des 26. Deutschen Rechtshistorikertages, Ius Commune Sonderheft* Vol. 30, (Frankfurt-am-Main 1987), p. 299; Filippo Ranieri, *'Eine Dogmengeschichte des europäischen Zivilrechts?'*, in: Reiner Schulze (ed.), *Europäische Rechts und Verfassungsgeschichte, Schriften zur Europäischen Rechts- und Verfassungsgeschichte*, Vol. 3, (Berlin 1991), p. 99 *et seq*.

subject-matter with this term, the question about historical similarities in the law in Europe, the aim of discovering these connecting elements in history: all this is determined by legal developments and questions in the present.

(2) The legal historian should not try to 'flee into the past' or 'submerge himself in the study of sources'; even with the latter he is only apparently defying the present. Instead he should look upon his engagement with the past as a way of dealing with the present, as a consideration of his own times. Instead of denying the preconditions and the interests of historical research in the present, he must reflect upon them and - with them in mind - understand and interpret the past for the present. Research work concerning European legal history is always therefore an expression and a consideration of a concept regarding today's European law.

(3) Denying the illusion of objectivism, of a pure (legal) history, should not result in an uncontrolled dedication to subjectivism either, because if one wanted to comprehend (legal) history with a radical subjectivism as a mere arbitrary construction of the present, one would consequently dispute that historical research has any sole informative value. History would reduce itself to a depiction of the present in the past tense.

(4) In the end, the legal historian, like any historian, cannot settle for either of the two extremes: neither for the moderation of submerging himself into 'pure history' nor for the comfort of placing historical testimonies completely into the arbitration of present-day demands. On the contrary, he will be forced to remain within the tension between the dependence of his work on the present and the simultaneous striving to understand an earlier (and therefore different) legal system. Doing so, he will always be conscious of the singularity of each historical era, of each course of events, of each occurrence and thereby of the differences between past and present states of law. For example, he will be aware that he is interested in the older common law of the European continent because the older common law can deliver stimulations and insights for a present or future common law. At the same time he will be aware that the older and the present common law are different[15]. He will recognise that the older common law, the *Usus modernus*, the science of pandects,

---

[15] Cf. recently Paolo Grossi, *Quaderni Fiorentini per la storia del pensiero giuridico moderno,* Vol. 23 (1994), p. 1 *et seq.*

are phenomena which are gone and are irretrievable and therefore historicity. They are not normative outlines or patterns for present or future law.

(5) In this field of tension, within which the legal historian must act, conceptions like 'European private law' and 'European legal history' are essential and legitimate as instruments of mediation between concepts and questions of our time and the mentality of earlier times, although they are not terms deriving from historical sources. They have corresponded with the aforesaid 'European' mentality since the nineteen-fifties and derive from the contrast of the prior, prevalent concepts of German (or respectively other national) private law and national legal history. 'European' legal history as a historiographical category hence aims to draw attention to legal developments which have affected a great deal of Europe and which are elements of a common legal tradition: for example, the older *ius commune* - the Roman and the canonical tradition (the latter also includes England), the customs of merchants - the basis of 'the law merchant' - contracts of matrimony and inheritance among the higher nobility in Europe and many other things. All of these research topics have been emphasised in Germany recently.

II LEGAL HISTORY AND CONTEMPORARY LEGAL PROBLEMS

(6) The awareness of historical similarities can help jurists of different national legal experience create a basis of understanding for the solution of contemporary legal problems. For example, if one takes into account that all continental European private law codifications in one fashion or another proceed from the system of Gaius *(res - personae - actiones)*; and if one further considers that many legal institutions on the continent - from the law of sale to unjust enrichment and tort law - have common roots in the *ius commune*[16], one cannot perceive different national worlds as opposed to each other. No, one can only perceive some variations of one development having a common historical reference and an open future.

---

16 Cf. Reinhard Zimmermann, *The Law of Obligations: Roman Foundations of the Civilian Tradition*, (Johannesburg 1990); Zimmermann, '*Das römisch-kanonische* ius commune *als Grundlage europäischer Rechtseinheit*', (1992) *Juristenzeitung* (*JZ*), p. 8; Helmut Coing, '*Das Recht als Element europäischer Kultur*', (1984) 238 *Historische Zeitschrift* (*HZ*), p. 1; Coing, *Europäisches Privatrecht, Vol. 1: Älteres Gemeines Recht*, (Munich 1985), *Vol. 2: 19. Jahrhundert*, (Munich 1989); Hein Kötz, '*Gemeineuropäisches Zivilrecht*', note 3 *supra*, p. 486 *et seq*.

(7) Another question which could fill books and symposiums by itself is that about the geographical area to which these thoughts apply; or in other words, whether Eastern Europe and England (and Wales, too) belong to 'Europe' in this sense.

There is some controversy concerning the position of the large part of Europe which in the Middle Ages was moulded not by the Latin church and language but by the Greek and Byzantine tradition. Until now the prevailing notion of Europe (in German research into legal history) has been restricted essentially to the Latin area, excluding the Greek and Byzantine east and south-east. This point of view may, however, excessively neglect the unifying elements of common European culture including the East - particulary the Christian and Roman tradition (perhaps because of the experience of the recent past, in which Russia, for example, had not yet opened up to the European idea).

Much more attention has been devoted to the historical connections between continental and English law. While the differences, largely determined by historical circumstances, between English (and American) common law and continental European law are well known, it is now clear that their historical relationships and common structural features are much greater than was previously assumed by most people. For example, a new series of publications, founded by Helmut Coing[17] has brought to light many historically-based common features of English and continental law. It seems that we can no longer think in terms of the isolated, completely separate development of the law on the continent and in England respectively.

At this point I cannot go further into these questions; many researchers from Great Britain would be more competent to speak on this subject anyway. In any case, we can summarise this for the Latin west of Europe on the continent: the common grounds of the premodern traditions, especially of the *ius commune*, may not be 'historical authorities' for a common European private law today. Yet they can be one of the starting points for a consensus extending beyond our national legal experiences and for finding solutions to fit the needs of our time.

(8) Nonetheless, it should not be forgotten: these solutions cannot deny the national legal experiences and thereby the legal developments of the last two centuries[18]. But the nineteenth century is regarded as the

---

17 See note 11 *supra*.

18 Therefore it is not justified to mark the different development as 'rubble', having covered the common tradition, see Reinhard Zimmermann, 'Heard melodies are sweet, but those unheard are sweeter...... *Condicio tacita*, implied *condition und die Fortbildung des europäischen Vertragsrechts*', (1993) 193 *AcP*, p. 171.

climax of the nation-state and the national law. Can it be considered an era of European legal history at all ?

A positive answer to this question is suggested in particular by two different approaches in Germany: firstly, some work is being done on the continued influence of the pre-modern, common jurisprudential tradition on the various modern national legal systems; secondly, research is beginning to focus on the new ways in which legal knowledge and experience were exchanged in the nineteenth century. It has become apparent that the age of the nation State, contrary to first impressions, was a period in which national legal systems in Europe drew on each other to a large extent and in which there were complex transfers of legal knowledge between them[19]. These new connections arose largely from the fact that different European countries faced comparable problems - particularly the demands of industrialisation.

(9) Under these new conditions the place of the older common jurisprudence was largely taken by comparative law, which covered wide areas of the legal systems and at the same time became a special discipline within legal science. Several recent studies on the nineteenth century have shown an intensive exchange of ideas and inspirations between countries like France, Germany and Italy. These exchanges were inflicted by the success of the French Civil Code and the outspread of the German '*Historische Rechtsschule*' (historical law school)[20].

I may add: the nineteenth and early twentieth century are for one further reason eminently important to research work dealing with European legal history: In this era of national law, the exchange of ideas and legal terms intensified, also with regard to Eastern Europe and England. But as I have mentioned, we cannot pursue this topic at this point.

Let us rather summarise the aims of European legal history.

(10) The legal historian working in the field of European legal history sees himself confronted with several challenges. One is to

---

19 Cf. Reiner Schulze, '*Vom* Ius Commune *bis zum Gemeinschaftsrecht - das Forschungsfeld der Europäischen Rechtsgeschichte*', in: Reiner Schulze (ed.), *Europäische Rechts- und Verfassungsgeschichte*, (Berlin 1991), p. 18 *et seq*., esp. at 20; Schulze, '*Gemeineuropäisches Privatrecht und Rechtsvergleichung*', in: Peter-Christian Müller-Graff (ed.), *Gemeinsames Privatrecht in der Europäischen Gemeinschaft*, (Baden-Baden 1993), p. 83; Müller-Graff, '*Allgemeine Rechtsgrundsätze und europäisches Privatrecht*', note 4 *supra*, p. 466 *et seq*.

20 Cf. Reiner Schulze, 'European Legal History - A New Field of Research in Germany', (1992) 12 *Journal of Legal History*, p. 276 *et seq*.

participate in the discussion of contemporary legal tasks. These include many matters from the common legal principles in the jurisdiction of the European Court of Justice to academic discussion of principles of European private law. Different methods of legal historical work - the more historical-descriptive and the more juridical-constructive - are equally legitimate. None can claim exclusivity with regard to the development of the discipline.

In these annotations, I have used the term 'European private law' several times. What does it mean and how will it develop ?

III LEGAL HISTORY, COMPARATIVE LAW AND JURISPRUDENCE

(11) With regard to European private law, our time seems to be more destined for jurisprudence than for legislation. Doubtlessly there will be further legislation by the EC for private law (for example on consumer law); but a completely different question is, whether a broadly laid out codification of private law, a civil law code for the EC, is possible and desirable under the current circumstances. It is true that the European parliament petitioned for the preparation of a private law code for the Community[21]. Hence, the pattern of a private law codification was to be transferred from the national to the European level. But it seems highly doubtful whether it is appropriate for the European private law of our time to proceed in a way which was once helpful for the creation of national private laws in many European countries[22].

There are not only the unanswered questions of authority for the Community but also those of political acceptance. The main problem seems to be the lack of scientific preparation and education of lawyers. Without a common scientific basis, without a combination of doctrine and legal education, the same law would be applied very differently in each country as a result of the respective legal traditions. The uniformly valid norms (if they could be made at all) would consequently only create the illusion of legal unity. So far, the *skepsis*, which Friederich Carl von Savigny expressed in Germany at the beginning of the last century regarding the vocation of his time for legislation, is also suitable for the entirely different circumstances of today's Europe.

---

21 Cf. Winfried Tilmann, *'Zweiter Kodifikationsbeschluß des Europäischen Parlaments'*, (1995) *ZEuP*, p. 534.

22 Cf. Reiner Schulze, *'Allgemeine Rechtsgrundsätze und europäisches Privatrecht'*, note 4 *supra*, p. 470 *et seq*.

(12) The comparison with the nineteenth century would be flogged to death, though, if one were to say that legal history has the same role for European private law today which it had for the common private law in Germany then. Unlike the situation in the nineteenth century, today the historical texts and authorities of Roman law cannot be considered the prominent foundation of the education of jurists in Europe any more. At the beginning of the nineteenth century, every jurist in Germany and in most other continental European countries was educated in Roman law. Furthermore the way of thinking in Germany was dominated by historicism and neohumanism. In contrast to that, the intellectual situation is completely different today: Most jurists in Europe have not even learned Latin, let alone studied Roman law. The path of the historical law school cannot be travelled again. Our time has to find its own way to a science of European private law.

(13) On this way it will be important to compare the national private laws of today, and thereby to use the methods of legal comparative work. Adequate for this is a comparative law which does not limit itself to the confrontation of codified rules. Moreover, it should include the solution of problems in juridical practice and ask whether common principles and institutions exist[23] . The elaboration of common principles of European contract law by an international commission headed by the Danish jurist Ole Lando[24] or the corresponding work on 'Principles of International Commercial Contracts' by 'Unidroit'[25] point in this direction. Recently, one of the leading German researchers of comparative law, Hein Kötz, has suggested 'an elaboration of a body of common principles of the law of obligations which can count on an international consent - at least in Europe'[26]. On this basis the making of 'textbooks on common European private law' is also being discussed. Thus a new perspective for the education of jurists could be

23 Cf. Hein Kötz, *'Neue Aufgaben der Rechtsvergleichung'*, (1982) 104 *Juristische Blätter*, p. 357 *et seq.*; Kötz, *'Gemeineuropäisches Zivilrecht'*, note 3 *supra*, p. 481 *et seq.*; Konrad Zweigert, *'Grundsatzfragen der Europäischen Rechtsvergleichung, ihre Schöpfung und Sicherung'*, in: Ernst von Caemmerer/Arthur Nikisch/Konrad Zweigert (ed.), *Vom deutschen zum europäischen Recht. Festschrift für Hans Dölle, Vol. 2*, (Tübingen 1963), p. 411; Axel Flessner, *'Rechtsvereinheitlichung durch Rechtswissenschaft und Juristenausbildung'*, (1992) 56 *RabelsZ*, p. 259 *et seq.*; Bernhard Großfeld/Karen Bilda, *'Europäische Rechtsangleichung'*, (1992) *Zeitschrift für Rechtsvergleichung* (*ZfRV*), p. 426 *et seq.*

24 Cf. Lando/Beale (ed.), note 3 *supra*.

25 Published Rome, 1994.

26 Hein Kötz, *Gemeineuropäisches Zivilrecht*, note 3 *supra*, p. 483 and p. 498.

established[27]: The common principles would be connecting starting points for the work of jurists in each country; the rulings of the national codifications and the respective case law would present themselves only as variations or as national peculiarities in contrast to these common starting points.

(14) Therefore legal history takes only the second rank in the process of building European private law; the first has to be taken by comparative law. What is nowadays incorporated in the body of common principles in the national laws, due to historical similarities, can be primarily established by comparing these national laws. We can only speak of a '*ius commune*, of a common European law, of our time' as far as the comparison of contemporary national laws can show that there really are common principles and legal institutions 'behind' the norms and the case-law of different countries today.

(15) Even if legal history must hand over the leading role to comparative law, its younger 'twin sister'[28], it has not become at all worthless for the contemporary science of European private law: It can help in discovering and understanding contemporary mutualities. By relativising historically national private law, by unveiling historical connections and mutual influences and by indicating earlier common solutions, legal history can support the comparison of the laws of different countries. This contribution would be directed at tackling the difficult task of comprehending the common grounds behind the different national regulations.

My conclusions are: legal historical research should seek and uphold contact with the contemporary problems of European private law and thus remain a legal sience. It cannot play 'the leading role' concerning the scientific engagement with European private law, but it can support its development. The core of European private law should be understood as an historically developed part of European legal culture with common principles and institutions. Our time for the moment seems to be less called to comprehensive legislation, but rather to jurisprudence. Jurisprudence is a form of juridical engagement -

---

27 Cf. Bruno de Witte/Caroline Forder (ed.), *The common law of Europe and the future of legal education*, (Deventer 1992); Dietmar Willoweit/Bernhard Großfeld, '*Juristen für Europa*', (1990) *JZ*, p. 605; Axel Flessner, note 23 *supra*; Hein Kötz, '*Europäische Juristenausbildung*', (1992) *ZEuP*, p. 268.

28 Hein Kötz, '*Was erwartet die Rechtsvergleichung von der Rechtsgeschichte?*', (1992) *JZ*, p. 20.

unlike legislation, not bound by political institutions and borders. No one can foretell the future development; and patience definitely will be needed for emergence of a European private law. Probably there will not be an European private law code in the near future. Whether there will be Europe-orientated textbooks on private law instead; whether such works will allow the Italian, the German, and perhaps even the English law of the twenty-first century to appear partly as only particular regional legal orders in Europe; whether the 'harmonisation' of private law will be left solely to the institutions and politicians of the EC or whether it will become a concern of the lawyers of the Member States - all these questions are still unanswered. But every legal historian can participate in answering them - due to his historical discipline as well as as a lawyer of today.

3

EUROPEAN LEGAL HISTORY AND THE EUROPEANISATION OF LAW

William M. Gordon

I. INTRODUCTION

The invitation to give this paper referred to a number of overlapping questions raised by Europeanisation of law, a phenomenon which, however inelegantly described, is now familiar to most lawyers. It was explained that the general theme of the colloquium was to be the Europeanisation of law and the legal curriculum and it was suggested that I might consider such questions as the Europeanisation of legal history itself, the use of legal history in bridging the gap between the common law and the civil law and the importance of legal history as a help to the understanding of legal forms and concepts coming to the United Kingdom from Europe. Clearly those parts of the United Kingdom which use the common law were particularly in view. Equally clearly it was no coincidence that the invitation was extended to one of the authors of a book somewhat ambitiously titled *European Legal History.*[1] It is worth noting by way of introduction that the history of how the second edition of that book came into being is something of an object lesson in the problems and opportunities which our closer ties with continental Europe create and which it is the object of this colloquium to examine. While it was not in publishing terms a best-seller the first edition, produced by Professional Books, did sell out within what seemed to the authors a reasonable period. What persuaded

---

1 O. F. Robinson, T. D. Fergus and W. M. Gordon, *European Legal History. Sources and Institutions*, 2nd edn (London, Dublin, Edinburgh, 1994). The first edition in 1985 had the more modest title *An Introduction to European Legal History*.

the successors of the original publishers to produce a second edition was not the potential student market, of which legal history is a relatively small part, but the potential market among those interested in European law who might wish to understand something of the history of those jurisdictions with which they were being brought into closer contact. European law seems to be a selling point where legal history is not, in that the modern lawyer must know about European law but the need for legal history is less urgent. Only so much can be done, which is a problem, and the present law has priority. But are students not the very persons who should be encouraged to regard the study of European legal history as a normal part of their education as lawyers who, if they do enter practice, will be practising in a part of the new Europe? There would then be the opportunity of a market to be made. Or should one take heart from the assumption that those who are using European law will be sufficiently interested to look into the history of European law and will not confine their attention to the latest regulations and directives? Do either students or practitioners have time to take a rounded view of the impact of Europe on the law and consider what history has to tell us of the development of the law?

II. EUROPEANISATION OF LAW

Europeanisation of law has been referred to above as a familiar concept and so it is in a general sense but 'Europeanisation' does have different connotations. Sometimes it is seen as a fact - much law now comes to us from Europe, directly or indirectly, through the organs of the European Union and the Council of Europe. European law can then be seen as meaning just what comes to us in various forms from Brussels, Luxembourg and Strasbourg, and particularly from the former two in increasing quantity. In a narrower sense European law can be seen as the law created on the basis of the treaties founding the European Union and so mainly by regulation, directive and the work of the European Court of Justice. But Europeanisation could also mean a policy, or rather a vision, in which more and more of the law is common throughout Europe. To achieve this the law might be made by a common legislature, whether federal or not, with a competence potentially covering the whole field of law, and the law being interpreted by a common system of courts - no doubt at present a logical extreme rather than a realistic policy or even realistic vision, if visions can be realistic. It is certainly not an immediate prospect. Europeanisation of law could also mean a union of legal method, legal science and legal education, a lawyers' union. This might be described as a new *ius commune* and is certainly on the agenda for some.[2]

These different conceptions of Europeanisation involve different conceptions or visions (or even nightmares) of the future shape of Europe. Will it become a unitary State or a federal union or a looser union? There are, indeed, different views on whether the countries in the European Union are already part of one Europe or just a grouping of separate States. In other words, Europeanisation of law involves political questions on the future structure and government of Europe. This is particularly clear with regard to the first two conceptions which concern the way in which law is most clearly 'made' by the act of a legislature and by interpretation of the relevant legislative acts. But questions of legal method, legal science and education involve political questions also, both the politics of the legal professions in the present States of the European Union and deeper questions of how the law is made and interpreted and operates and how lawyers should be educated so that they can handle legal problems most effectively in the best interests of the society in which they practise. Can there be - now or in the future - a truly European lawyer who is completely at home throughout a European Union which at present is inhabited by lawyers of different species?

The relevance of these different ideas of Europeanisation to European legal history is that European legal history has different relationships to these different ideas and a European legal history as opposed to national legal histories might well have a different impact depending on what sort of Europeanisation is in issue. The different ideas about Europeanisation of law might indeed call for different versions of European legal history because there is room for discussion what 'European legal history' is. Whether the issue is an urgent one or not will in turn depend on the sense in which Europeanisation is understood. Europeanisation in the first sense is an actual problem, issue or opportunity and what effect it has or should have demands immediate attention. The same could be said of the third sense because if the ideal of a European lawyer can be achieved it should be possible to achieve it without awaiting political developments which may never come or may come in unexpected ways. It is quite clear, for example, that a unitary State will be a long time in coming and the United Kingdom, if still united, will not be part of it if Eurosceptics have their

---

2 Witness the foundation of new journals such as *European Review of Private Law* or *Zeitschrift für Europäisches Privatrecht*.

way. That does not prevent lawyers from understanding better their different traditions and drawing on the strengths of all.

III. EUROPEAN LEGAL HISTORY

If European legal history is thought to have some possible part to play in Europeanisation of law it may be as well before going further to consider what the term 'European legal history' does or may mean. It is not a subject so well established that it has a recognised content and there are questions both of what can and what should be covered which impinge on the wider question of Europeanisation in its various senses.

Simplistically European legal history might be defined as the history of law in Europe. But even without going into the vexed question of what amounts to 'law' for this purpose it is clear that it is a tall order to attempt to deal with the history of all undoubted manifestations of law within Europe or with the history of all the legal systems found in the various States which compose Europe, including the law of jurisdictions within States, such as Scots law within the United Kingdom. Put bluntly, it is impossible within normal constraints of time and space where teaching or writing is concerned. Is it then possible to pick out some common features which can count as European or does European legal history necessarily consist of a series of local or national histories of law? Or is there perhaps a European phase of legal history which is superseded when local or national histories begin which may be at different times for different systems? Whatever the answer to these questions may be thought to be, it affects the relevance of European legal history to the Europeanisation of law in any sense. For example, on a view that European legal history ceases to be meaningful or even possible after about the thirteenth century when local or national systems of law begin to be more clearly discernible, the study of European legal history is not going to make much *immediate* impact on understanding the law at the present day, and especially the law emanating from Brussels, whatever value the study may have in educational terms. I stress the 'immediate'; I do not doubt the value of such study nor the possibility that it has a relevance but I would have to agree that the study of French public law would be of more immediate value.

For myself, while I admit the practical impossibility of covering the whole history of law within Europe, I take a less pessimistic view of the possibility of a European legal history on a selective basis. There do appear to be influences, events and movements which have had an effect on the local or national systems of law which we accept as forming the existing pattern of legal systems within Europe. Some of them at least can be and should be dealt with in anything described as European legal history. Canon law, the civil law based on the *Corpus iuris civilis,*[3] rational natural law are obvious examples. All have affected pretty well all the systems of western Europe, and eastern Europe, in a greater or lesser degree and all of them could claim to be European systems of law.

It does become increasingly difficult to follow out the European theme as one progresses in time from, say, the thirteenth to the nineteenth century as national elements predominate over the European elements and some systems close their boundaries by codification, at least in part. It becomes less easy to identify the common themes which do seem still to be there but exerting a more general influence, such as economic factors in the industrial revolution and political factors in the move to greater democracy. The difficulty is compounded by the fact that the quantity of material grows and it is all the more tempting to pursue national or local history and leave the possible European themes out of account. There is certainly a danger of superficiality if one tries to keep up a European coverage by the nineteenth century. Again, if one concentrates on broad influences does one learn enough of the detail to be helpful? It is one thing to see the common background to the move towards greater democracy but does that help in understanding the particular response in different legal systems? There is a recognition of this difficulty in that actual discussions or accounts of European legal history do tend to focus on a particular country even if they are European in outlook.[4] This seems inevitable at this stage as they are, and have to be, written primarily for a readership from one country or jurisdiction.

---

3 In this context 'civil law' is preferable to 'Roman law' because the civil law as developed on the basis of the *Corpus iuris* is not necessarily the same as what a modern Romanist would understand the Roman law to have been, and in particular is not the same as the pre-Justinianic law on which modern Romanists tend to concentrate. For example, texts might be generalised by civilian lawyers even beyond the generalisations already found in the *Corpus iuris* (such as the text which says that the emperor is not bound by the laws, D. 1,3,31) or applied in a different context where the idea contained in them was seen as providing a possible solution to a problem.

4 An example would H. Hattenhauer, *Europäische Rechtsgeschichte* (Heidelberg, 1992) which deals with European legal history from a German standpoint. This might be regarded as step forward from treatments of German legal history against a European background such as G. Wesenberg, *Neuere deutsche Privatrechtsgeschichte*, 4th edn by G. Wesener (Wien, Köln, Graz, 1985). See also R. Schulze, 'European legal history - a new field of research in Germany', (1992) 13 *J. Leg. Hist.* 270.

But assuming that there are European themes which can be pursued in a meaningful and scholarly way how do they help in dealing with the various kinds of Europeanisation which have been envisaged? If one looks only to the European law which is created by the organs of the European Union it is doubtful how far European legal history in the sense of study of the development of law in Europe is directly helpful. It is probably not essential anyway because one may ask how far this law is 'European' in content, so that a general knowledge of European legal history is helpful in coping with it, and how far it comes from the laws of individual countries, including countries in the English common law tradition. For example, in the case of competition law, are we dealing with 'European' concepts or with American ones? How much traditional learning is there in the employment law of modern times or in social security provisions? The ECJ tries to form its own legal concepts. European legal history in the sense of a history of the Common Market and the European Union might be more apposite in this context than a broader view, given also constraints of time.

If one conceives of Europeanisation as meaning the formation of some kind of supranational State or super-State then European legal history in the sense of study of the development of law in Europe or the pursuit of European themes in legal history is perhaps more helpful at the present stage because it seems necessary to be able to say that the various legal systems in the European Union as it exists or may become are sufficiently compatible to come together or to live with one another, say, in a federal structure. One can argue from the existence of a sufficient common heritage, if that can be established, to the possibility of a European State as a viable aim, rather as some of those favouring union of Scotland and England in the early seventeenth century argued that their legal systems had common roots.[5] The issue is not one of finding common rules but enough common ground to see a future State of some kind as possible. Being unable or choosing not to pursue too much detail is then not such a serious problem as if one is hoping for help in finding or constructing specific rules.

On the third conception of Europeanisation as involving a European legal science, European legal history can offer some encouragement in that it is possible to look back to a past in which there was a considerable sharing of legal thought, even between civil law and

---

5 B. P. Levack, 'The proposed union of English and Scots law in the seventeenth century', 1975 *Jurid. Rev.* 97, esp. at p. 105.

common law systems.[6] This might be better expressed as a sharing between civil law systems and the English common law which was beginning to be exported to the former British Empire about the time when national or local systems were growing away from their roots in the *ius commune*.[7] There is no doubt that the idea of a common European legal science is attractive and such a legal science did exist at least until the seventeenth century and even into the eighteenth century. When one takes the Pandectists into account, there was much common ground still in the nineteenth century. But there is one great difference from the present day. The lawyers of the *ius commune* shared a common language, Latin, and a common style of legal education founded on texts which were often themselves in Latin. That community was breaking down in the eighteenth century and it is much less easy to have common ground without such a common medium of expression shared by the great majority of lawyers. National legal systems make it all the more difficult to think in common terms. A common European legal science may come but do we not need to limit the choice of languages as happens in the Council of Europe and in practice in the ECJ? It would seem essential that the greater European Union should bite the bullet on the language issue in that it does not make sense to try to work with all languages, unless the intention is to provide employment for translators and improve the unemployment figures.

So far as European legal history is concerned there is also a problem in that one needs so many languages to do justice to the whole of Europe, although one can get by with the major languages by choosing to concentrate on the legal systems which use them. And, of course, one needs Latin as well as modern languages and Greek to deal with the Humanists. It is difficult to turn the clock back to an ideal world of law in which lawyers could move across Europe and quickly be at home in any country in which they chose or were allowed to settle. Nor should it be forgotten that before the Reformation there was a European institution, the Roman Catholic Church, which facilitated the

---

6 R. Zimmermann, '*Der europäische Charakter des englischen Rechts*' (1993) 1 *Zeitschr. für Europäisches Privatrecht* 4, makes a strong, but in the writer's view not wholly persuasive, case for placing English law within the tradition of the *ius commune*. He does make it clear that English law owes more to the civilian tradition than has sometimes been thought.

7 K. Luig, 'The institutes of national law in the seventeenth and eighteenth centuries', 1972 *Jurid. Rev.* 193, a revised English version of his article, '*Institutionenlehrbücher des nationalen Rechts im 17. und 18. Jahrhundert*', (1970) 3 *Ius Commune* 64.

movement of lawyers using what was almost a European law, the canon law, which applied everywhere, albeit with variations.

Certainly European legal history can help to bring home to lawyers and others that there is a deal of common ground between the separate legal systems found within Europe and even between the civil law systems and the English common law. If they could talk together in the past could they not talk together again? The fact of Europeanisation in any form is one very good reason for looking in legal history outside the borders of the jurisdiction with which it is primarily dealing and trying to give the broader perspective which is needed if there is to be rapprochement within Europe. Here we enter the field of politics. Do people want rapprochement? At a recent conference in Aberdeen celebrating the European legal tradition it was noted that ideas of Europeanisation of civil procedure based on styles of procedure which were at one time familiar to Scots lawyers, whose system owed a good deal to Romano-canonical procedure, were being viewed with suspicion as continental innovations. There is much need for lawyers of every jurisdiction to become aware of what is truly peculiar to their own system and what reflects a common heritage of which they may not have been made fully aware in the course of their education. In that sense European legal history could have a vital part to play.

IV. EUROPEANISATION AND THE LEGAL CURRICULUM

When it comes to consideration of the effect of Europeanisation on the legal curriculum and the place of European legal history in that context the first question is how far legal history is necessary at all as a separate subject. Legal history does not often figure as a separate compulsory subject in curricula, at least in the United Kingdom. It may, of course, be taught at an elementary level as part of introductory courses. Insisting on European legal history as a separate subject would add to the existing problem of fitting in European law. This seems generally to claim a place as a necessary subject if not for graduation then for entry to the legal profession. Any necessary subject creates problems of time within the limited period available and while it was rightly pointed out in discussion that one need not think of new knowledge in terms of new subjects in the curriculum there is still a problem of presenting new knowledge on top of the increasing range of knowledge which ought to be brought to the attention of law students at the present time.

And so, is European legal history now to claim a separate place alongside any local or national legal history that is already taught? Or should the European dimension be injected into legal history courses, separate or not, in order to broaden students' perspectives? The debate seems to me rather like the debate on European law: is it simply part of the system to be taught as such or does it deserve a special place? In my view it certainly ought at least to be injected into the curriculum in some way in order to make students realise that what has happened in country X has not necessarily only happened there but may well be a reflection of developments elsewhere. But that in itself puts pressure on the curriculum, desirable as it may be to thus broaden students' horizons - or it puts pressure on the students to master a greater body of knowledge. That, however, may well be an argument for Europeanisation of the curriculum by making it longer - as it commonly is in Europe - so that all that it is desirable to present to students can be presented better, with more time for absorption of what they should know.

The difficulty of including European legal history in the curriculum in any form is compounded by other pressures coming from membership of the European Union, such as the desire to include languages in the legal curriculum and the desire to expose students to a knowledge of other particular systems in the Union, such as French or German law. At the present stage of Europeanisation there is no doubt of the potential value of knowing other systems either for the purpose of communicating with lawyers from that system in the course of practice here or for the purpose of establishing oneself elsewhere as permitted by European legislation. The benefit of such study is not in question but it does also impinge on study of one part of the European heritage which could offer an area of common ground, namely, Roman law. This is losing ground as a subject studied by the generality of students, as it once was in some universities, although Roman law is preeminently a European subject and can help to exercise or acquire linguistic skills because of the great variety of languages in which contributions to scholarship have been made. And Roman law, in the sense of the civil law, is undoubtedly part of European legal history and a necessary part for the full understanding of how the legal systems of Europe, including the English common law, have developed.

It has been suggested that there ought to be a European law school.[8] It can be said that there is no urgent need for one as opposed to national or local law schools merely because of the European Union, as knowledge of the legal history even of the United Kingdom would indicate. The union of Scotland and England, much closer than anything immediately envisaged for the European Union, whatever may

---

8 R. Goode, 'The European law school', (1993) 13 *Legal Studies* 1.

ultimately emerge, did not lead to the creation of British law schools as opposed to law schools in Britain. National or local law schools can cope relatively easily with the European dimension of law at the undergraduate level. European law schools at the postgraduate level have more to be said for them at this stage. But again, something depends on one's vision for Europe and of the functions of law schools and if European law schools should develop an element of history would be highly desirable. What form that should take might depend on the precise function of the schools. But should not all law schools simply be European in outlook if one is to look back to what used to obtain within legal education as a guide to the future?

V. CONCLUSION

Whether any conclusion to these reflections can be positive or not depends on one's expectations of Europe and one's views on the importance of legal history in general, and European legal history in particular. There is no easy answer to what European legal history can contribute towards Europeanisation or how it can do so because much depends on what is regarded as European legal history and what form of Europeanisation is in mind. At a very general level lawyers and others should have some notion of the development of law within Europe, particularly at the present time, but from an educational point of view this would hold even if the European Union were to dissolve tomorrow. Any legal historian can benefit from knowledge of what happened elsewhere at the time with which he or she is concerned and a sound and rounded perspective is scarcely possible without knowledge of what went on elsewhere. Ignorance of that is likely to distort the picture and may lead to claims that some phenomenon which is found elsewhere is peculiar and special to one system. Comparative legal history can illuminate the history of one's own legal system as comparative law can illuminate its rules and institutions.

At a more detailed level the help given depends on how European legal history is conceived and presented and what aspect of European law is in issue. Does history ever give an answer to questions of application of law, unless it is the legislative history of an enactment in a system in which the legislative history is a legitimate aid to interpretation?

European legal history in the sense of a study of the development of law in Europe shows that a common law across Europe is possible and that Europeanisation is not necessarily an impossible dream. It should, at the same time, also serve as a warning against undue optimism because the past trend of development has been away from Europeanisation and that trend has left a legacy of nationalism or particularism which is not easily overcome. Circumstances, too, are different. The common law of the past was founded on a common language as well as a common law. It was supported by common institutions, the Church and a recognised community of scholars operating in universities whose views carried weight whatever their origin. The question is how far such a community can be recreated and that is a major challenge for lawyers everywhere in Europe of the present day.

4

LANGUAGE LEARNING IN EUROPE

Professor Rudolf Carpanini

First of all, I should like to thank Professor Wylie and Professor Watkin for inviting me, a language and literature specialist, to address such a distinguished gathering of lawyers. This reflects not so much any personal merits of my own as the sensitivity with which the Cardiff School of Law has, for a long time now, regarded the problem of language learning within the context of legal studies. And this sensitivity itself, I feel, stems from the recognition that language is the single most important factor not only in the Europeanisation of law, but, indeed, in the process of Europeanisation as a whole.

To say that language precedes law is to state the obvious. The social, economic and cultural process implied in the term 'Europeanisation' depends on the interaction of people, on people communicating and understanding each other and, therefore, on the peoples of Europe having the will and the opportunity to learn languages other than their own. From this point of view, it seems to be particularly appropriate to be speaking about such matters here in Cardiff, since Wales, and South Wales in particular, provides what must be an early example of successful European integration. And I am sure that any study of the way in which the large Italian emigrant population integrated with the Welsh community in Cardiff and elsewhere in Wales in the course of the last hundred years or so would show how important a factor language was, besides revealing a surprising number of early Italian emigrants who learnt not only English but Welsh as well. The motivation was, of course, prevalently economic, which, on second thoughts, may not have been so very different from what it is today. Since then, however, the social, cultural and educational framework of language learning has changed completely, and I shall be concentrating on the contemporary problems of language training in Europe, or, at least, in four of the major European countries, paying special attention to what is done for language learners at an institutional level in Britain, France, Germany and Italy. In other words, I shall be looking at some of the opportunities that exist, or will exist in the not too distant future, for the foreign language learner in Europe, and for the EC scholarship-holder in particular.

If one looks first at Britain, one is immediately struck by the number, variety and flexibility of the English Language courses available to the foreign learner. A foreign student preparing to learn English outside of, or parallel to his or her university studies, can turn to any one of the ten different major Examination Boards (eleven, if one includes the American-based, but now international TOEFL course) and study English at any level, and in exactly the way that most corresponds to his/her individual needs. The importance of such an availability cannot be over-emphasised. For the foreign student, and for the Erasmus student in particular, obtaining a certificate or diploma of this kind has at least two benefits: it signifies the acquisition of an added valuable job qualification, and it provides a much-needed and objective assessment of progress made during the year in which the scholarship is held. It is very satisfying to know that more and more Italian Erasmus students visiting Britain study for a Cambridge First Certificate, or even attempt the Cambridge Proficiency Examination, while also sitting examinations for four or five different courses at their host university. This is a trend that deserves every encouragement and, where the opportunity exists, British Erasmus students too, should be made aware of the advantages of studying for a certificate in the language of their host country, even if this takes them outside the confines of the university.

A long pedagogical tradition has clearly made Britain a leader in the organisation (and, of course, commercialisation) of EFL, in the theoretical and practical aspects of language teaching and applied linguistics, and in the training of effective language teachers. It has been largely responsible for the almost universal acceptance of the communicative method in schools and universities throughout the world, and this in spite of considerable resistance on the part of both teachers and students, who often remain tied to the more traditional grammar-based methods adopted in their home countries. The learner of English as a second language will find an abundance of course-books, dictionaries, grammars and texts for special skills and special purposes. The problem for the student is not so much where or how to find the suitable text, but which text, course or methodology to choose out of an embarrassment of riches. The foreign learner of English is pedagogically privileged. What is more, the foreign student can finalise his/her studies in accordance with individual needs within a reliable system of graded certification.

Though France and Germany may not offer as great a number of differentiated language courses as Britain does, both countries have made significant contributions to language policy and planning at an institutional level. In Germany, the *Volkshochschulen* (VHS) were established by the German Federal Republic with the intention of providing courses in languages and other subjects for adults, within the context of a programme for continuous education. The *Deutscher Volkshochschulen-Verband* or German Federation of Popular Universities, has made, and continues to make a considerable contribution to European plurilinguism by providing all strata of the population, of whatever social extraction or degree of education, with the opportunity to study and, in particular, to study foreign languages. The *Volkshochschulen* are non-profit making bodies, though they are sometimes registered companies, supported financially by the State and the regional *Länder*, as well as by a small enrolment fee paid by the student. There are some 4,000 of them located in almost every important German city or town, and they are obliged by the laws of the *Länder* to provide a specific number of teaching hours per inhabitant annually. They are now part too, of the International Certificate Conference, which includes members from all over Europe (including Britain), so that the certificates they now release reflect a larger European syllabus common to the partner members of the ICC.

From a didactic point of view, what distinguishes the *Volkshochschulen* is the particular attention given to the receiver of language instruction, who is analysed according to age, study objectives, linguistic skills, and to the future he/she intends to make of the language learned. The didactic objectives are then fixed in relation to the development of the four basic skills: listening/speaking, reading/writing. No reference is made, however, to integrated skills. 80% of the programme is set out in published lists, which provide the students with a clear idea of what they are expected to do before they obtain the certificate. These are lists of communicative acts or phrases, of subjects, of written and oral tests, of words chosen not for the frequency with which they are used but for their usefulness in verbalising communicative intentions and day-to-day situations, and of basic grammatical structures, again chosen from among those most used in real-life situations. The teachers at the *Volkshochschulen* are urged to bear in mind, above all, the linguistic needs of the students and to speak the foreign language at a natural speed at all times. At the end of the course, there is a separate examination for each of the four skills, and these are assessed by means of a points system that leaves little room for error or subjective evaluation.

Just as the *Volkshochschulen* have done in Germany, so the French Ministry of Education has formulated precise instructions for the teaching of foreign languages in French secondary modern schools. It urges the adoption of a communicative method aimed at achieving three basic objectives, which are communicative, cultural and linguistic. The teacher is encouraged to practise a kind of '*pédagogie differenciée*', or personalised didactic approach for each student, with the purpose of attaining the following objectives:

- comprehension of written and spoken language;
- knowledge of the most significant aspects of the culture and contemporary life of the country whose language is being studied;
- knowledge of the ordinary everyday use of the language;
- a capacity for self-correction and self-assessment;
- a knowledge of the formal aspects of the language, that is, of those that appear in written texts and which enable one to deduce grammatical rules.

Clear instructions are provided as to the didactic methodology that should be adopted, the didactic aids to be employed (particular reference being made to audiovisual equipment and computers), the examinations to be set, the objectives to be established, to the use of films and other visual material suitable for the illustration of the life of the country whose language is being studied, and to the teaching of culture by means of a comparative method. For the first elementary level a list of a minimum number of words to be learnt is set, some of them exemplified by accompanying phrases, and a short list of grammatical structures with instructions indicating the exercises best suited to learn them is also provided. For the three successive levels even more precise directives are set out regarding the use of texts and documents, the contents of the lessons on culture, the reading of entire works in the target language, readings on history, literature, economics, science and art, films in their original language, types of written and oral exercises, the use of personal computers, and the behaviour and didactic activity of the teacher. All this abundance of precise instruction is clearly aimed, first and foremost, at the teachers themselves, whereas that of the *Volkshochschulen* is aimed at both teachers and students studying for a certificate.

As far as Italy is concerned, on the other hand, there is as yet no widely shared idea as to how the teaching of Italian as a second language should be planned and graded from an elementary to the 'threshold' level indicated by the Council of Europe, and then on through the acquisition of study skills to Italian for special purposes. There are few Italian language texts that deal with these different phases of learning, just as there are very few effective Italian language course books. And though the number of Italian grammar books suitable for class-room study has greatly increased of late, their didactic effectiveness is often limited by their authors' lack of pedagogical experience in the field of language learning, and by an excessively metagrammatical emphasis. Thus, the learning and teaching of Italian as a second language awaits not only the formulation of clear targets, but also the elaboration and publication of valid instruments of study.

More important still is the lack of language policy and detailed language planning in both the public and private sectors of Italian education. Unlike the French Ministry of Education, the Italian has never specified the contents and objectives of the two levels of foreign language learning officially recognised in the secondary modern schools; elementary and advanced. It has only provided general indications as to what should be known at the end of each course, so that teachers are left to improvise on a personal, intuitive basis.

Nevertheless, there are signs of a change of attitude to the problems of foreign language teaching in Italy, and they are to be found mainly in the universities, and in those of Perugia, Siena, Rome and Pavia in particular. Perhaps the best known of these, to foreign language students at least, is the *Università Italiana per Stranieri* in Perugia, which, in 1987, inaugurated two kinds of diploma: an Italian Language diploma, and another in Italian language and culture. These correspond to two different levels, though both are fairly advanced. The University of Perugia has since become a member of the Association of Language Testers in Europe, commonly known as ALTE, which began its life as a European Economic Interest Grouping, that is, as one of the first legal international organisations in Europe. The association operates under the aegis of the Council of Europe, and its members include the Generalitat of Catalogna, the University of Cambridge Local Examination Syndicate, the Goethe Institute, the Alliance Francaise, the

University of Lisbon, the University of Salamanca, the Cervantes Institute, and the Dutch foreign-language centre, CITO. The aim of the group is to draw up a project capable of leading to a common form of certification for all the languages of the EEC. ALTE has established five distinct levels of language learning, and each member of the group has pledged itself to setting examinations for all five levels, which have been denominated as follows:

1. Waystage
2. Threshold
3. Independent User
4. Competent User
5. Good User

As a result of this experience of European co-operation, the University of Perugia now confers an Italian Language diploma at five different levels. What is more, two recent publications of the University set out in detail the specific objectives of each of the five levels, the contents of the examination tests that lead to the certificate, and the way in which these are assessed. Perugia has been something of a pioneer not only in the publication of invaluable study guides of this kind, but also in the publication of effective Italian language course books. In all this, while the dominant influence has clearly been British, one can also find traces of the *Volkshochschulen* experience and of the French ministerial directives.

While the Department of Modern Languages at the University of Rome '*La Sapienza*' is also studying a plan for its own form of certification, the University for Foreigners of Siena introduced its ministerially approved Certificate of Italian as a Foreign Language (CILS) in 1993, when its first examinations were held in Siena and in Italian Cultural Institutes throughout the world. On 19 December 1994, an agreement was signed between the universities of Siena and Pavia with the purpose of forming a joint study group between the two universities in order to elaborate a Certificate of Italian as a Foreign Language for University Students (CILSSU). The aims and contents of this certificate are already present in an experimental form in the Italian language courses Pavia provides for Erasmus students, and foreign students should be able to sit the examinations for this certificate in the fairly immediate future. The realisation of such a project is of considerable importance for the Erasmus student studying Italian as a foreign language, since it enables him/her to sit an examination for a nationally recognised certificate in Italian in northern Italy, instead of having to travel to Siena, Perugia, or Rome.

The purpose of this brief interlude in the discussion of the Europeanisation of law has been to draw attention to what must necessarily be prior to legal, or comparative legal studies in Europe: the need for European lawyers, law students and ordinary citizens to acquire skills in European languages other than their own. Given the limited time at my disposal and the vastness of the subject, I have chosen to look at some of the attitudes and traditions behind language training at an institutional level in four major European countries. I have deliberately avoided any detailed comparison of the curricula of the different language programmes mentioned, as this would have entailed an excessively lengthy, specialist treatment of the subject. Instead, I have preferred to approach my subject in such a way as to be able to stress what is common to the European experience of language training. This may be summarised as follows:

1. The prevalence of a communicative approach to the teaching of foreign languages.

2. The need for graded language acquisition and, therefore, for carefully differentiated language courses.

3. The desirability of language courses that provide for an integration of the four basic skills.

4. The study of a foreign language should be paralleled by that of the principal political, social, economic and cultural institutions of the country where that language is spoken.

5. The programming of foreign language study should set itself clearly defined objectives, both for teachers and students.

6. Finally, every encouragement should be given to the creation and publicisation of national systems of language certification - wherever these do not exist - based on European criteria for foreign language learning and assessment.

These didactic principles are the fruit of a multi-lingual and multi-national experience and, as such, constitute a valuable point of departure for all those responsible for the future planning and programming of foreign language studies in the European Community.

5

THE EUROPEANISATION OF CONSTITUTIONAL LAW

John Bell

I INTRODUCTION: HOW FAR IS THERE EUROPEANISATION OF CONSTITUTIONAL LAW?

In many ways the title I have been given is a fraud. One can legitimately ask whether there is a serious 'European' dimension to constitutional matters. On the one hand, many constitutional issues are common across liberal democracies throughout the world. On the other hand, constitutional arrangements are often rather specific to national traditions. As a result, one might think that Europeanisation is limited in this area to the constitutional implications for Member States of their participation in a supra-national, yet hierarchically superior, legal order. But my contention will be that Europeanisation goes further in that examples from the constitutional systems of other EU and Council of Europe States will increasingly provide our point of reference in constitutional matters, and that the European context is the one in which we will find appropriate principles of good government. Despite the large literature on the subject, my concern is not with whether we have or should develop a constitution for the European Union. Undoubtedly, a more structured constitution for the EU would provide a focus for reconsidering national constitutions, particularly if it were to stipulate the limits of the competences of Member States. I would not wish to deny that the EU structures create a common framework for the adjustment of national constitutional arrangements. But my focus in this article is simply to reflect on the European dimension as a part of a focus for comparative reflection on national constitutions, an exercise in comparative law. Although much of my discussion focuses on the importance of influence from our Western European neighbours, I would not equate 'Europeanisation' with what Van Gerven has described as 'communitarisation', a form of harmonisation (if not homogenisation) of the citizen's experience throughout the European Community.[1] I would see the concept of 'Europeanisation' as involving an integration of lessons and influences from across Europe into the national constitutional agenda, but this may not generate the same results across different countries in the way that Van Gerven's concepts would imply. A constitution is as much a dialogue with the past of a nation's constitutional history and institutions as an attempt to provide an ideal institutional solution. As a result, the national solutions will often be different as a result of different starting points, however close the similarity of values which inform them.[2]

II PRELIMINARIES

A. The nature of a constitution

I have argued elsewhere[3] that a constitution should be seen in part as 'what we do', a set of practices, rather than just a document. Conventions and practices form part of a constitutional order, so that the line between constitutional law and constitutional morality is, as Geoffrey Marshall suggests, merely one of gradation.[4] But in addition, a constitution is not just descriptive but prescriptive. It thus sets out the values we proclaim (but by which we do not always abide). These values inform what we do. Ian Harden has written that a constitution contains both 'an official map of power' and 'a set of principles of legitimate government'.[5] Such values are concerned principally with the manner in which power is exercised and the procedures involved, not just with those fundamental human rights which are to be defended. As a result, any discussion of Europeanisation must go beyond the commonplace discussion of the influence of the European Convention on Human Rights on national laws. The values we proclaim embrace a whole range of principles of good government of which the protection

---

1 See W. Van Gerven, 'Bridging the Gap between Community and National Laws: Towards a Principle of Homogeneity in the Field of Legal remedies?'[1995] *CMLRev* 679 at p 698, note 62.

2 See R. David, *International Encylopaedia of Comparative Law*, vol. 2, ch 5, paras. 58 and 65-8.

3 *French Constitutional Law* (Oxford 1992), pp 2-4.

4 G. Marshall, *Constitutional Conventions* (Oxford 1984), pp 10-18.

5 'The Constitution and its Discontents' (1991) *British Journal of Political Science* 489.

of human rights is only a part. The 'principles of legitimate government' are concerned more frequently with issues about the allocation of power and the participation in decision-making.

There is a tendency to focus on the constitution as a document enacted once and for all, defining thereby constitutional action. I think there is more value in Dario Castiglione's description of the constitution as 'a form of structured polity' [6] in which there is not just an isolated constitutional moment, but a series of distinct moments over time. There are key points at which, for internal or external reasons, the constitutional arrangements of a country need to be reconsidered. It is the present state of events in Europe - the end of the Cold War and the need to redefine relations with Eastern Europe, the development of the European Union, the place of Europe within the global economy and political stage, as well as a certain loss of confidence in existing political structures which offer many countries a moment for redefining constitutional arrangements.

I am also concerned to give priority to constitutional law (*droit constitutionnel, Verfassungsrecht*) rather than constitutional litigation (*contentieux constitutionnel, Verfassungsgerichtsbarkeit*). Constitutional law covers the full range of procedures and practices in government, not just the matters which are the subject of constitutional litigation. There is much written on the growth of constitutional litigation across Europe in recent years.[7] But the increasing importance of such courts is only one feature of constitutional change. The key issues are less who should exercise control (courts, ombudsmen, select committees), but how the power of government should be exercised, and that is the province of constitutional law and constitutional morality.

B Europeanisation and globalisation

The issues of what are good values to guide and legitimate government and what are the best procedures to adopt are not of peculiarly western European concern. Constitutional and political theory knows no bounds. For instance, two of the most widely read contemporary theorists, Rawls

---

6 In R. Bellamy, V. Bufacchi, D. Castiglione, *Democracy and Constitutional Culture in the Union of Europe* (London 1995) at p 69.

7 A.R. Brewer-Carias, *Judicial Review in Comparative Law* (Cambridge 1989), M. Cappelletti, *Judicial Review in Comparative Perspective* (Oxford 1989), L. Favoreu & J.A. Jolowicz (edd.), *Le contrôle juridictionnel des lois* (Paris 1986).

and Habermas, are discussed in most liberal democracies.[8] To go back further in time, the sources of ideas for Paine and de Tocqueville were not limited to Europe. There has been a fruitful cross-fertilisation of ideas from many liberal democracies, even though it would be true to say that the United States has been the major source of ideas in recent times, not only for the English language reader, but in other countries. Such an intellectual globalisation of liberal political issues is reinforced by the ascendancy of liberal values at an international level through organisations such as the UN, the ILO, the World Bank and so on. European countries participate strongly in these institutions, but they also are subject to the criticism of such organisations.

The problems which confront contemporary constitutions are not peculiar to Europe. The increasing interconnection of international business, finance and social movements, together with rapid communications give rise to notions such as globalisation. By their very nature, such problems do not stop at Europe, nor do they have a markedly distinct impact on this small part of the globe. The question of how centralised and local decision-making should be structured is one faced by many in this world. Furthermore, the problems of democracy today such as corruption, the low esteem of politicians, and the ability of governments to achieve policies are just as much felt in Japan or the US, as in Western Europe. In a sense, the very universality of problems is what has enabled western European countries to offer advice to the fledgling democracies of central and Eastern Europe.

C Europeanisation and national traditions

Constitutional practice is very divergent from one country to another, much more so than commercial practice (especially in a Single Market). As two French lawyers wrote:

> 'at a period when French lawyers are forced to prepare very actively for European competition, there is one area in which national lawyers should occupy a privileged position, that is public law, which related to mechanisms which are altogether specific to French society.'[9]

---

8 J. Rawls, *A Theory of Justice* (Oxford 1972) and *Political Liberalism* (New York 1993) and J. Habermas, *Legitimation Crisis* (London 1975) are translated into a number of languages.

9 Jessau & Huglo, *AJDA* 1988, at 129.

On this view, public law is about the constitutional and political order of a country. Since national traditions and history have an important impact on how government in a particular country is organised and conducted, there are centrifugal forces which work against European uniformity in constitutional matters. In Steffan Zetterholm's collection on *National Cultures and European Integration*[10] the editor defines 'culture' as 'beliefs, norms, institutions and traditional ways of "doing things" in a society' and suggests that culture is among the major features which create a sense of community identity[11]. To the extent that political and constitutional activities and practices impinge on that common self-identity, then there is likely to be resistance to change and a divergent impact of common policies[12]. In the same collection, Stephen George points out the particularity of the British political culture and how British political parties have changed.[13] But the British culture here is distinct from that of France.[14] If there are political cultures, there are also significant differences between countries in terms of legal culture as Pierre Legrand has pointed out.[15]

After all, 7 of the 15 member States of the EU are monarchies, and 5 are federal States of some kind. French ways of organisation are different from those in Ireland in a way which is more pronounced than in commercial matters. In nation States, constitutional practices (and a number of other matters such as religion and language) may well form part of national identity and cannot be ignored in any account of 'Europeanisation'. The history of Germany leads to a federal system which worries about central power for different reasons from Spain, where language and culture are stronger elements in encouraging diversity. One could multiply examples, but the point is that there are no uniquely right answers in the design of constitutional systems, and the specific experiences, history, culture and traditions of particular countries may lead them to make choices of governmental structure

---

10 (Oxford & Providence, USA 1994)

11 *Ibid*, pp 2 and 71 respectively.

12 *Ibid*, p. 74.

13 S. George, *ibid*, ch 3.

14 V. Wright, *The Government and Politics of France* (3rd edn 1989), esp. ch. 13, J. Ardagh, *France Today* (London 1990), pp. 28-51.

15 For example in 'Legal Traditions in Western Europe: the Limits of Commonality' in R. Jagtenberg, E. Örücü and A.J. de Roo, *Transfrontier Mobility of Law* (The Hague, 1995), 63, esp. pp. 73-5. While I would quibble with the idea that there is a '*summa divisio*' between civil law and common law, at least as far as public law matters is concerned, Legrand forcefully makes the case for a lack of a common legal culture across Western Europe.

which mark them out from others. It is also true that constitutional debate often focuses on the past experience of that country, rather than on comparative analysis of other systems. Thus the current French constitution was really a mix of elements which had been drawn from France's previous 14 constitutions, rather than a conscious modeling on other systems. Similarly, the German Basic Law involves a dialogue with the past, both to build on features such as federalism and to correct problems in the areas of fundamental rights and presidential power.[16] It is in terms of its national tradition that the UK sees itself as constitutionally distinct from most other Member States in terms of its way of handling matters.

While it is true to say that there is such a thing as an economic culture of a country, its weight is less easy to demonstrate, and its effect as a barrier to integration or an incentive to diversity is probably less significant than the political culture.[17]

III HOW SHOULD WE UNDERSTAND 'EUROPEANISATION'?

The analysis thus far might suggest that there is little scope for Europeanisation. I think we have to see Europeanisation as involving a range of different things:

(1) *A common experience*: As I have said, I think most of the experiences of liberal democracies are either of a global dimension or are specifically national. The common experience between European States relates mainly to the problems encountered by liberal democracies in general, though there are some features such as membership of the Council of Europe, the EU, NATO, as well as experiences of co-existence over the centuries which provide a focus for most European countries in a special way. Some issues such as the provision and privatisation of public services and downsizing the civil service which have more common echoes within Europe than outside. To be more accurate, there are influences from across the world to which the

16 See D. Currie, *The Constitution of the Federal Republic of Germany* (Chicago 1994), 8-30.

17 See H. Plaschke, 'National Economic Cultures and Economic Integration', in S. Zetterholm, above note 10, ch 6.

response within Europe may more closely mirror our own experience than that elsewhere.[18]

(2) *Common principles*: For the most part, the common principles of legitimate government are not peculiarly European. There are, however, some values which are shared in a close way through membership of the EU and the European Convention on Human Rights and these provide some basis for a common and distinctive set of values. In the sphere of private law, Markesinis has suggested that there is a convergence occurring in the principles adopted by different European countries, in order to confront common problems.[19] Much of the commonness of the principles stems from long common legal and political traditions. These have a centrality for Europe, even if they have also been exported to other countries.

(3) *European institutions as the cause of constitutional problems*: For many countries, European Union has been the cause of constitutional problems. The Maastricht process involved a significant number of constitutional amendments to enable it to occur. Issues such as the relationship of national and European Parliaments, the role of regions, and the democratic control of EC decisions are constitutional questions which the fledgling structures of the EU have forced onto the agenda in all countries and which we need to solve together. For example, individual constitutions and practices have been amended to give national parliaments a greater say in the development of European Community legislation and decisions.

(4) *Europe as a locus of comparison*: My primary interest is, however, in another, more subtle aspect of the common experience of working together, notably in the European Union. It is the suggestion that the constitutional experience of our European partners will increasingly be a focus for comparative reflection and for inspiration in our national constitutional debates.

Traditionally, the UK has prided itself on having a long-standing constitutional system which had evolved without the revolutions, dictatorships, invasions and written constitutions of those in western Europe. It is in Teubner's term autopoeitic (self-generating). At

---

18 See W. Müller, 'Political Traditions and the Role of the State' (1994) 17 *Western European Politics* 32.

19 *The Gradual Convergence* (Oxford 1994), ch.1.

most, the experience of other Commonwealth countries such as Canada, New Zealand and Australia have offered insights into how that common tradition might evolve. If one looks at any constitutional textbook, then those countries will provide some examples in areas such as conventions of the constitution and principles of parliamentary supremacy, and even in handling a Bill of Rights.

All the same, critical reflection often is stimulated by comparison with other countries.[20] If the UK lawyer wanted a critical contrast to our way of doing things, then the USA offers the standard comparison to the present day. Paul Craig, Norman Lewis, Martin Loughlin[21] are among leading contemporary thinkers on constitutional law who have offered powerful analysis of the present British constitution using the US as a comparator. In part this is simply a matter of language. But also the philosophy behind the US constitution is shared with the UK in writers like Locke and Paine (or more recently Dworkin). There is also the fact that the US and the UK are part of the common law tradition and share ways of explaining constitutional rules and practices which are easily understood.

By contrast, European legal systems are less well know, are written in another language, with different assumptions and philosophies in many cases and with very clear constitutional histories which are distinctive. The features mentioned above provide reasons to think this commonplace *locus* of comparison will gradually shift.

IV WHY SHOULD EUROPE BECOME A LOCUS *OF COMPARISON FOR PRINCIPLES OF GOOD GOVERNMENT?*

There are powerful linguistic and legal cultural reasons for British constitutionalists not to look first to Europe for inspiration, that go beyond any simplistic distinction between 'civil law' and 'common law' countries. The United States and Canada in particular offer examples of a variety of constitutional debates and illustrations within the common law family and in English. These are often seen as sufficient 'external' viewpoints for examining our constitutional arrangements. There are also important differences in the character of constitutional arrangements which are long-standing. As Dicey pointed out in his

20 M. Loughlin, 'The Importance of Elsewhere' (1993) 4 *Public Law Review* 44.

21 See P. Craig, *Public Law and Democracy in the United Kingdom and the United States of America* (Oxford 1990); M. Loughlin, *Public Law and Political Theory* (Oxford 1992); I. Harden and N. Lewis, *The Noble Lie* (London 1986).

comparison with the Belgian constitution of 1830[22], European constitutions and constitutional freedoms are based on texts, the British on the common law. This is a difference not just a matter of formulation, but of the character of constitutional debate within the legal order as a whole. Stephen George has more recently drawn attention to the way in which we rely on political consensus and informality, the bedrock of conventions, while our European partners have more rule-based procedures and arrangements between parties.[23] There is almost a cult of informality and convention which contrasts with the more legalistic character of other constitutional orders within Europe. In brief, if we want contrasts and challenges, then we can find them within the common law family. If we want to refine our own system, its character has markedly distinct features which makes any other European constitution a difficult comparator.

Any analysis of 'Europeanisation' cannot suggest intelligently that these features are going to disappear quickly. At most one can suggest that other European comparisons will be supplemental. (Indeed, the Irish example of a more structured, common law constitution may provide more of a bridge than other European constitutions[24].) At the same time, wider European comparison is not unhelpful or unnecessary.

In the first place, like any analysis of legal families in private law, the classification of the British constitution as idiosyncratic or part of the common law family is too simplistic. As an established constitutional system in the 18th century, it provided inspiration for a range of reforms from jury trial in press cases in Sweden[25] to constitutional monarchy in Belgium. But it was also subjected to currents of ideas from the rest of Europe - from reform of suffrage in the 19th century to the Ombudsman in the 20th century. There have been a variety of mutual influences which have shaped European systems in particular over time. It has been rather the language and cultural specificity of other systems which has made them less of a point of reference in the past than they might usefully have been. Within a context of greater dialogue and comparison, a greater mutual understanding arises which serves as a foundation for comparison.

---

22 *An Introduction to the Study of the Law of the Constitution* (10th edn by ECS Wade, London 1959) pp. 196-9.

23 See note 10 *supra*.

24 See J.Temple Lang in D. Curtin and D. O'Keefe (edd.), *Constitutional Adjudication in European Community and National Law* (Dublin 1992) 237 at p. 244.

25 See T. Vallinder, 'The Swedish Jury System in Press Cases' (1987) 8 *Journal of Legal History* 190.

Similarity of experience: I would argue that there are certain features of British society which make its government much more similar to the rest of Europe than to the US. The length of historical traditions and institutions have given rise to cultural features which cannot be ignored in the same way as newer States. In addition, the small size of countries with distinct languages and cultures (and often religions) provide special features which have to be recognised as part of the framework for government in ways which are not true of the US, Canada and Australia. Such similarities of constitution-making are reinforced by the experience of having to make common European institutions work. That common experience on the task will focus attention on common problems and ways forward.

Similarity of citizen expectations: Globalisation has reinforced the similarity of expectations among the citizens of different countries. If expectations depend to some extent on prior experience, then the experience of working and living in a common community will reinforce common expectations. If media push our frame of reference towards the US, and our work for multinationals will provide other benchmarks. The EU will not necessarily be a primary context for expectations about how government will act, but it will provide an additional point of reference which will gradually have an influence on what we expect by way of government. To date, the idea of European citizenship is relatively formal, but it provides a basis for expectations not merely from EU institutions, but also from the Member States. The very mobility which the European Community has sought to facilitate over nearly 40 years generates both the desire for and the expectation of a degree of 'homogeneity'[26] within the basic experience of the individual moving from one country to another - expectations about how one will be treated by Government and officials, expectations about the freedoms one will enjoy, and expectations about the ability to participate in decisions which affect one's life.

Similarity of critical values: The enlightenment and utilitarianism have had a major influence in terms of liberal political values within Europe. The common heritage extends beyond the European Convention to include a number of values. Mario Chiti has argued for a set of values in terms of the conduct and control of the administration which reflect an 'administrative patriotism', a commitment to working together in a common enterprise through the

---

26 Van Gerven, note 1 *supra*.

administration.[27] Representativity , transparency, participation and so on might reflect similar ideas with regard to the relationships between the citizen and the State. The common values are reflected in how we relate to the common European enterprise and serve to reinforce (or sometimes to change) our attitudes to the way good administration should work.

Diversity of traditions and solutions: While there may well be different traditions and practices, we have to recognise that, as Stephen George suggests, a political culture may contain more than one strand which has to be reconciled.[28] On that analysis, the scope for comparison is greater in that, though the solution reached in another country may be different, similar forces may be at work. To take George's examples, liberalism and collectivism are at work in many countries, but lead to different institutional solutions. How far liberalism requires recognition of diversity of religious practice within schools is something on which the Americans and French may take a different position from the Germans and British, but the character of the arguments can be compared fruitfully.

V WHAT WOULD THE BENEFITS OF ANY COMPARISON BE?

I want to be perhaps rather chauvinist (or at least restrictive) in examining the way in which such a Europeanised comparative constitutional agenda would work, and I will concentrate on the way this will help to improve constitutional analysis and debate in Britain. Any significant use of European comparisons would work in three directions:

greater insights into shared problems
greater articulation and formality of principles
greater willingness to make use of rules and law.

I think the idea that there are common problems is well acknowledged. Martin Loughlin has argued that 'public law should adopt as its principal focus the examination of the manner in which the normative structures of law can contribute to the tasks of guidance, control and evaluation in government'.[29] That task is one which has been developed in other European constitutions as well as in the common law

---

27 'Are there Universal Principles of Good Governance?' (1995) 1 *European Public Law* 241 at p. 258.

28 *Supra* note 13 at p 51.

29 *Public Law and Political Theory*, p 264.

constitutions with which we are perhaps more familiar. Cassese also argued that public law is about principles of good government[30]. The British constitution has been strong on practice and procedures - who decides and how they go about the process, but less good in articulating principles - what are the standards for judging whether the job has been done well.

The other feature is the rise of formality which will break down the idiosyncracy of the British constitution and its methods. In a recent article, Norman Lewis and Di Longley have argued that too much in the field of norms of conduct in government is based on 'sentiments and understandings'.[31] The Nolan Committee offers an alternative perspective. Mark Freedland also suggests that in the area of the civil service, our lack of formality needs replacing, notably as choices and services move into the private sphere.[32]

VI SOME ILLUSTRATIONS: PUBLIC SERVICES, CORRUPTION, SUBSIDIARITY

The core of what is proposed as an agenda for the European influence on constitutional law is the development of principles of good government. Many of these principles are not peculiar to Europe, but are being developed in ways which will be commonly developed. If we look at principles of government, I would identify the following: openness/transparency, accountability, participation, efficiency, probity, public service, proximity, subsidiarity, and the British might add responsiveness.[33] Such principles of good government go beyond the protection of fundamental rights and serve to shape the behaviour of government. The agenda is being developed at national level. Comparison serves to expand the horizons of the national approach and to offer a critical dimension.

I would divide the specifically European influence through comparison into three: (i) often common experiences, not necessarily through EU activity; (ii) a distinct European understanding of the constitutional values, or (iii) a way of formulating principles which can serve as a model for us to formalise our own (perhaps idiosyncratic) understandings.

---

30 *Le basi del diritto amministrativo* (Turin 1989), p 53: where the focus of administrative law is the control of the administration.

31 'Ethics and the Public Service'[1994] *PL* 596 at 597.

32 M. Freedland, 'Government by Contract and Private Law'[1994] *PL* at 104.

33 *The Citizen's Charter. Second Report: 1994* (Cm 2540; 1994) p 2.

A Shared experiences

As Braibant has pointed out, government everywhere has become more complex in terms of activity and forms of regulation[34]. There are many similar approaches to the handling of this complexity.

Redefining government: In a number of countries there has been an attempt to narrow the scope of government in its classic form. In the Deregulation and Contracting Out Act 1994, the core activities of government which cannot be contracted out are restricted to justice, actions affecting civil rights, and lawmaking (presumably as well as certain classic areas of foreign affairs and public order). The Italian law on the civil service of 1993 takes similar lines protecting the judiciary and lawmaking civil servants from the transfer of jurisdiction over civil service litigation to the private law courts. There are obvious debates about the core of governmental activity which are shared and which go to the heart of the nature of government.

Limiting budget deficits: Many countries are concerned about the deficits which accumulate through Parliament's reluctance to set budgets with taxation set high enough to cover expenditure. Both France and Italy have established formal mechanisms to cover this problem. In Italy, Article 81 of the Constitution as amended has tried to restrain Parliament requiring it to vote enough money to cover the expenditure and restricting the authorisation of loans.[35] This requirement is then protected by the Constitutional Court which has struck down budgets as invalid for lack of adequate provision to cover expenditure. In France, the reforms of 1959 have also restricted the way in which a budget can be voted and encourage a balance[36], though are less restrictive than in Italy on the content of the budget. The law, through the *Conseil constitutionnel*, is brought in to restrict the freedom of Parliament in procedural terms. By contrast, we have no formal mechanisms, either in Parliamentary standing orders or law to require a balanced budget, merely that various distinct laws on supply and estimates are voted. The consolidated budget introduced recently does not go very far to ensure this. What we see in this are different ways of handling the same problem. By comparison of the way restrictions work in the different systems, we are able to reflect critically on whether our reliance on non-

---

34 *'Du simple au complexe quarante ans de droit administratif (1953-1993)'* *EDCE* 1994, 407.

35 See S. Cassese & A.G. Arabia, *L'amministrazione e la Costituzione* (Bologna 1993), pp 115-128 and 145-8.

36 J. Bell, *French Constitutional Law*, section 4.4.

legal, political methods of controlling the expenditure process continue to be, indeed, the most suited to our own situation and traditions.

Corruption and probity in government is a serious problem in Europe. It may be to the fore now in Britain with the Nolan Committee, but it has been of major significance in Italy, France and Spain, as well as Belgium. There are two areas for the handling of the problem which are of interest: the form of investigation and the character of the rules set. In Italy, France, Spain and Belgium, the principal procedure for uncovering corruption has been the work of public prosecutors and the investigating magistrate. The Italians such as Di Pietro are the most famous prosecutors, but there is a range of equally eminent figures in other countries. By contrast, in the UK, we have relied on journalists and parliamentary pressure to sanction wrongdoing.[37] The vogue for legal investigation is on the wane in Italy and France.[38] All the same, there remains scope for regulation by law. The role of committees which rule on the eligibility of civil servants or ministers to take up posts in France and Italy is more formal and has more legal authority than much of what is likely to be brought into being in England.[39]

B Distinctly European principles

There can be seen to be a distinctly European understanding of principles such as proximity, subsidiarity and participation. The evolution of European institutions brings more facets of life within the remit of EU institutions. At the same time as this sucks power and decision-making into the centre, there is a concern that the increasing Europeanisation and globalisation needs to be counterbalanced by greater involvement of the regions and localities. The idea of subsidiarity within the Maastricht Treaty is one recognition of this. But the idea can be taken not simply to be a principle governing the workings of EU institutions. It can also be understood as a principle which affects the operation of the constitutions of Member States, which is, after all, its origin in German constitutional law.

The constitutional principles in this area have been developed, for example, in the Pujol report for the Committee of the Regions, the fledgling Maastricht institution which brings together the regions of

---

37 See my 'English Law and French Law - Not so different?' [1995] *CLP* 63.

38 See D. Nelken, 'A Legal Revolution? The Judges and *Tangentopoli*' in S. Grindle and S. Parker (edd.), *The New Italian Republic: From the Fall of Communism to the Rise of Berlusconi* (London 1995).

39 See my note in (1995) 1 *European Public Law* 16 at pp 20-22.

Europe (except from the UK). The Committee of the Regions resolved in May 1995 that the IGC should amend the subsidiarity Article 3b of the Treaty to include an explicit reference to regional or local authorities as an alternative to Member States.[40]

The explanatory memorandum states that:

> 'On the constitutional front, the Committee proposes a new formulation of Article 3b that defines the principle of subsidiarity not only as a criterion for exercising shared powers between the Union and the Member States, but also as a criterion for sharing powers and responsibilities among all levels of government in the European Union.'[41]

The interpretation offered by the Committee makes clear that subsidiarity should be taken as a general constitution value:

> 'The principle of subsidiarity implies that the public authorities do not take action when this can be done adequately and effectively by citizens. The principle also introduced the concept of gradation, i.e. higher levels of government act only when lower levels cannot do so satisfactorily.'[42]

Understood in this way, subsidiarity involves a notion of proximity, that decisions are made as close to citizens as possible, and that thereby they feel more involved in them.[43] This analysis corresponds with what Scott, Peterson and Millar have characterised as the substantive principle of subsidiarity.[44] It goes beyond the merely procedural principle set out in Article 3b that the lowest possible level should be given powers to

---

40 Opinion of 21 April 1995, *Institutional Reform* (Committee of the Regions May 1995), p 39.

41 *Ibid*, p 33.

42 *Ibid*, p 32.

43 See the interventions of Dr Hans Katschalter (Austria) and Knud Andersen (Denmark), *ibid* pp 19 and 13.

44 'Subsidiarity: A Europe of the Regions *v.* the British Constitution' (1994) 32 *Journal of Common Market Studies* 47.

achieve determined objectives. There is clearly an agenda of a Europe of the Regions in the Committee's approach.[45]

Now this is a constitutional approach which does not reflect practice in Britain or France, and is a bone of contention in Spain and Italy. I am not suggesting that this principle will necessarily succeed, but I am suggesting that the European dimension to our constitutional order brings into play ideas which can spread from their original home in the constitutional practice of the EU to influence the constitutions of Member States[46]. Indeed, as Scott, Peterson and Millar point out, the trends within British government over the last 20-30 years have been towards centralisation, which runs counter to the substantive principle promoted by the Committee of the Regions. It must not be forgotten that at least the SNP (if not *Plaid Cymru*) would endorse the devolutionary approach which this idea of subsidiarity involves, and Mrs Thatcher's 'rolling back the frontiers of the State' approach also has echoes in the idea of limiting State interference. The constitutional agenda will be partly transformed and certainly reinforced by the very presence of a European Union constitutional debate and by the practice of the European Union which gives mechanisms for regions to obtain financial support for their policies without recourse to national governments. Certainly, the existence of the European dimension has transformed the impact of the 1982 decentralisation reforms in France.[47]

C *European examples as models for normalisation*

The European Union process brings us into contact with the ideas of other Member States either because they provide a setting within which issues are formulated or because their ideas are actually proposed as the basis for new European regulations. To take an example, the whole area of public contracts was not addressed as a coherent whole in the UK despite the seminal analysis by Colin Turpin and Sue Arrowsmith[48]. Yet EC directives on public works and public services have now built into a

---

45 Though see J. Steiner, 'Subsidiarity under Maastricht', in D. O'Keefe and P.M. Twomey, *Legal Issues of the Maastricht Treaty* (London 1994) 49 which brings out the legal ambiguity of the subsidiarity concept in terms of its consequences for centralisation or decentralisation.

46 See N. MacCormick, in R. Bellamy et al., above 6 *supra*, ch. 7.

47 See R. Ladrech, 'Europeanization of Domestic Politics and Institutions; The Case of France' (1994) 32 *Journal of Common Market Studies* 69.

48 C. Turpin, *Government Contracts* (London 1972); C. Turpin, *Government Procurement and Contracts* (London 1989); S. Arrowsmith , *Government Procurement and Judicial Review* (London 1988).

substantial code regulating public contracts. The concepts of the public sector used in EC law are not really those which arise out of our own constitution. The notion of an emanation of the State which is used in the *direct effect* cases such as *Marshall* and *Foster v. British Gas* rests on ideas which are found in French or German law, but which lie outside our constitutional experience, focused as it was on the Crown as the touchstone of government. These illustrations point to the ways in which we have to view our own system with different eyes and formalise rules which are to govern it.

My own favourite example is the idea of *public service* on which Patrick Birkinshaw and I have been doing some consultancy for the French government as it prepares for the IGC at which it wishes to propose the regulation of public services as part of the revisions to the EU treaties.

The first thing to state is that we have no *legal* concept of 'public service'. We do have political statements of principle. Thus, even the Thatcher Government was driven to write in 1988:[49]

> 'Comparison with the private sector has to be treated with caution. In the private sector there is a direct relationship between commercial success - as measured by profitability and market share - and the standard of customer service. The public sector position is more complicated and in many circumstances distinctly different. In general the reasons for providing a service in the first place, the nature of that service and the manner in which it is delivered, are not dictated by markets. In these circumstances the balance between public expectations and the level of service to be provided is decided on the basis of political judgments about economic and social priorities.'

The Citizen's Charter identifies the following principles of public service: standards, information and openness, choice and consultation, courtesy and helpfulness, putting things right, and value for money.[50] But these are operational principles which influence the performance of public service tasks, but they do not match the more

49 Cabinet Office, *Service to the Public* (London 1988), para. 1.5.

50 Second Report, note 33 *supra*, at p 1.

general, organisational principles which are offered in other legal systems.

European examples show us both the way of developing legal principles and how they might be formulated. A more formalised system, such as classical French public law argues that there are two main strands to governmental activity: public order and public services. The very definition of public law matters hinges around the identification of public service missions. The *Conseil d'Etat* argued in an advisory opinion that there is a constitutional principle that 'bodies of civil servants can only be created and maintained in order to implement public service missions'[51] and that privatisation must define the public service missions which those retained in the civil service are to perform. A similar idea lies behind *Foster v. British Gas* and its interpretation of vertical direct effect, which defines an 'emanation of the State' in terms of the provision of a public service.[52]

The French see four basic and distinctive values as governing the performance of the public service. *Continuity* requires that the service must continue in order to provide for a public need and so, for example, public sector strikes should be restricted. *Adaptability* requires that a public body must be able to adapt the provision (e.g., the terms of a concession) in order to meet changed demands of the public interest. *Equality* requires that users ought to be treated with equality by the service (not in the unequal way frequent in ordinary business). Finally, *neutrality* requires that the service is impartial in its treatment of individuals.

I do not believe that these principles are idiosyncratic to French law. I think we could easily take such principles and see them exhibited in English law. Indeed, such principles might make more sense of how we apply our law.

To illustrate the point, neutrality requires the public service to refrain from favouring or disfavouring political or religious views. If we examine *Wheeler v. Leicester City Council*[53] (a refusal to allow a club to use a local authority sports ground if it did not publicly condemn players lawfully going to play in apartheid South Africa), *R v. Barnet LBC, ex parte Johnston*[54] (anti-nuclear protesters prevented from having a stall at a local authority funday), *R v. Coventry City Council, ex parte Phoenix*

51 See above 39 *supra*.

52 [1990] 3 All ER at p 922, para. 20.

53 [1985] AC 1054.

54 [1989] COD 538.

Aviation[55] (exporters of veal calves refused use of a local authority airport), and *R v. Somerset County Council, ex parte Fewings*[56](ban on hunting on council land), we see that the decisions are really unlawful because they breach the injunction of neutrality. An attempt was made by the local authorities in each case to refuse access to a public service or public property because of the opinions of the potential user. In each case, the English courts resorted to the notion of 'unreasonableness' in a rather amorphous sense to justify the decision. If we can actually articulate the structural principles of public service, then we can have a more coherent enforcement of the principles of good government. This would prevent 'unreasonableness' becoming an unwieldy and amorphous idea, and would give a greater coherence to our practice.[57]

The case of neutrality merely illustrates that comparison and greater formality can help us understand our own system better, and get round the frequent lack of clarity in the way our law is expressed.

D *Can this lead to common European principles?*

It might be thought that we can do better than simply use comparative law to help clarify our understanding of our own legal system. The approach of Jürgen Schwarze, an academic with a strong European pedigree and a former judge of the ECJ, Yves Galmot, suggest that European principles can be developed. Such a process goes beyond the mere collation of distinct rules and approaches, and a reflection on one national system. What they argue should be sought are the most progressive (*performant*) solution in terms of the direction of EU institutions and the protections which they offer to citizens. In his work, Schwarze draws on K. Zweigert to suggest that the method of determining the content of principles is not simply minimalist, based on what is actually common between systems, but is maximalist, based on the best solution involving a critical analysis of the various solutions offered from a comparative survey.[58] Schwarze notes that the documentation service of the ECJ produces a number of comparative reports for the court and this is borne out by its practice. In similar words to Schwarze, Y. Galmot, a French former member of the Court, relates how it looks for the most progressive solution (and how that is

55 [1995] 3 All E.R. 37.

56 [1995] 3 All E.R. 20.

57 For a similar line of argument, see my colleague Ian Cram, 'Public Authorities, Political Protest and Judicial Review' 1995 *SLT* 213.

58 *European Administrative Law* (London 1992), pp 71-72.

not often found in English public law).[59] They suggest that comparison is used in a critical sense to distill the most effective legal protection. If we are to contribute to this process, we have to be able to offer certain positive statements, which is a stimulus to us to refine the principles we believe in.

VII CONCLUSION

The argument may appear rather diffuse, but I hope it helps to illustrate the multi-faceted character of the question of Europeanisation in constitutional law. In brief, I have argued three main points. First, 'Europeanisation' is not a dominant trend within constitutional reflection on principles of good government. The tension between global and distinctly national features of the debate on what are the best organs of government suggest that the regional aspect of the question is limited. There is an appropriate European dimension to the debate, but the points of reference, especially in the common law world will remain predominantly elsewhere. Secondly, Europe offers both a number of discrete constitutional issues and a *locus* for comparison. Discrete issues arise in matters such as the national parliamentary control of European Community legislation and the incorporation of the European Convention on Human Rights. These are topics which any national system must confront. But in addition and more importantly, Europe offers a range of different perspectives which can be used to understand and evaluate existing institutions and principles. Finally, this *locus* of comparison can offer dimensions which are not available within the common law family, notably by offering examples of how principles might be formalised and by encouraging critical evaluation as one considers whether other approaches are more effective in achieving the objectives for which our constitution strives. Of course, there are the changes to constitutional institutions and practice brought about by the European Convention and the European Union, but these have an impact principally on fundamental rights and on the competence of Member States in particular fields. The development of governmental structures and principles of good government in the broad sense remain rooted in national traditions and subject to global pressures. Europeanisation is an important, but not exclusive aspect of the comparative work which needs doing to enable us to put in place institutions and principles which will encourage better government.

---

59 Y. Galmot, *'Réflexions sur le recours au droit comparé'* Rfda 1990, 255.

6

THE PERVASIVE INFLUENCE OF EUROPEAN COMMUNITY LAW IN THE UNITED KINGDOM

Nicholas Grief

Much has been written about the uniqueness of Community law and the significance of the fact that the European Community is a supranational system, its hallmark being the creation of rights and duties for individuals and the supremacy of Community law over national law in the event of a conflict.[1] It is clear that Community law reaches parts of the domestic legal system which other kinds of international law[2] cannot reach. Lord Denning once stated:

> 'The treaty does not touch any of the matters which concern solely the mainland of England and the people in it. They are still governed by English law. They are not affected by the treaty. But when we come to matters with a European element, the treaty is like an incoming tide. It flows up the estuaries and up the rivers. It cannot be held back.'[3]

---

1 See John Usher, *Plender and Usher's Cases and Materials on the Law of the European Communities* (3rd ed. 1993) p.3.

2 In Case 26/62 *Van Gend en Loos v. Nederlandse Administratie der* Berlastingen [1963] ECR 1 at 12, the European Court of Justice observed that 'the Community constitutes a new legal order of international law'.

3 *H.P. Bulmer Ltd.* v. *J. Bollinger S.A.* [1974] 2 All E.R. 1226 at p.1231hj.

More than twenty years on, however, it is apparent that the domestic impact of Community law is not confined to cases with a European element. Already there are several examples of what might be called the pervasive influence of Community law in the United Kingdom, particularly in the sphere of public law.

I. STATUTORY INTERPRETATION AND DRAFTING

Ever since the entry into force of the European Communities Act 1972,[4] British judges have been required (in the absence of a reference to the European Court of Justice under Article 177 EC) to determine 'any questions as to the meaning or effect of any of the Treaties, or as to the validity, meaning or effect of any Community instrument ... in accordance with the principles laid down by and any relevant decision of the European Court'.[5] A similar requirement is laid down by s 3(1) of the Civil Jurisdiction and Judgments Act 1982[6] in respect of the 1968 Brussels Convention on Jurisdiction and the Enforcement of Judgments in Civil and Commercial Matters, which the European Court regards as part of the Community legal order.[7]

Above all, this means adopting a schematic and purposive (teleological) approach to interpretation rather than a literal and historical approach.[8] As David Pannick Q.C. has put it:

> 'To examine where the commas have been placed in the relevant provisions of the treaty in an effort to identify their precise meaning is to misunderstand the

---

4 1972 c.68. The Act (which was amended in 1993 in order to pave the way for ratification of the Maastricht Treaty) gives the force of law to those provisions of Community law which are intended to have direct effect. Under British constitutional law a treaty cannot of itself be a source of domestically enforceable rights and obligations.

5 s.3(1) of the European Communities Act (as amended). This obligation would exist as a matter of Community law even without the statutory provision. See the Rt. Hon. the Lord Slynn of Hadley, 'Looking at Community Texts' (1993) 14 *Statute Law Review* p.12 at p.23.

6 1982 c.27. The 1982 Act was amended by the Civil Jurisdiction and Judgments Act 1991 (1991 c.12), which gives effect to the 1988 Lugano Convention.

7 The Convention was concluded pursuant to Art. 220 EEC. See A. Layton, 'The Interpretation of the Brussels Convention by the European Court and the English Courts' (1992) 11 *Civil Justice Quarterly* 28, p.32; R.H.H. White, 'The Government Role - Negotiation, Legislation and Litigation', (1992) 11 *Civil Justice Quarterly* 52, pp.60-61.

8 Slynn, see n.5 *supra*, at p.23. See e.g. Case 283/81 *CILFIT* v. *Ministry of Health* [1982] ECR 3415.

> way in which Community law operates. The role of the European Court is to add spirit to the words of Community texts. When interpreting those provisions of the treaty from which the United Kingdom has not opted out, the court will consider itself entitled ... to assess what the concept of a community requires having regard to the social, economic and political realities of the day.'[9]

Not surprisingly, judicial adjustment to purposive interpretation was not without its difficulties.[10] The Court of Appeal's approach to the construction of Article 30 EEC in *R.* v. *Henn and Darby*[11] remains one of the best examples of how not to interpret Community law. When that case came before the House of Lords, the error of the Court of Appeal - and ultimately, of course, of counsel[12] - was identified and explained by Lord Diplock:

> 'In the Court of Appeal considerable doubt was expressed by that court whether an absolute prohibition on the import of a particular description of goods could amount to a quantitative restriction or a measure having equivalent effect, so as to fall within the ambit of Article 30 at all. That such doubt could be expressed shows the danger of an English court applying English canons of statutory construction to the interpretation of the EEC Treaty or, for that matter, of regulations or directives. What is meant by quantitative restrictions and measures having equivalent effect in Article 30 of the treaty has been the subject of a whole series of decisions of the European court to which the attention of the Court of Appeal ought to have been drawn.'[13]

---

9 David Pannick Q.C., 'An alien legal tradition', *The Times*, 8 Oct. 1992.

10 See Layton, see n.7 *supra* at p.36: 'The unfamiliarity of English courts and English practitioners with purposive interpretation has proved something of an initial stumbling block in the assimilation of the Brussels Convention into our procedural law'.

11 [1978] 3 All E.R. 1190.

12 See D.F. Pugsley, 'The Advocate's Duty to the Court', in D. Lasok et al. (eds.), *Fundamental Duties* (1980) p.113; reprinted in D.F. Pugsley, *Lawyers and Precedents* (1989).

13 *Supra* n.11 at p.196f. See also Slynn, n.5 *supra* at pp.23-24.

His Lordship continued:

> 'The European court, in contrast to English courts, applies teleological rather than historical methods to the interpretation of the treaties and other Community legislation. It seeks to give effect to what it considers to be the spirit rather than the letter of the treaties; sometimes, indeed, to an English judge, it may seem to the exclusion of the letter. It views the Communities as living and expanding organisms and the interpretation of the provisions of the treaties as changing to match their growth.'[14]

The distance which British judges have travelled since the early years of Community membership is illustrated by *Litster* v. *Forth Dry Dock and Engineering Co. Ltd.*,[15] which concerned the interpretation of domestic regulations designed to implement the Business Transfer Directive. Lord Oliver stated:

> 'If the legislation can reasonably be construed so as to conform with [Community] obligations - obligations which are to be ascertained not only from the wording of the relevant Directive but from the interpretation placed upon it by the European Court of Justice at Luxembourg - such a purposive interpretation will be applied even though, perhaps, it may involve some departure from the strict and literal application of the words which the legislature has elected to use.'[16]

The obligation to interpret Community law - and national measures intended to implement Community law - purposively is now established and understood. What is interesting is that this has led judges to adopt a purposive approach to the interpretation of statutes outside the Community law context. In *Pepper (Inspector of Taxes)* v. *Hart*[17] the

---

14 *Ibid.*, at p.196h.

15 [1989] 1 All E.R. 1134.

16 *Ibid.*, at p.1140. The House of Lords implied provisions into the regulations so that they complied with the Directive. In *Webb* v. *E.M.O. Air Cargo (UK) Ltd.* [1995] T.L.R. 525, it construed the Sex Discrimination Act 1975 in accordance with the ECJ's interpretation of the Equal Treatment Directive.

17 [1993] 1 All E.R. 42.

House of Lords relaxed the general judge-made rule, probably first stated in 1769, that parliamentary material cannot be used as an aid to statutory interpretation. Judges can now refer to such material where (a) legislation is ambiguous or obscure, or leads to an absurdity; (b) the material relied on consists of one or more statements by a Minister or other promoter of the Bill, together with such other parliamentary material as is necessary to understand such statements and their effect; and (c) the statements relied on are clear.[18] Although this relaxation of the exclusionary rule was not expressly influenced by Community law, it represents approval of the purposive approach to statutory interpretation[19] and there can be little doubt that judicial experience of Community law was a contributing factor.

As Lord Browne-Wilkinson observed,[20] a major inroad on the exclusionary rule had already been made in *Pickstone* v. *Freemans plc.*[21] where, in interpreting a statutory instrument designed to implement the Equal Pay Directive as construed by the ECJ,[22] the House of Lords had regard to what had been said by the Minister who initiated the debate on the regulations in question.[23] His Lordship also pointed out that in *Factortame Ltd.* v. *Secretary of State for Transport,*[24] where Spanish applicants challenged the legality of certain provisions of the Merchant Shipping Act 1988 and the Merchant Shipping (Registration of Fishing Vessels) Regulations 1988[25] on the ground that they infringed Community law,[26] the House of Lords referred to a Law Commission report not only for the purpose of ascertaining the mischief which the Supreme Court Act 1981 was intended to cure, but also for the purpose of drawing an inference as to parliamentary intention from the fact that

---

18 *Ibid.*, at p.69de (Lord Browne-Wilkinson).

19 See [1993] *I.R.L.R.* 1 at p.3: 'This can be regarded as the final triumph of the purposive approach to statutory construction over more literal techniques' (Michael Rubenstein).

20 *Supra* n.17, at p.61g.

21 [1989] A.C. 66.

22 In Case 61/81 *Commission* v. *United Kingdom* [1982] E.C.R. 2601.

23 *Supra* n.17, at p.61eg.

24 [1990] 2 A.C. 85.

25 The Act and the Regulations radically altered the statutory regime governing the registration of British fishing vessels in order to stop the practice known as 'quota hopping'. The British government considered that the United Kingdom's fishing quotas were being plundered by fishing vessels flying the British flag but lacking any genuine link with the UK.

26 In particular, Arts. 7, 52, 58 and 221 EEC.

Parliament had not expressly implemented one of the Law Commission's recommendations.[27]

The adoption of a purposive approach to statutory interpretation clearly commends itself to some of our judges. In *R.* v. *Newham London Borough Council, Ex parte Dada*,[28] Sir Louis Blom-Cooper Q.C.[29] quashed a decision that it was unreasonable of the applicant to refuse the offer of permanent one-bedroom accommodation as being unsuitable, holding that an unborn child was a 'person who might reasonably be expected to reside' with a pregnant woman for the purposes of s.75 of the Housing Act 1985.[30] In the light of the statute's purpose, which is to confer rights on the homeless person and benefit members of his (her) family, his Lordship concluded that Parliament had intended the term 'person' to include the unborn child. He stated that it would be odd if the homeless person had to occupy accommodation which would be rendered unsuitable almost immediately after taking up occupancy and to await a transfer to suitable accommodation when the child was born, with all the delay and domestic disruption which that would involve. On appeal, however, the decision was overturned. The Court of Appeal held that a child *en ventre sa mère* was not a 'person who might reasonably be expected to live with' the mother for the purposes of s.75 of the 1985 Act. Glidewell L.J. said that the term 'person' should be given its ordinary and natural meaning, i.e. a person who was alive (sic) when the offer of accommodation was made.[31]

---

27 *Supra* n.24, at p.149GH. Lord Bridge used this to explain why s.31 of the 1981 Act did not allow injunctions to be granted against a Minister of the Crown. See below.

28 [1994] T.L.R. 438.

29 Sitting as a deputy judge of the Queen's Bench Division of the High Court.

30 According to s.75, 'accommodation shall be regarded as available for a person's occupation only if it is available for occupation both by him and by any other person who might reasonably be expected to reside with him'.

31 [1995] T.L.R. 51. In *R.* v. *Brown*, [1996] 1 A.C. 543, the House of Lords held that the mere retrieval of information from a computer database did not constitute the use of data under s.5(2)(b) of the Data Protection Act 1984. Lord Goff said that the term 'use' had to be given its natural and ordinary meaning. As Lord Griffiths observed in his dissenting speech, however, unless 'use' is given a broad construction the purpose of the Act is not achieved. Under Directive 95/46/EC of 24 Oct. 1995 on the protection of individuals with regard to the processing of personal data and on the free movement of such data (O.J. 1995 L 281/31), 'processing' includes retrieval. In accordance with the judgment of the ECJ in Case C-106/89, *Marleasing S.A.* v. *La Comercial Internacional de Alimentación S.A.* [1989] E.C.R. I-4135, UK courts will be required, as far as possible, to interpret the Act in conformity with the Directive after the expiry of the deadline for the latter's implementation.

Undeterred, Sir Louis tried again in *R.* v. *Bristol City Council, Ex parte Bradic.*[32] In holding that a person who was unlawfully evicted and who applied to a housing authority as a homeless person was capable of qualifying for priority need as an emergency under s.59(1)(d) of the Housing Act 1985, his Lordship said that the council's argument that an unlawful eviction of a single household could not constitute an emergency within the meaning of s.59 could not prevail because 'it negatived the purpose of priority groups'. Once again the Court of Appeal disagreed, holding that unlawful eviction did not give rise to priority need.[33]

In *R.* v. *Moore,*[34] however, the Court of Appeal took advantage of *Pepper* v. *Hart* in order to discover and give effect to the policy underlying an Act of Parliament, the Criminal Justice Act 1991. The question was whether an offence (shoplifting) committed during the operational period of a suspended sentence and which, in the opinion of the justices, merited only a conditional discharge could activate the suspended sentence of imprisonment. According to s.1C of the Act, it could do so: it followed from the literal reading and location of s.1C that an offence committed during the operational period of a suspended sentence and for which the justices gave a conditional discharge created a 'conviction' which could activate the suspended sentence. However, the Court of Appeal held that a major element of the policy of the Act had been to prevent the imposition of imprisonment for minor offences, even if repeated. Furthermore, under the Powers of Criminal Courts Act 1973 as amended, a conditional discharge can be imposed only where 'it is inexpedient to inflict punishment'. Although the 1991 Act was neither ambiguous nor obscure, therefore, since loyalty to the literal wording would have frustrated the plain legislative intent (by activating the suspended sentence), the Court construed the Act so that it did not frustrate that intention. This amounted to treating s.1C(1)(a), which read 'under the following provisions of this Act', as if it said 'under the preceding provisions of this Act'.

But it is not only certain members of the judiciary who are thinking purposively. Those concerned with the drafting of legislation also seem to be aware of the advantages of such an approach. For example, the Civil Jurisdiction and Judgments Act 1982[35] provides for

---

32 [1995] T.L.R. 57.

33 [1995] T.L.R. 443.

34 [1994] T.L.R. 666.

35 *Supra* n.6.

its own modification by Order in Council[36] as occasioned by agreed revision of, in particular, the 1968 Brussels Convention[37] or by decisions of the ECJ as to the Convention's meaning or effect.[38] Rightly described as the Act's most important dynamic element,[39] this power was extended by the Civil Jurisdiction and Judgments Act 1991 to enable statutory modifications to be made to give effect to future revisions of the 1988 Lugano Convention.[40]

Even more significant because it has no connection with Community law is the Courts and Legal Services Act 1990.[41] The objective of Part II of the Act[42] is defined in s.17(1):

> 'The general objective of this Part is the development of legal services in England and Wales (and in particular the development of advocacy, litigation, conveyancing and probate services) by making provision for new or better ways of providing such services and a wider choice of persons providing them, while maintaining the proper and efficient administration of justice.'

The statutory objective having been defined, s.18 of the Act imposes a statutory duty. Any person exercising any functions with respect to, for example, the granting of rights of audience, the granting of rights to conduct litigation, or the approval of qualification regulations or rules of conduct[43] shall act in accordance with the general principle[44] and, subject to that, shall

> '(a) so far as it is possible to do so in the circumstances of the case, act to further the statutory objective; and

36 Subject to an affirmative resolution of each House of Parliament - see s.14(2).
37 See s.14 of the Act.
38 See s.47 of the Act.
39 See White, *supra* n.7, at p.56.
40 *Ibid.*, at p.58.
41 1990 c.41.
42 Part II is headed 'Legal Services'.
43 s.18(1).
44 See s.17(3).

> (b) not act in any way which would be incompatible with the statutory objective.'

Not only is the objective of Part II of the Act defined in the Act itself, therefore, it is also used to construct remedies. This was highlighted during debate in Parliament on the Courts and Legal Services Bill, when the Attorney-General made the following statement with reference to the new arrangements concerning rights of audience and rights to conduct litigation:

> 'The Government consider that those arrangements[45] continue ... the long-established involvement of the judiciary in the control of proceedings in the courts in which they sit. However, the arrangements regulate the exercise of judicial involvement in that area by reference to the statutory objective and the general principle ... For example, if a designated judge[46] were to refuse to concur with the Lord Chancellor's proposal to approve an alteration to the rules of conduct of, say, the Law Society,[47] his refusal would have to be compatible with his specific duty ... to act in furtherance of the statutory objective and in accordance with the general principle. If it were not so, it would be subject to judicial review.'[48]

II. REMEDIES

The pervasive effect of Community law is also evident in the area of remedies. The law of restitution provides a good example. In *Woolwich Equitable Building Society* v. *Inland Revenue Commissioners*,[49] the House of Lords held that money paid to a public authority in the form of

---

45 See Schedule 4 to the Act: 'Authorisation and Approval'.

46 The Lord Chief Justice, the Master of the Rolls, the President of the Family Division or the Vice-Chancellor: see s.119(1) of the Act.

47 s.29(3) of the Act provides that where an authorised body (e.g., the Law Society) alters any of its rules of conduct, those alterations shall not have effect, so far as they relate to any right of audience or rights to conduct litigation granted by that body, unless they have been approved under Part II of Schedule 4. Para. 10 of Schedule 4 states: 'If the Lord Chancellor or any of the designated judges refuses to give the required approval, the alteration in question shall not have effect'.

48 *Hansard H.C. Debs.* vol.170 col.1448: 18 April 1990.

49 [1993] A.C. 70.

taxes or other levies pursuant to an *ultra vires* demand is *prima facie* recoverable as of right. Lord Goff regarded the ECJ's decision in *Amministrazione delle Finanze dello Stato* v. *SpA San Giorgio*,[50] which established that a person who pays charges levied by a Member State in breach of Community law is entitled to repayment, as 'a sixth reason which favours this conclusion'. He continued:

> 'The *San Giorgio* case is also of interest for present purposes in that it accepts that Community law does not prevent a national legal system from disallowing repayment of charges where to do so would entail unjust enrichment of the recipient, in particular where the charges have been incorporated into the price of goods and so passed on to the purchaser. I only comment that, at a time when Community law is becoming increasingly important, it would be strange if the right of the citizen to recover overpaid charges were to be more restricted under domestic law than it is under Community law.'[51]

For his part, Lord Slynn[52] considered that if Parliament found that limitations on the common law principle of recovery were needed for reasons of policy or good administration, they could be adopted by legislation, presumptions of validity,

> 'even ... a power in the courts to limit the effects of any order for recovery comparable to that conferred on the European Court of Justice by Article 174 of the EEC Treaty.'[53]

The pervasive influence of Community law is even more striking in the context of public law remedies. In *Factortame Ltd.* v. *Secretary of State for Transport* the House of Lords held that, as a matter of English law, the courts had no jurisdiction to grant interim relief in terms which

---

50 Case 199/82, [1983] E.C.R. 3595.

51 *Supra* n.48, at pp.177C-E. Lord Browne-Wilkinson agreed with Lord Goff: see p.196H.

52 Formerly an Advocate General and then a Judge at the European Court of Justice.

53 *Supra* n.48, at p.200DE. According to Art.174, the European Court can state which of the effects of a Regulation which it has declared void shall be considered as definitive.

would involve either suspending the operation of Part II of the Merchant Shipping Act 1988 in advance of any decision by the ECJ that the statute infringed Community law or issuing an injunction against the Crown.[54] However, the question whether Community law either obliged or empowered an English court to grant such relief in order to protect putative Community rights was referred to the European Court under Article 177 EEC.[55] Emphasising the obligation of national courts to ensure the legal protection which persons derive from the direct effect of Community law,[56] the ECJ ruled that

> 'a national court which, in a case before it concerning Community law, considers that the sole obstacle which precludes it from granting interim relief is a rule of national law, must set aside that rule.'[57]

In other words, irrespective of the position under national law, British courts must be prepared to grant appropriate interim relief in order to protect rights claimed under Community law.[58]

Then came *Re M*,[59] a case which had no connection with Community law. A Zairean citizen (M) claimed political asylum on arrival in the United Kingdom. The Home Office rejected M's claim and made directions for his removal to Zaire, whereupon his lawyer sought leave to apply for judicial review. The judge in chambers (Garland J.) considered that an application should be made the following day to a nominated Crown Office list judge and, believing that counsel for the Home Office had undertaken that M would not be removed pending the application, adjourned the application overnight. Meanwhile, the applicant had been put on board a flight to Zaire via Paris. Later that evening the judge issued a mandatory order requiring the Home Secretary to return M to the United Kingdom but the Secretary of State failed to comply with it.

---

54 [1990] 2 A.C. 85, at pp.142E-143B and 150H. The Divisional Court (Neill L.J. and Hodgson J.) had made an order granting interim relief but that order had been set aside by the Court of Appeal.

55 *Ibid.*, at pp.151-152.

56 Case C-213/89, *R.* v. *Secretary of State for Transport, Ex parte Factortame Ltd (Factortame No.1)* [1990] E.C.R. I-2433 at paras. 19-20.

57 *Ibid.*, at p.2475.

58 In the light of the ECJ's ruling in *Factortame No.1*, interim relief was granted by the House of Lords. See [1991] 1 A.C. 603, at p.663C.

59 [1993] 3 All E.R. 537.

The main issue in the case was whether the courts have jurisdiction to make coercive orders, such as injunctions, against the Crown or Ministers of the Crown. The House of Lords unanimously held that there is jurisdiction and that if a Minister acts in disregard of such an order the court can make a finding of contempt against him or his government department.[60] Broadly speaking,[61] it based its decision on the need to enforce the rule of law,[62] the fact that the Crown Proceedings Act 1947 was designed to preserve pre-existing remedies against the Crown,[63] and the inapplicability of the prohibition of injunctive relief to judicial review proceedings because, by virtue of s.38(2) of the Act, Crown side proceedings are not civil proceedings.[64] Nevertheless, it is evident that the House was strongly influenced by Community law. Lord Woolf described the European Court's decision in *Factortame No.1*[65] as an 'important development', observing that

> 'the unhappy situation now exists that while a citizen is entitled to obtain injunctive relief (including interim relief) against the Crown or an officer of the Crown to protect his interests under Community law he cannot do so in respect of his other interests which may be just as important.'[66]

Conscious of that anomaly, the House of Lords closed the gap which had opened up as a result of *Factortame No.1* by raising the standard of protection for individuals outside the Community law context. *Re M* is thus an excellent example of the pervasive influence of Community law, which has extended its reach into areas of English law which have no Community law dimension.

---

60 Lord Templeman observed that the argument that there is no power to enforce the law by injunction or contempt proceedings against a Minister in his official capacity would, if upheld, establish the proposition that the executive obey the law as a matter of grace and not as a matter of necessity. See n.59 *supra*, at p.541ab.

61 See Law Commission Consultative Paper No.226, *Administrative Law: Judicial Review and Statutory Appeals*, at para. 2.10.

62 *Supra.* n.59, at pp.540-541.

63 *Ibid.*, at pp.555j-556d.

64 *Ibid.*, at p.555eg.

65 *Supra* n.56.

66 *Supra* n.59, at pp.550j-551a.

In Scotland, however, the gap closed in *Re M* still exists. In *McDonald* v. *Secretary of State for Scotland*,[67] where a prisoner sought interdict against the Secretary of State or anyone on his behalf from searching him without lawful authority, the Court of Session[68] held that the views expressed in *Re M*, to the effect that an injunction could be granted against officers of the Crown, were based on peculiarities of English law and were not binding upon a Scottish court. Lord Ross, the Lord Justice Clerk, stated:

> 'It appears from the speech of Lord Woolf that jurisdiction to grant injunctions against the Crown was to be found in the provisions of s.31 of the Supreme Court Act and Order 53 of the Rules of the Supreme Court. In the course of his speech Lord Woolf comments upon the provisions to be found in s.21 of the Crown Proceedings Act 1947. That section applies to both England and Scotland but Lord Woolf's views are expressed in the context of English law. I am therefore satisfied that what was stated in the House of Lords regarding the interpretation of this section for the purposes of English law is not binding upon this court.'[69]

The Court of Session held that the action constituted civil proceedings against the Crown[70] and was therefore covered by s.21(1) of the Crown Proceedings Act 1947, which had deprived litigants in Scotland of the right to obtain interdict and interim interdict against the Crown.[71] However, the judgment does not actually determine whether such relief would be available in judicial review proceedings. Counsel appearing as *amicus curiae* in *McDonald* considered that if the pursuer had applied to the Court of Session for judicial review, instead of raising an action for damages in the sheriff court, he might have been able to seek interim

---

67 1994 *S.L.T.* 692.

68 Second Division.

69 *Supra* n.67, at p.696I-J. See also p.700I-L (Lord Sutherland).

70 The pursuer had raised an action for damages against the Secretary of State in Stirling sheriff court.

71 Lord Sutherland accepted that the construction of s.21 preventing an individual from obtaining relief by way of interdict against the Crown was a restriction of the remedies available in Scotland prior to 1947 and observed that, if there were any doubt or ambiguity, *Hansard* showed that the Lord Advocate had been aware that the right of interdict against the Crown was being removed in Scotland. See n.67 *supra*, at p.701F.

interdict on the basis that an application to the Court's supervisory jurisdiction does not constitute 'civil proceedings' against the Crown within the meaning of s.21(1) of the 1947 Act.[72] Without deciding the point, the Court of Session concluded that 'there would be formidable difficulties in the way of any (such) submission'.[73]

III. PROPORTIONALITY

As applied by the European Court of Justice, the principle of proportionality essentially involves asking whether a given measure is appropriate and necessary to achieve its stated aims and objectives:

> 'This requires [the ECJ] to consider whether the measure actually achieves or is likely to achieve the end claimed for it, whether or not a measure less restrictive of individual freedom would achieve the same result and finally, whether the objective of the measure justifies even that minimum level of interference with individual liberty.'[74]

In English law, lack of proportionality is not a separate ground for judicial review,[75] except as part of Community law in cases involving Community law issues.[76] Unlike the European Court, an English court will confine itself to asking whether any reasonable administrative body could have reached the decision in question.[77] Under the influence of

---

72 *Ibid.*, at p.698H.

73 *Ibid.*, at p.698L (Lord Ross). See also p.701HI (Lord Sutherland).

74 Gordon Slynn, *Introducing a Legal Order* (1992), p.36.

75 But see e.g. *R.* v. *St. Albans Crown Court, Ex parte Cinnamond* [1981] Q.B. 480 and *R.* v. *Admiralty Board of the Defence Council, Ex parte Coupland* (18 July 1995), where penalties which were out of proportion to the gravity of the offence were quashed.

76 In *R.* v. *Secretary of State for the Home Department, Ex parte Gerard Adams* [1995] All E.R. (EC) 177, counsel for the applicant argued that since Community rights were in issue (freedom of movement), Community law required respect for the principle of proportionality as illustrated by Case 222/84, *Johnston* v. *Chief Constable of the R.U.C.* [1986] E.C.R. 1651, and that the principle had been violated by the exclusion order prohibiting Mr Adams from entering Great Britain. The High Court referred four questions to the E.C.J. under Art.177 but the reference was withdrawn after the exclusion order was revoked. With regard to the principle of legitimate expectation, cf. *R.* v. *M.A.F.F., Ex parte Hamble Fisheries (Offshore) Ltd.* [1995] 1 *C.M.L.R.* 533.

77 See *Associated Provincial Picture Houses Ltd.* v. *Wednesbury Corporation* [1948] 1 K.B. 223.

Community law, however, lack of proportionality will almost certainly come to be recognised as such a ground,[78] probably sooner rather than later, and those who advocate such a development seem to be pushing at an open door. Ten years ago, in *Council of Civil Service Unions* v. *Minister for the Civil Service*,[79] Lord Diplock stated:

> 'One can conveniently classify under three heads the grounds on which administrative action is subject to control by judicial review. The first ground I would call "illegality", the second "irrationality" and the third "procedural impropriety". That is not to say that further development on a case by case basis may not in course of time add further grounds. I have in mind particularly the possible adoption in the future of the principle of "proportionality" which is recognised in the administrative law of several of our fellow members of the European Economic Community.'[80]

Reference to that dictum was made by Lord Roskill in *R.* v. *Secretary of State for the Home Department, Ex parte Brind*:[81]

> '[Lord Diplock] clearly had in mind the likely increasing influence of Community law upon our domestic law which might in time lead to the adoption of [the principle of proportionality] as a separate category and not merely as a possible reinforcement of one or more of these three stated categories such as irrationality.'[82]

Recalling the suggestion of case by case development, his Lordship continued:

> 'I am clearly of the view that the present is not a case in which the first step can be taken for the reason that to apply the principle in the present case would be for

---

78 See P. Walker, 'Irrationality and Proportionality', in M. Supperstone QC and J. Goudie QC, *Judicial Review* (1992), pp.119, 137.

79 [1984] 3 All E.R. 935.

80 *Ibid.*, at p.950hj.

81 [1991] 1 A.C. 696.

82 *Ibid.*, at p.750A.

> the court to substitute its own judgment of what was needed to achieve a particular objective for the judgment of the Secretary of State upon whom that duty has been laid by Parliament. But so to hold in the present case is not to exclude the possible future development of the law in this respect, a possibility which has already been canvassed in some academic writings.'[83]

For his part, Lord Ackner observed that a total lack of proportionality would lead to a decision which was Wednesbury unreasonable. Short of this, however, he felt that application of the proportionality test would involve an enquiry into the merits for which there was then no basis in English law.[84]

The issue was further considered in 1992 by the Court of Appeal in *N.A.L.G.O.* v. *Secretary of State for the Environment.*[85] Recognising that in cases where European Community law is directly enforceable an English court must assess the validity of a domestic regulation by reference to the principle of proportionality, and that a principle akin to the principle of proportionality is applicable where an appellate court is considering the exercise of a judicial discretion or the appropriateness of a penalty,[86] Neill L.J. considered that it was

> 'less clear whether, and if so in what circumstances, a court could apply the the principle of proportionality when it was exercising the function of judicial review and when there was no substantive rule of Community law by which the relevant decision was to be measured.'[87]

---

83 *Ibid.*, at p.750EF.

84 *Ibid.*, at pp.762-763. Cf. the strong reservations expressed by Lord Lowry at p.767G: 'there can be little room for judges to operate an independent judicial review proportionality doctrine in the space which is left between the conventional judicial review doctrine and the admittedly forbidden appellate approach. To introduce an intermediate area of deliberation for the court seems scarcely a practical idea, quite apart from the other disadvantages by which, in my opinion, such a course would be attended'.

85 [1992] T.L.R. 576.

86 See *supra* n.75.

87 *Supra* n.85, at p.577.

In the light of *Brind*, his Lordship was satisfied that it was not open to a court below the House of Lords to depart from the traditional *Wednesbury* grounds of reasonableness when reviewing the decision of a Minister who had exercised a discretion vested in him by Parliament. On the other hand, he thought there was much to be said for the view that the courts in the European Community should apply common standards in the field of administrative law.[88] His Lordship felt that, in time, the English courts would become familiar with the principle of proportionality[89] and that in cases involving the judicial review of decisions made below government level the lack of proportionality might be recognised as a separate ground for intervention. In view of the delicate balance between the courts and the executive, however, he saw greater difficulty in applying the principle of proportionality to the decisions of government ministers.[90]

Re M[91] has surely made it easier for that to happen. Now that the English courts, at least, are able to grant mandatory injunctions against ministers of the Crown, even outside the Community law context, acceptance of the proportionality principle would require only a small step further on the part of the judiciary. It is arguable that allowing injunctive relief against the Crown is potentially as intrusive, and therefore as disturbing of the balance between the courts and the executive, as enquiring into the merits of administrative action. Besides, administrators would be entitled to a 'margin of appreciation' which could vary according to the subject-matter or even according to the remedy sought.[92] As Steyn L.J. (as he then was) observed in *R.* v. *Secretary of State for the Home Department, Ex parte Gerard Adams*:[93]

---

88 See further Jürgen Schwarze, *European Administrative Law* (1992), cited by Sedley J. in *R.* v. *M.A.F.F., Ex parte Hamble Fisheries (Offshore) Ltd., supra* n.76.

89 They are already using the principle in some non-EC contexts. For example, in *T.* v. *Secretary of State for the Home Department* [1994] T.L.R. 568 the Court of Appeal held that in deciding whether an asylum-seeker's crime is non-political for the purposes of Art.1F(b) of the 1951 Convention and Protocol relating to the Status of Refugees, regard must be had, *inter alia*, to whether the offence is disproportionate to a genuine political objective. It concluded that an airport bombing was 'grossly out of proportion to any genuine political objective' and therefore did not constitute a political offence.

90 *Supra* n.85, at p.577.

91 *Supra* n.59.

92 As in Community law. In Case 114/76, *Bela-Mühle Josef Bergmann K.G.* v. *Grows-Farm GmbH & Co. K.G.* [1977] E.C.R. 1211, the ECJ annulled a Council Regulation because it violated the principle of proportionality. However, in Joined Cases 83/76 and others, *Bayerische H.N.L. Vermehrungsbetriebe GmbH and Co. K.G.* v *Council and Commission of the European Communities* [1978] E.C.R. 1209 the Court dismissed an action for damages involving the same Regulation. It held that 'in the context of Community

> '... it seems to us that explanations of the principle [of proportionality] span a spectrum of views from a narrow doctrine not essentially very different from *Wednesbury* unreasonableness to a *de novo* review of the administrative decision ... Even in respect of proportionality there may be a margin of appreciation. And it is not self-evident that the principle of proportionality may not need to be adapted to the special circumstances of a case involving a tension between freedom of speech and national security.'[94]

The growing acceptance of the principle of proportionality in judicial review proceedings outside the Community law context is further illustrated by *R.* v. *Governors of St Gregory's R.C. Aided High School, Ex parte Roberts.*[95] Turner J. held that although an exclusion hearing before school governors had been flawed, the procedure adopted at a subsequent hearing by the appeals committee was fair and therefore the exclusion decision was valid. Significantly, he added:

> 'The decision would have been the same even if the principle of proportionality formed a part of the domestic law of the UK courts.'

Paradoxically, by drawing attention to the principle and observing that it would have made no difference to the outcome of the case, his Lordship may well have facilitated its emergence.

IV. FUNDAMENTAL RIGHTS

Some years ago David Pannick asked whether, in determining the substantive principles of judicial review, the English courts would move towards a theory based on proportionality and fundamental rights.[96] The

provisions in which one of the chief features was the exercise of a wide discretion essential for the implementation of the Common Agricultural Policy, the Community does not incur liability unless the institution concerned manifestly and gravely disregarded the limits on the exercise of its powers'.

93 *Supra* n.76.

94 *Ibid.*, at p.192. See also n.81 *supra*, at p.762H.

95 [1995] T.L.R. 28.

96 David Pannick, 'What is a Public Authority for the Purposes of Judicial Review?' in J.L. Jowell and D. Oliver (eds.), *New Directions in Judicial Review* (1988), pp.23, 34.

European Convention on Human Rights, which is not yet part of domestic law,[97] has long been recognised as an aid to the construction of ambiguous legislation.[98] However, ministers are considered to be under no legal obligation to take the Convention into account in exercising their statutory powers. In *R.* v. *Secretary of State for the Home Department, Ex parte Kirkwood,*[99] for example, Mann J. rejected the applicant's submission that the Home Secretary's decision to extradite him to the USA would be Wednesbury unreasonable in the light of Article 3 ECHR,[100] since there was no legal obligation upon the minister to take the Convention into consideration.[101]

Like the principle of proportionality, of course, the rights and freedoms enshrined in the European Convention demand protection by British judges in all cases where Community law issues arise. This is because fundamental rights form part of the general principles of Community law,[102] constraining not only the Community institutions themselves[103] but also national authorities whenever they act within the framework of Community law - in other words, whenever they are applying, obliged to apply or seeking to justify derogation from, Community rules.[104] Even outside the Community law context,

---

97 The Convention will shortly be incorporated into UK law. The Human Rights Bill was published in October 1997.

98 See e.g. *R.* v. *Chief Immigration Officer, Heathrow Airport, Ex parte Salamat Bibi* [1976] 1 W.L.R. 979; *R.* v. *Secretary of State for the Home Department, Ex parte Brind, supra* n.82; *Derbyshire C.C.* v. *Times Newspapers Ltd.* [1992] 3 All E.R. 65. But cf. the judgment of the Court of Session (Outer House) in *Kaur* v. *Lord Advocate* 1981 S.L.T. 322.

99 [1984] 1 W.L.R. 913.

100 The applicant, who was wanted for murder in the USA, argued that extradition would be likely to expose him to the 'death-row phenomenon' and so violate Art.3 of the Convention, which prohibits torture and inhuman or degrading treatment or punishment. The European Court of Human Rights subsequently upheld that argument in *Soering* v. *United Kingdom (A/161):* [1989] 11 E.H.R.R. 439.

101 See also *R.* v. *Secretary of State for the Home Department, Ex parte Brind*, n. 81 *supra*.

102 Indeed, by virtue of Art.F(2) of the Treaty on European Union they are part of the constitutional order of the EU.

103 See Case C-404/92P, *X.* v. *Commission* [1994] E.C.R. I-4737, where the ECJ annulled a Commission Decision because it infringed the applicant's right to privacy which is enshrined in Article 8 E.C.H.R. He had been subjected to an AIDS test without his consent.

104 David A.O. Edward and Robert C. Lane, *European Community Law* (2nd ed. 1995) para.153; Nicholas Grief 'The Domestic Impact of the European Convention on Human Rights as Mediated through Community Law' [1991] *Public Law* 555. See e.g. Case 5/88, *Wachauf* v. *Federal Republic of Germany* [1989] E.C.R. 2609; Case 260/89, *Elliniki Radiophonia Tiléorassi A.E.* v. *Dimotiki Etairia Pliroforissis and Sotirios Kouvelas* [1991] E.C.R. I-2925; Case C-62/90, *Commission of the European Communities* v. *Federal*

however, English courts have sometimes treated the Convention as 'an articulation of some of the principles underlying the common law'.[105] This bears comparison with the ECJ's longstanding willingness to regard it as a source of Community law principles.

Such an approach also appears to be a developing feature of Scottish jurisprudence. In *Irfan Ahmed*,[106] an immigration case involving a petition for judicial review of a decision of the Home Secretary, counsel referred to the European Convention and to cases under it in order to emphasise that serious consideration had to be given to the impact of any decision upon the petitioner's family life.[107] Lord Coulsfield stated that

> '... if the policy of the Home Office were one which ignored the obvious humanitarian principle of respect for family life, that would be a factor in favour of holding the policy to be unreasonable and subject to the Court's review. I do not think that, so far as this case is concerned, the Convention or the cases decided under it take matters any further ...'[108]

V. CONCLUSION: THE CHALLENGE FACING LAW SCHOOLS

According to a recent Law Commission paper,[109]

Republic of Germany [1992] E.C.R. I-2575; Case C-159/90, *S.P.U.C. Ireland Ltd.* v. *Grogan* [1991] E.C.R. I-4685 (especially the Advocate General's opinion).

105 *Rantzen* v. *Mirror Group Newspapers and Others* [1993] T.L.R. 206, at p.207 (Neill L.J.). See e.g. *Attorney-General* v. *Guardian Newspapers Ltd. (No.2)* [1990] 1 A.C. 109; *Derbyshire C.C.* v. *Times Newspapers Ltd.* [1993] 2 W.L.R. 449; and *R.* v. *Cambridge Health Authority, Ex parte B.* [1995] T.L.R. 159, in which Laws J. observed that the 'rights occupying a central place in the European Convention ... and obviously including the right to life ... were to be vindicated as sharing with other principles the substance of English common law'. In *R.* v *Secretary of State for the Home Department, Ex parte Norney* [1995] T.L.R. 500, Dyson J. held that the Home Secretary's policy of not referring the cases of discretionary life prisoners to the Parole Board until after the expiry of the tariff period of their sentences 'flouted the principles of common law and the European Convention on Human Rights'. Cf. *Wheeler* v. *Leicester C.C.* [1985] A.C. 1054 at p.1064B, where Browne-Wilkinson L.J. (as he then was) observed that the Universal Declaration of Human Rights and the European Convention on Human Rights 'do not extend the rights any further than those established by our domestic law'.

106 Court of Session: Outer House, 26 Oct. 1994.

107 See Art. 8 of the European Convention.

108 At pp.24-25 of the transcript. See also the judgment of Lord Morison in *Budh Singh* 1988 S.C. 349.

109 *Supra* n.61.

> 'senior judges have pointed to a divergence from EC law as a justification for changing domestic law. On this approach, our membership of the Community gives EC law a greater role as an indicator of possible avenues of reform than other systems of law which might be considered in a comparative manner.'[110]

One reason is that European law is 'habit forming': a practice or principle enters into the judicial consciousness within the framework of Community law; judges grow accustomed to it and come to appreciate its value, and eventually they find a use for it in cases without any European element. The impact of legal education is also clearly relevant: the judges and lawyers of today are generally much more conversant with European law than their predecessors.[111] But perhaps it is the impact *upon* legal education which poses the greatest challenge:

> 'Today, no lawyer can risk being ignorant of European Community law.'[112]

That is certainly true, not merely because of its obvious impact in matters with a European dimension but also because EC law is pervasively (some would say insidiously) re-shaping our legal order. British law teaching and legal research must respond by tracking its domestic influence and investigating the underlying reasons, seeking to anticipate developments and suggest reforms, and critically assessing whether in this regard Community law is a corrective (like equity to the common law?) or a contaminant.

---

110 *Ibid.*, at para. 2.10.

111 See e.g. [1994] *I.R.L.R.* 149 where, in relation to *R.* v. *Secretary of State for Employment, Ex parte Equal Opportunities Commission* (*ibid.* at p.176), Michael Rubenstein refers to 'the dramatic changes in the composition of the judicial committee of the House of Lords'.

112 L. Neville Brown, 'New Judicial Architecture on the Kirchberg', in *Lecturers' News*, Sweet & Maxwell, Autumn 1994. See further Francis G. Jacobs, 'Preparing English Lawyers for Europe', (1992) 17 *E.L.Rev.* pp.232, 233.

7

EUROPEANISATION AND ECCLESIASTICAL LAW

Hanns Engelhardt

As Professor Gordon mentioned, quite rightly, it may be contended that canon law was the first corpus of law which could be regarded as European in the sense that its force was not limited to individual European countries. Throughout the Middle Ages, there were, of course, canons which could claim local or regional force only; we need only look in Johnson's collection of *The Laws and Canons of the Church of England*[1], beginning with the canons of the Council of Hertford (673). But the great canonical works - e.g. of Ivo of Chartres and others - intended at least to reproduce what had general authority in the Church at large. The *Decretum* of Gratian (1140) was regarded as containing norms which had to be obeyed throughout the Catholic Church, and the official collections of decretals published by several popes, as the *Liber Extra* of 1234 and the *Sext* of 1298, claimed universal authority. The Roman Catholic Church lived under this corpus of canon law, to which other collections were added, until 1917, when the *Codex Iuris Canonici*, a modern codification after the example of the important codifications of secular law like the French *Code civile*, the Austrian *Allgemeines Bürgerliches Gesetzbuch*, the German *Bürgerliches Gesetzbuch* - to name but a few - was promulgated.

But the unity of Latin canon law was lost at the Reformation. The Churches which accepted the Reformation appear not to have been able to maintain, even among themselves, a common Church law. So

---

1 Oxford 1850/51 (new ed.).

national Church laws developed, and - more and more - the laws governing the relationship of the Churches to the States in which they lived grew to be different as the national opinions regarding this relationship developed. Some more or less common principles may have survived; but their binding force did not rest on any common basis but on the legislation in the several States concerned. (In Germany this holds good even with regard to the single territories until 1918). This was - the Ecumenical Movement of the twentieth century notwithstanding - the state of affairs when the States of Europe began to get closer to each other after the end of World War II.

1. If we look at the law concerning the relationship of Church and State in the European States, we may form three groups. There are, firstly, the States which have preserved the system in which there is one State Church, which does not mean that there is no religious liberty for those citizens who do not want to conform to the rules of this State Church. The most prominent members of this group are the Scandinavian States - Sweden, Norway and Denmark - with their Lutheran State Churches which command, if only formally, the loyalty of the vast majority of their citizens. The United Kingdom belongs to this group as far as England and Scotland are concerned, while there are no State - or established - Churches in Wales and Northern Ireland since the Church of Ireland and the Church in Wales were disestablished in the nineteenth and twentieth centuries. It is rather interesting to note that Péter Erdö in his recent book on Church and Religion in today's Hungarian law finds a certain similarity between the English system of Church and State and the Hungarian one up to the end of World War II[2].

At the other end of the spectrum we find those States which have introduced a total separation of Church and State, e.g., France and Portugal as well as most States which belonged to the former Soviet bloc. Again, this does not mean that there are no legal relationships whatever between Church and State. Even in France - where the separation of Church and State was introduced with considerable hostility at the beginning of this century - in the course of time some new connections have been built up with regard, for example, to State assistance for private Church schools[3].

Between these two groups we find a third one comprising those States which have abolished the traditional State Church without totally

---

2 Cf. Péter Erdö & Balázs Schanda, *Egyház és vallás a mai magyar jogban*, (1993), p.22 seq.

3 Cf. A. v. Campenhausen, *Staat und Kirche in Frankreich*, 1962, *passim*.

severing the connections of State and Church. It is to this group that Germany belongs.

The relationship between the State and the Church(es) in Germany is characterised by what one might call 'semi-disestablishment'. In Germany it has been called '*hinkende Trennung*' - claudicant separation. What is meant by this is shown by a brief retrospect on the development of the relations between Church and State in Germany since the time of the Reformation.

(a) In the time after the Reformation of the sixteenth century the relationship of State and Church in Germany was, on the whole, rather the same as in England. One major difference, however, derived from the fact that the German Reich of that time was not a unitarian State, but - for all practical purposes - a federation of more or less independent princes and cities. So the Peace Treaty of Augsburg of 1555 decreed that the decision as to which confession should be binding on the Church was to lie with the single (princes of the) territories, not any longer with the central imperial authority of the Reich. In part of the territories the Lutheran confession was introduced, or had been introduced already; other territories remained under allegiance to the Pope. Only the princes spiritual had to resign if they converted to the Lutheran confession..

In the territories in which the Reformation was introduced, the jurisdiction of the bishops, who remained - in most cases - Roman Catholic, was suspended by the Peace Treaty (§20); in these territories the secular ruler was at the same time supreme governor of the Church. In the territories which remained Roman Catholic the status of the Church remained as it had been before the time of the Reformation. But in these territories the external affairs of the Church were governed by the State, too. In both cases the Church was 'by law established' in the sense that only one Church was allowed, and the State decided which one. The Augsburg Peace Treaty did not accord religious liberty to individual subjects. They had to conform to the decision of the respective princes. But there was a beginning. Subjects who did not feel able to conform were to be permitted to leave the territory (*beneficium emigrandi*, §24).

These regulations were recognised as valid by the Peace Treaty of Westphalia of 1648 by which the Swiss Reformed, who had been excluded from the Peace of 1555, were included, too (Article VII §1).

In the course of the seventeenth and eighteenth centuries, not all territorial changes which occurred were followed by a religious change. More and more, the princes began to tolerate other religions in the territories which they acquired. When in the beginning of the nineteenth century the spiritual territories were abolished by the *Reichsdeputationshauptschluß* of 1802/3 - formally a decision of the Diet and the Emperor - and transferred to other States, the freedom to exercise the former religion was guaranteed. So the majority of the larger German States had a mixed population, partly Roman Catholic and partly Protestant, i.e. either Lutheran or Reformed. Church property was transferred, to a large extent, to the State also; at the same time the State became obliged to make certain payments to the Churches (*Staatsleistungen*) as an aid to the fulfilment of their financial needs.

In the course of the nineteenth century, the close connection of State and Church was loosened. The Churches gained a certain autonomy. The princes remained the supreme governors of the Protestant Churches; but parallel to the constitutional parliaments in the States, synods were introduced for Church legislation. The Churches were regarded as 'corporations under public law', distinct from, but under the supervision of, the State.

(b) In 1918/19 the monarchy was abolished in Germany. Thus, the protestant Churches lost their supreme governors. The Constitution of the German Reich of 1919 declared that no State Church existed any longer. It guaranteed to all Churches - and indeed to all religious communities - the right of self-government without interference from the State or the municipality, but within the framework of the general laws which are binding on all citizens (*innerhalb der Schranken des für alle geltenden Gesetzes*). By virtue of this the Churches can legislate with regard to their own affairs though there are, from time to time, disputes with regard to the extent and limits of 'their affairs'. Church law needs no approval by the State; on the other hand, the State is obliged to recognise the decisions of the Church without being able to review them. Only insofar as the Churches exercise public powers delegated by the State (*hoheitliche Befugnisse*) - as when they levy Church tax or maintain and administer public cemeteries - their decisions may be made the subject of judicial review in the State courts. The Church has the right to appoint incumbents and other officers without influence from the State. There is, for all practical purposes, no resort to the courts of the State in disputes about the labour relationships of the clergy.

In practice, however, the State retained some influence, especially - to a certain degree - with regard to the superior offices of the Churches. This influence derived in part from the elevated status of corporations under public law, which the great traditional Churches enjoyed, and which was held to be necessarily connected with a certain degree of government supervision (*Staatsaufsicht*), in part from agreements between Church and State.

This special status of corporations under public law was guaranteed to the Churches by the Constitution as far as they had had this status before 1919 (Article 137 section 6 clause 1). By this status the Churches enjoy an important position in public life, and at the same time the State appears to recognise this position[4]. So we have a three tier system of religious congregations in Germany: in the upper drawer - so to speak - we find the Churches and religious communities which are corporations under public law, among them the Roman Catholic dioceses and the Protestant *Landeskirchen*, the former State Churches, and the Jewish congregations. On the second level we find a great number of small Churches or religious communities which are associations of private law, among them a number of Anglican chaplaincies, which may obtain the status of corporations under public law under certain conditions - appearance of stability by virtue of their constitution and of the number of their members (Article 137 section 6 clause 2), and some of them have, as Methodists, Baptists, or - by far the largest body among them - the so-called New Apostolic Churches. On the third level, we find religious communities which have no legal personality (*Rechtsfähigkeit*).

The property rights of Churches and religious communities were guaranteed by the constitution too (Article 138 section 2). Payments by the State (*Staatsleistungen*) to the Churches based on law, treaties, or special legal titles, should be redeemed or commuted (*abgelöst*) (Article 138 section 1); this regulation had, however, the effect of a guarantee as no agreement with regard to the form and extent of this redemption or commutation could be achieved. These payments are made even today, though in a consolidated form.

The right to levy Church taxes from their members had already been granted to the Churches in the course of the second half of the nineteenth century. The motive of the State was that it avoided the necessity of increasing State payments for the stipends of the clergy. Other than in England, where compulsory Church rates were abolished in 1866 because it was felt undesirable to give cause to an exodus of people unwilling to pay[5], the State granted to everyone the legal

4 Cf. P. Kirchhof in: *Handbuch des Staatskirchenrechts der Bundesrepublik Deutschland*, 2nd ed., Vol. 1 p. 655.

5 Cf. S M Waddams, *Law, Politics and the Church of England*, 1992, p. 249-269 (253).

possibility to withdraw from Church membership (*austreten*) by a declaration made to the local court or register office (*Standesamt*) of the State. These Church taxes have for nearly a century made the German Churches rather affluent. At the same time there has indeed been a steady flow of members leaving the Churches, not least because they did not see any advantage for themselves in the payment of Church tax. It remains to be seen whether this decrease in membership will continue in the future.

In some other respects, too, the interests of the Churches are protected by the constitution. The observance of Sundays and recognised holidays is protected; the constitution itself requires that these days be not treated like normal days of work. While only a small number of schools are Church schools, religious education in State schools according to the principles of the religious communities is guaranteed; pupils - or their parents - may opt out, however. A very hot debate has been roused by a recent decision of the Constitutional Court according to which a crucifix may not be displayed in the classroom of a State school - as prescribed at least in Bavaria - if a pupil or his parents object.

So one can regard the separation of State and Church in 1919 as a sort of disestablishment; but it was in no way a disendowment. The Churches retained their status in public law and their property rights, and obtained constitutional guarantees for the future.

A very important role among the sources of law concerning the relationship between the State and the Churches in Germany is played by treaties between Church and State. For the Roman Catholic Church, concordats (i.e., treaties) between the Holy See and secular powers, are an old and well-established tradition. As long ago as 1122, the election of bishops in the Holy Roman Empire was regulated by a concordat between Pope Calixtus II and the emperor Henry V. In the early nineteenth century, the relations between the Kingdom of Bavaria and the Roman Catholic Church were determined by the concordat of 1817. In other territories affairs of mutual interest were regulated by parallel agreed legislation of State and Church. After 1918, the Holy See succeeded in concluding concordats with Bavaria - again -, Prussia and Baden, and at last, with the German Reich. The *Reichskonkordat* has gained a special notoriety because it was the first international treaty concluded by the Hitler government, and helped to achieve international reputation for that regime. For this purpose, the German government made concessions to the Roman Catholic Church - especially in the law relating to schools - which former republican governments hadn't been prepared to make. The validity of this concordat has been an object of continuous discussion since 1945. The three States mentioned before - Bavaria, Prussia and Baden - concluded similar treaties with the evangelic Churches of their territories for reasons of parity[6]. The contents of these treaties are very similar and cannot all be recounted here. One rather important point is the regulation of State payments to the Church. With regard to these payments, which serve - in part at least - for the augmentation of clergy stipends, Church and State agreed on certain preconditions for the appointment of parochial clergy, e.g., German nationality and theological study at a German university for at least three years. The so-called 'political clause' gave the State the right to object to candidates for the office of bishop for political reasons.

Another important subject of these treaties is the guarantee to the theological faculties in the State universities. Many German State universities include faculties of theology which are - unlike in England or America - either Roman Catholic or Protestant. The Roman Catholic Church has - by the concordats - acquired a strong position with regard to the appointment of professors of theology. Nobody may be appointed without the consent of the bishop. Even if he has been appointed - with the bishop's consent - the bishop may afterwards complain about the teaching or the lifestyle of the professor. Then, the State is obliged to appoint another one and to remove the original holder of the chair from the theological faculty, without prejudice, however, to his rights as a university professor, i.e., he remains a professor, but not in the Roman Catholic faculty.

After World War II the position of the Churches in the State was strengthened considerably. For the Churches had got over the war and the general breakdown far better than the civil authorities. Their political influence increased, not least by the political predominance - during the early years of the Federal Republic of Germany - of a Christian party. The relevant Articles of the Constitution of 1919 were incorporated in the Basic Law of 1949; so basically, the system remained the same, and what was said about the relationship of Church and State under the Constitution of 1919 is true even now. But the new political context strengthened the position of the Churches in the State.

---

6 If a remark on terminology is permitted I should like to point to the fact that there are two different words in the German language, '*evangelisch*' and '*evangelikal*'. The first one means largely the same as 'protestant' and is found in the official names of the Churches deriving from the Reformation; the second one denotes the ecclesio-political tendency which is called 'evangelical' in the English language. These are, of course, two different things. So you may find rather 'catholic' tendencies in Churches which are called '*evangelisch*'. Therefore I should think it might be useful to translate '*evangelisch*' by 'evangelic', not 'evangelical'.

The former superiority of the State faded away nearly totally. A new series of treaties was concluded by German *Länder* with their evangelic Churches, beginning with the famous treaty of Loccum of 1955 between the State of Lower Saxony and the Lutheran and Reformed Churches, which became a model for a number of treaties with other *Länder*. The juridical status of all these treaties has been an object of dispute. The concordats have been regarded either as treaties under international law or as quasi-international treaties. As the evangelic Churches are not subjects of international law, it has been rather difficult to find a legal basis other than State law on which to found the treaties. Some lawyers have assumed a legal order (*Rechtsordnung*) which is *sui generis*. But one may suspect that this theory only leads into ever more difficult problems.

In the German Democratic Republic we find a different development, of course. As in other States of the so-called 'really existing socialism', the position of the Church in State and society was curtailed as much as possible. The Churches had to live on the voluntary contributions of their members, and, as this was not sufficient, on financial assistance from the Churches of the Federal Republic. In 1990, when Germany was united again, this dependence on Western assistance forced the East German Churches to take over the Western system of Church-State relations and, above all, the Church tax system, though many churchmen in the new member States of the Federal Republic felt quite uneasy about this. The re-unification of Germany in 1990 and the re-structuring of ecclesiastical law in the so-called new *Länder* initiated a new time of treaties, too. The first of them - between the Land Sachsen-Anhalt and six evangelic Churches (*Landeskirchen*) was signed on 15 September 1993 at Wittenberg. It has been called a Loccum for the new *Länder*[7]. In the meanwhile, three more treaties were concluded between the Länder Mecklenburg-Vorpommem, Sachsen and Thüringen and their Churches[8].

(c) I should like to add some remarks on the relationship of Church and State in Hungary, for this country provides a significant example of developments in the former socialist countries of Central and Eastern

---

7 Cf. Hermann Weber, '*Der Wittenberger Vertrag - Ein Loccum für die neuen Bundesländer?*' in: *Festschrift Emst Gottfried Mahrenholz* (1994), p. 99 sqq.

8 Cf. A. v. Campenhausen, '*Vier neue Staatskirchenverträge in vier neuen Ländern*', [1995] *NVwZ* (*Neue Zeitschrift für Verwaltungsrecht*) 757.

Europe[9]. Until the end of World War II, ecclesiastical law in Hungary consisted of a mass of regulations which had developed in the course of history, and were rather complicated[10] The Churches in Hungary enjoyed only a limited liberty. There was a distinction between the so-called 'received' (*bevett*) and the 'legally recognised' (*törvényesen elismert*) Churches and religious communities. The former group comprised the Roman, Greek and Armenian Catholic, the Reformed, the Lutheran, the Serb and Romanian Orthodox and the Unitarian Churches as well as the Jewish communities. The foundation of new legally recognised religious communities was controlled by the State, which also set the preconditions for such foundation. The received Churches and religious communities enjoyed a privileged position, for instance they could send representatives to the Upper House of Parliament. After the war, the distinction between received and legally recognised religious communities was abolished. In the course of the establishment of communist rule, a hostile separation of Church and State came into being. However, the State, which had expropriated most Church property, granted limited financial assistance to the Churches and concluded agreements with the Roman Catholic, Reformed, Lutheran and Unitarian Churches[11]. But on the whole, State policy was directed at a suppression of Church influence in society. For example, the numerous Church schools were taken over by the State with few exceptions; teachers were not permitted to officiate as cantors in Churches as they usually had done before. Of course, many Church people were prosecuted, and detained. But unlike other socialist countries, the Hungarian regime had already lost much of its strictness and rigidity before the great change. New regulations were prepared in order to improve the religious liberty of the individual and of religious communities. Eventually, with the collapse of the communist system, the sections of the constitution concerning religion were changed too, and a new law concerning the liberty of conscience, religion and the Churches was enacted. This law, No. IV of 1990, and the revised constitution, emphasise these liberties, although in the framework of a pronounced separation. The normative foundations of the relationships between the State and the Churches are regulated not by concordats in

---

9 For what follows cf. Erdö & Schanda, see n.2, *supra*, *passim*; Erdö, in: 29 *Essener Gespräche zum Thema Staat und Kirche* (1995), p. 134 sqq.

10 Cf. Erdö & Schanda, see n.2 *supra*, *passim*, p. 20.

11 Cf. H Engelhardt, '*Die Vereinbarungen des ungarischen Staates mit den Kirchen*', in; *Verantwortlichkeit und Freiheit. Festschrift für Willi Geiger* (1989), pp. 722 sqq.

the first place, but by parallel legislation. Agreements between State and Church are possible, however, and there are two so-called 'partial agreements' (*részleges megállapodások*) with the Roman Catholic Church. Churches get their money by way of voluntary contributions from their members, and by considerable annual payments from the State which are, however, not guaranteed by law. There are no theological faculties in the State universities; but the Churches have begun to extend their own theological academies into ecclesiastical universities, for example, the Roman Catholic Church as well as the Reformed Church are at present organising faculties of law in the Péter Pázmány University and the Gáspár Károli University. I have been told that the present coalition government of socialists and liberals is not very happy and helpful in this respect; but one has the impression that the Churches are very successful in recruiting prominent teachers, and this seems to be the most important precondition for their eventual success.

2. As we are talking about Europeanisation of the law I trust you will permit me some words about ecclesiastical law on the transnational level, too. In the Europe of today, ecclesiastical law is no longer governed exclusively by national law. It is not surprising that the Council of Europe should have been active in this area. But the law of the European Union has begun to influence religion and the Churches, too. Even the work of the Conference on Security and Co-operation in Europe begins at least to extend into this realm.

(a) The first important step to European unity was the foundation of the Council of Europe in 1949. This oldest of the important European institutions of our time was instrumental in bringing about and implementing the European Convention for the Protection of Human Rights and Fundamental Freedoms. These rights and freedoms, as guaranteed by the Convention and protected by the European Human Rights Commission and the European Court of Human Rights, include the freedom of religion. Article 9 of the Human Rights Convention says[12]:

> '(1) Everyone has the right to freedom of thought, conscience and religion; this right includes freedom to change his religion or belief and freedom, either alone or in community with others and in public

---

12 [1952] 2 BGBl (*Bundesgesetzblatt*) 689.

> or private, to manifest his religion or belief, in worship, teaching, practice and observance.
>
> (2) Freedom to manifest one's religion or beliefs shall be subject only to such limitations as are prescribed by law and are necessary in a democratic society in the interests of public safety, for the protection of public order, health or morals, or for the protection of the rights and freedoms of others'.

Contrary to most State constitutions the Convention expressly protects the right to change one's religion or belief. This was rather important as some State regulations, as in Sweden, did not permit the withdrawal from the State Church without at the same time becoming a member of some other religious community. This Swedish regulation was repealed only in 1951, after the coming into force of the Convention[13].

Another important aspect is that Churches and religious communities can invoke Article 9 as such, and not only individuals.

The establishment of a State Church is not forbidden by Article 9; the Convention does not impose on the Member States the separation of Church and State[14]. But it need not be explained at length that any compulsion with regard to membership of such a State Church, or to an observance of its rites, would be at variance with the Convention. The individual must have the right to withdraw from any connection with the State Church, or any other Church, whenever he so chooses.

(b) If we turn to the European Union, formerly the European Communities, we may say: 'In the beginning was the economy'. For more than thirty-five years, what is now the European Union, was an economic community. Religious questions were of no importance for that new supranational entity. But as the Churches live in the world, the Europeanisation of the law concerning commerce, industry, and labour could not but affect the Churches also. The free movement of workers in the Community extends to employees of the Churches. The freedom of (commercial) establishment may be an advantage for ecclesiastical activities. The EC Council Directive concerning television says that religious services and other religious transmissions of less than 30

---

13 Frowein, '*Die Bedeutung des die Gedanken-, Gewissens- und Religionsfreiheit garantierenden Artikels 9 der Europäischen Menschenrechtskonvention*', 27 *Essener Gespräche zum Thema Staat und Kirche* (1993), p. 46 sqq., at p. 50.

14 Frowein, see n.13 *supra*, p. 49.

minutes length must not be interrupted by advertising. Advertising on TV must not offend religious feelings.

Accordingly, the European Court of Justice has been seised with matters of religious concern.

In the *Van Roosmalen* Case[15] a Dutch Roman Catholic priest had worked as a missionary in Zaire. He was a member of a religious order; though during his time of missionary work he received maintenance not from his order, but from the congregation he served. There was no contract of employment. The court held that he rendered independent personal services, and so he was accorded the benefits of freedom of establishment and of social security.

In the *Steymann* Case[16] the complainant, a German, had settled in the Netherlands and worked, at first, as an employee. Later on, he became a member of the *De Stad Rajneesh Neo-Sannyas Community*, also called Bhagwan Community, a religious community which secures its economic independence by running a disco, a beverage shop, and a laundry saloon. In the framework of his participation in the life of this community, Mr Steymann supplied plumbing and domestic services. He received no fixed payment, but maintenance. He applied for a stay permit in the Netherlands. It was denied. The Court held that religious activities belong to the scope of Common Market Law only insofar as they may be regarded as part of economic life. Paid services are a part of economic life. Thus, services of a member of a religious community rendered in the framework of the economic activities of this community form part of economic life insofar as what the member gets from the community can be regarded as a remuneration for actual services by the member.

It was only in 1975 that the European Court of Justice had to deal with a question of religious liberty when it had to decide on a complaint concerning the contest for a position in the European civil service by a Jewish lady who felt unable to take part in an examination held on the first day of the Jewish feast of Pentecost[17]. The court held that religious impediments of that kind had to be respected if they were notified to the European authorities in due time.

European law may also affect what, from a secular point of view, appears to be the law concerning labour relations between the Churches and their ministers: for instance, in Germany there are clauses

---

15 Judgment of 23 Oct 1986, Case 300/84, *Slg.* (*Sammlung* (German)) 1986 p. 3097.

16 Judgment of 5 Oct 1988, Case 196/87, *Slg.* 1988 p. 6159; *NVwZ* 1990, p. 53.

17 27.10.76, *Rs.* 1'30/75, *Slg.* 1976, 1589.

in concordats and treaties between the State and the Churches which require that priests are, as a rule, German citizens and have undertaken theological studies for a certain time at a German university. These regulations seem to be questionable under the European law of free movement of labour in the Community and the Council Directive concerning the mutual recognition of university diplomas.

(c) Even in the work of the Conference on Security and Co-operation in Europe, the Churches play a role, however small. Among the ten principles for international relationships, in principle seven the Member States subscribed to the human rights and fundamental freedoms, expressly including religious liberty, and they have undertaken to recognise the freedom of the individual to avow and to practise, alone or in communion with others, his religion or conviction (persuasion) in accordance with what his - or her - conscience commands him - or her. It goes without saying that the freedom to practise one's religion in communion with others is of fundamental importance for the life of the Churches. It must be kept in mind, however, that the final document of Helsinki is no binding international treaty; its significance, therefore, is not legal, but political.

3. On the whole, European law has exerted only a limited influence on the internal law of the Member States of the European Union regarding the relationship of Church and State. Even this limited influence, however, has caused considerable anxiety in some people, who fear that their inherited and cherished traditions may be overturned. In order to prevent this, I have tried to show that our own system in Germany may well serve as a model for other, allegedly less developed - in this part of the law - countries. The results of all this remain to be seen.

8

THE EUROPEANISATION OF PUBLIC LAW: ECCLESIASTICAL LAW

A RESPONSE BY AUGUR PEARCE
TO BUNDESRICHTER DR HANNS ENGELHARDT

I should like to add my voice in thanking Dr Engelhardt for a very full and wide-ranging introduction to the church-State relationship across the European spectrum, and to some of the issues affecting the churches which European institutions and common legal standards may throw up.

Germany, where I have lived for the past four years, is a particularly fruitful source of ideas in the area of ecclesiastical law, offering as it does two large denominations with their own legal systems, many smaller ones with a quite different legal régime, a history in which every conceivable permutation of the church-State relationship has featured, and a wealth of recent constitutional cases, some of which have had direct material effect on the ordinary citizen. In his remarks on his own country Dr Engelhardt has given us a taste of this variety of subject-matter, and I hope inspired us to pursue particular areas more closely.

But I feel that a note of caution must be sounded as regards taking the modern German system as a model for a wider European approach. This is partly because, as I suggest, there are areas in which no such wider approach is necessary; but also because in other areas, those in which the Europeanisation of law will undoubtedly affect the churches, Germany appears to me to be going against the general trend.

The distinction I would draw is between, on the one hand, those fields in which the views of the churches themselves (together with regional or national history and culture) can be determinative, and on the other, those which involve necessarily universal concepts like human rights or environmental protection.

Let me illustrate what I mean. The heading of this session brings together the two expressions: 'ecclesiastical law' and 'public law'. To some, inclined to think of churches as voluntary associations of people pursuing a common activity even this juxtaposition may have an anomalous ring. But they are thinking in very modern terms. Historically there have been three ways in which ecclesiastical law has either been or brushed against public law.

I THE REFORMATION APPROACH

One such way I shall call the Reformation approach - more to place it chronologically than to attribute it to any Protestant Reformer. On this approach, ecclesiastical law is public in nature because it stems from public authority in the form of the temporal ruler. It is, as a leading English decision[1] put it, 'the King's ecclesiastical law'.

Various attempts have been made to justify this. The most modest theory is that of the *jus reformandi*, by which a Christian prince has the right and duty to intervene in the affairs of the church in order to set it right and check abuses which the church's own organs are failing to deal with. Having done so, he must sit back and allow the now-reformed church to govern itself once more. On a more permanent basis, the temporal ruler (Council or King) may be seen as the church's 'principal member', who perforce needs to take over as such those functions which bishops can no longer be trusted to perform. Yet more drastic is to see the church as nothing more than the nation 'wearing its spiritual hat', subject therefore by simple logic to the nation's sovereign head.

The 'principal member' theory was long dominant in the Lutheran territories of the Holy Roman Empire and still holds today in Scandinavia. The 'identity with the nation' theory can be seen in the religious legislation of some Swiss cantons, but is above all clear from the Preamble to the English Ecclesiastical Appeals Act 1532[2].

Both theories have their drawbacks in modern ecclesiology and in pluralistic democratic societies. But I believe the role for State organs which has resulted from them is something that - even in a more united Europe - the churches themselves can be left to sort out. History offers several precedents for political federations leaving religious matters to the constituent units: the Swiss Confederation (where local autonomy preceded the Reformation), the Holy Roman Empire in the Religious

1 *Caudrey's Case* (1591) 5 Co. Rep. 1.

2 24 Hen. VIII c.12.

Peace of Augsburg (1555), the United Kingdom of Great Britain in the Treaty and Acts of Union (1706/7). And speaking of Switzerland, there is evidence that such relics of State authority in church matters as remain today are by no means automatically resented: in ten days' time the people of Canton Zürich will be voting in a referendum aimed at severing the church-State links in the canton, but both the churches concerned and the cantonal government have declared themselves emphatically against such a step.[3]

Ways have been found of getting round the difficulty of a national church in a pluralistic society. Germany and Switzerland accord every citizen the right to dissociate him- or herself formally from a religious body, with consequences in the secular legal sphere such as freedom from church taxation[4]. England, though continuing to regard everybody as potentially a member of the national church, now attaches benefits but no burdens to this assumption: Englishmen may seek the church's ministrations, appear before its courts, elect some of its officers, but must no longer attend its services perforce or support it with their tithes[5].

II THE MEDIAEVAL APPROACH

Let us look at another approach to ecclesiastical law as public law. It is older than the one we have considered, and flourished throughout the Middle Ages; but is in some ways mirrored in modern Germany. The underlying motivation here is the idea of a public interest in religion; that a religious country is a fortunate country.

For the Emperor Constantine, this was expressed as an interest in promoting true religion. He was just as concerned that Heaven should be properly worshipped and smile accordingly upon his government as that the Christian Church's administrative structure should contribute to the unity of his Empire. The rulers of the

---

3 In fact the Zürich electorate voted against a dissolution of the church-State link by a substantial majority.

4 This right is regulated by *Land* legislation in the federal *Grundgesetz* of 1949, Art. 4(1).

5 E.g., Canon B22 (duty to baptise), *Argar v. Holdsworth* (1758) 2 Lee 515 (duty to marry), Canon C38 (duty to bury), *Cole v. Police Constable 443A* [1937] 1 KB 316 (right to attend divine service), Faculty Jurisdiction Rules 1992, r. 15 (*locus standi* of parishoners in faculty cases), Churchwardens (Appointment and Resignation) Measure 1964, s.3 (parsioners' participation in choice of churchwardens); Toleration Act 1688, ss.1, 2 (relief from prosecution for failure to worship with established church), Tithe Act 1936, s. 1 (abolition of tithe rentcharge).

mediaeval period, had they stopped to consider the place of ecclesiastical law in their systems, would have concurred without thinking twice.

Modern, confessionally neutral Germany cannot speak in the same way of 'promoting true religion', and no longer purports to determine which religion is true and which is not. But the 1949 *Grundgesetz* still recognises the important role which religious (and humanist) bodies play in society by the special treatment which it gives them[6]. At the same time it acknowledges that they have an autonomous lawmaking capacity in their own affairs, to which the temporal courts will (without more) give effect. State organs concluding so-called 'church treaties' deal with the churches more as equals than in a sovereign/subject relationship. All these factors imply the churches having a 'public' function which is seen as original and not derivative, and which does not necessarily bow before the ordinances of the temporal power.

III PUBLIC LAW AND THE CHURCHES' RULES

In both the approaches we have considered the emphasis has been on rules made for the churches, whether by themselves or by State organs. Public law affecting the churches need not, however, present itself as law *of* the church; it may equally well be law *about* the churches, or law which impinges upon them accidentally, in the course of providing for some more general good.

This is largely a modern development. It dates in part from a time after 'promoting true religion' had ceased to be an unquestioned social good, a time when the churches were more likely to be seen as rivals to the State and tyrants over its citizens. To this era belong guarantees of religious liberty and free withdrawal from church membership, political vetoes over ecclesiastical appointments, provision for civil marriage, perhaps even constitutional bans on State funding of religious bodies. But today it can equally be planning and environmental protection law, or employment and discrimination law, which clash with ecclesiastical self-determination. Some of you may recall cases in which the needs of a living church have conflicted with the public interest in an historic building, or church bells have been branded as noise pollution, or a congregation's worship has been dubiously enhanced by the presence of a protected species of bat.

6 *Grundgesetz*, Art. 140, read with *Verfassung des Deutsches Reiches*, 1919, Art. 137.

Others may think of the incompatibility of employee participation in decision-making with a church's hierarchical constitution, or of issues thrown up by female or divorced and remarried staff.

I would suggest that it is in these last areas, where the motivation for a State's legislation is to be found in naturally universal concepts like human rights or the environment, that public law affecting the churches is most likely to - and perhaps should - see increasing standardisation on a European basis.

IV CONCLUSION

Yet such a development implies that it is legitimate for States to regulate such matters even in a church context; and this threatens to collide with what I have called the 'mediaeval' (or modern German) approach, which sees the church's lawmaking capacity as an autonomous one with which the temporal power has no business interfering, a species of public law in its own right.

Dr Engelhardt has referred to the *Rahmen der für alle geltenden Gesetze,* the 'framework of statute law applying to all'. which limits ecclesiastical autonomy under the German constitution. The wide or narrow construction of such limitations will determine how far European standardisation may in future impinge upon areas of ecclesiastical law. The German expression has been interpreted by the Federal Constitutional Court in a very narrow way[7], so leaving the churches with a wide field of independence from the sort of provisions I have mentioned. It remains to be seen whether European institutions will be prepared to concede as much.

---

7 See in particular (1976) 42 *Entscheidungen des Bundesverfassungsgerichts* 312 at 334, (1985) 70 *Entscheidungen des Bundesverfassungsgerichts* 138 at 172.

9

THE INFLUENCE OF EUROPEAN LAW ON FRENCH ADMINISTRATIVE LAW

Jean-Claude Helin

I INTRODUCTION

Time has now run out for a French doctrinal position which was based on ignorance, a reductionist vision according to which European law only has a minor impact on French Administrative law. Even more so for the more chauvinistic position which was sometimes taken - that French law, from its position of perfection, was able to offer European law notions and methods of which it was in need.

An analysis of the substance of this doctrinal debate which has been taking place over the last ten years clearly shows the change of position. The phenomenon of the Europeanisation of administrative law is now analysed, in a fuller and more measured way, as being a phenomenon which affects national law profoundly, and not just on the surface.

This change of thought was inevitable. Firstly, because the 'Europeanisation' of French law is a fact. A 1992 report of the *Conseil d'Etat* confirmed that 'Each year, the Community introduces more rules into our body of law than the French government does ... and today in national law, there is more than one new statute which has its origins in Community law'. Secondly, because, within the French legal order, Administrative law has been subjected to the challenge of deregulation, and several waves of privatisation. Liberal ideology has been at the heart of an increasingly critical view which is being taken of the myth of public service *(le service public)*. As J-F Flauss correctly points out (*Les Petites Affiches*, 9.1.95) 'the recent exogenous changes which have affected Administrative law are such as to favour a greater receptivity of exogenous influences' - in particular European influences. Finally, this change of thought is part of a broad movement towards an externalisation of sources of French law (which can particularly be seen in Environmental law).

I do not intend here to enter into the debate as to whether it is the law of the European Convention on Human Rights or Community law which has had the greatest impact on French Administrative law. On this, see the excellent analysis of J-F Flauss (*supra*). Even less will I look at the extent of the changes brought about. Nor will I dwell on the issue of origin and paternity of the developments, as the relationship between national and European law is very complex, and European law is itself largely inspired by national law. Confrontation between the two legal systems is inevitable: each national legal system is the fruit of history, and the product of a culture. European law, on the other hand, cannot claim to be rooted in history in this way; indeed it aims to supplant the diversity of national cultures.

In this address I will seek to show how Europeanisation is nowadays affecting, in extremely diverse ways, not only the sources of Administrative law, but also its content, as well as the way the Administrative courts exercise control over the Administration.

II THE INFLUENCE OF EUROPEAN LAW ON THE SOURCES OF FRENCH ADMINISTRATIVE LAW.

In this matter we are concentrating on the status of European law itself. Louis Dubouis correctly reminds us of the importance of this issue, and the fact that 'the status of community norms as a source of Administrative law largely governs the influence of Community law'. It is on this point that the dialogue between the French *Conseil d'Etat* and the European Court has been the most difficult, and yet subject to the greatest development.

To get to the heart of the matter - if you are willing to accept a certain degree of simplification inherent in this type of communication - the reception of Community law into French Administrative law has met with a strong three-pronged defence strategy by the *Conseil d'Etat*: the rejection of the primacy of Community norms which post-date national statutes; the rejection of the theory of direct applicability of directives, and the critique of what is regarded as excessive use of the *acte clair* theory. What is the position on these issues?

A *The Primacy of Community Norms*

On this first point it is necessary to remember the long adherence of part of the French political class to the dogma of the sovereignty of parliamentary statute, as well as to the idea of the *Conseil d'Etat* that, despite the provisions of Article 55 of the Constitution (which admits the supremacy of duly ratified treaty law over internal law), it is not for the administrative courts, who are the servants of the law, to refuse to apply the law. Without going into the complex reasons why the *Conseil d'Etat* modified its position on this issue (such as increasing marginalisation within the Community, even marginalisation of its position within France, and the progressive arrival of new generations of *Conseillers d'Etat* who are more open to the externalisation of sources of law), the *Nicolo case,*[1] in which the *Conseil d'Etat* for the first time accepted the primacy of treaty provisions over a later French parliamentary statute, rapidly opened up the way to Community law being more fully taken into account. In particular, it enabled the confirmation one year later that Community regulations have primacy over national laws[2]. Then in two decisions of the plenary court given on the same day in 1992, the *Conseil d'Etat* recognised the primacy of a Community directive over a subsequent national statute, and held the State liable in respect of an administrative regulation which was based on a parliamentary statute which was void through incompatibility with a European directive[3]. A good number of French writers are today awaiting what could be the final stage of these developments: making the State as legislator liable on the basis of fault for failing to keep to its community obligations[4].

B *Direct effect of directives*

On this second point it is well known that in the case of *Cohn-Bendit*[5], a formal sitting of the *Conseil d'Etat,* basing itself on the terms of Article 189 of the Treaty, clearly rebelled against the case-law of the Court of Justice by refusing to recognise the direct effect of directives, a position

---

1 CE 20.10.1989, Rec CE p.190, G.A.J.A. 106me Ed, 1993, p.742.

2 CE 24.9.1990, Boisdet, Rec. p251, A.D.J.A. 1990, p.863, chr. Honorat et Schwarz, *R.F.D.A* 1991, p. 1 72, note Dubouis, *R.G.D.I.P.* 1991, p.964.

3 CE Ass. 28.2.1992, *SA Rothmans International France*, Rec p.80.

4 See Dubouis, *supra*.

5 CE Ass 22.12.1978, *G.A.J.A.* p.692.

it subsequently maintained[6]. Despite the clear blue water between the positions taken, this did not prevent dialogue between the two courts. Thus the Court of Justice took care not to close down dialogue, on the one hand, by making it clear that only precise and unconditional dispositions of a directive could be invoked, and, on the other hand, by reaffirming (in the *Faccini Dori* case of 14.7.94) that a directive could be invoked only *vis-à-vis* the State, and not private persons[7]. For its part, a division of the *Conseil d'Etat* has just held that the State cannot invoke against individuals dispositions of a directive which have not been implemented[8]. According to commentators of authority[9] this could set the scene for the court developing its case law more in line (in its effect, if not its reasoning) with that of the Luxembourg court.

C *The* 'acte clair' *theory*

On this third point it should be noted that the circumstances in which the *Conseil d'Etat* apply the dispositions of Article 177 of the treaty are rare, and there are still a fairly large number of cases which use the *acte clair* theory. M. Larzul noted that out of 60 cases involving Community law this theory was used, either expressly or impliedly, 20 times[10]. Undoubtedly the *Conseil d'Etat* is taking care to ensure that Article 177 is used by the plaintiff as a subordinate remedy, and not merely as a supplementary remedy just to keep the matter dragging on. However, the use of the theory of *acte clair* undeniably offers the *Conseil d'Etat* the means to retain its jurisdiction to hear the case as the appropriate national jurisdiction, and to avoid the dynamic of the preliminary ruling procedure as an instrument for the integration of Community law into internal law.

Overall, the criticism of legal nationalism which has long been made against the *Conseil d'Etat*, and indeed a part of the French political class, is increasingly less justified, and is giving way to a more measured debate on the real and serious legal questions which are being asked, and on the ways in which these should be faced.

---

6 See for example CE 23.7.1993, *Compagnie Général des Eaux*, Rec. p.255, *R.D.F.A.* 1994 p.252, note Ph Terneyre.

7 Aff c.91/92, Rec. pi3325 - contrary to the recommendation of Advocate General Lentz.

8 (CE sect. 23.6.1995, SA Lilly France, *A.D.J.A* 1995, p.496).

9 See the comments in the *A.D.J.A.* (*supra*) of J-H Stahl and D. Chauvaux, *Maîtres des Requêtes* at the *Conseil d'Etat*.

10 *Les mutations des sources du Droit Administratif*, ed. l'Hermes, p.226.

The reception of Community law by the Administrative courts no doubt still has some grey areas, but the most important barriers are now down, and the debate within the *Conseil d'Etat* itself has since 1980 moved on to examine how the court should cooperate, and adjust its case law[11]. The *Conseil d'Etat* remains attached to the idea that it is because of the internal constitutional provisions[12], and not because of the specificity of the Community legal order, that the court may henceforth refuse to apply statutes which are incompatible with previous international norms. Furthermore, the debatable thesis is still sometimes put forward that the national court which is called upon to intervene to apply Community law is exercising a competence not as an internal jurisdiction but as a Community jurisdiction.

Politically, there has been sensitivity to the fact that this enrichment of the norms of legality has had as a corollary effect the weakening of the role of the legislator, which not only has no role in the elaboration of regulations and directives, but often has little role in their implementation in the internal legal order.

The cases of *Nicolo* and *Boisdet* gave rise to a passionate debate, which led to a constitutional amendment being put down with a view to specifying that the primacy of treaty law was only recognised in respect of parliamentary statutes 'which predated the treaty'[13]. This proposal never went to Parliament for debate. Of greater importance, however, are two reforms which have recently been carried out. The first relates to the information-receiving capacity of Parliament. The parliamentary delegations which communicate the opinion of the French Parliament on draft European legislation have, since the passing of the law of 10 May 1990[14], had more possibilities to participate in the preparatory work of the deliberations of the European authorities. The second results from the law of 25 June 1992 which revised the Constitution, and which in a new Article 88-4 requires the government to transmit to Parliament proposals of the European Commission which contain dispositions of a legislative nature. This makes it possible for Parliament to pass resolutions on the proposals, even outside of regular parliamentary sessions. Here the issues of sources relates to the content of Administrative law. Finally, the *Conseil d'Etat*, in its consultative

---

11 See the study of B. Genevoix *'Le Conseil D'Etat et l'ordre juridique communautaire'*, *E.D.C.E.* 1979-1980 p73.

12 Art. 55 of the Constitution.

13 Proposal of Deputies Mazeaud and Debré on 9.10.1990, *R.F.D.A.* 1991, p.177, taken up again by Deputy Mazeaud on 7.4.93.

14 *R.F.D.A.* 1991 p.179.

function rather than its judicial function, has systematically intervened in respect of the draft regulations so as to 'ensure in advance better compatibility with our internal law'[15]. In application of a Prime Ministerial Circular of 31 July 1992 which implements the provisions of the new Article 88-4 of the Constitution, the *Conseil d'Etat* is broadly associated with the elaboration of Community norms[16]. In respect of the elaboration of draft laws and regulations the *Conseil* looks closely at the issue of the conformity of French law to our European and indeed international obligations.

C *Influence on the content of Administrative law*

Virtually no area of Administrative law has escaped from the process of Europeanisation. Institutional law, the law relating to unilateral acts and decisions, the law of public procurement contracts, and the law of legal liability have all evolved, and continue to evolve, in their different ways, under the impact of the Europeanisation of sources of law. It is therefore not possible to draw up a full list of these developments in the context of this presentation, even less an exhaustive analysis. Instead, I will take just two examples which show the very differing ways this process is working, as well as the lively debate and sometimes resistance to which it has given rise.

II. LA FONCTION PUBLIQUE *(CIVIL SERVICE)*

Jean-Francois Flauss rightly notes[17] that France took a long time to come into line with the case law of the Court of Justice. The law of 9 January 1986 which opened up the possibility of employment as nurses in public hospitals to non-French EU nationals was only passed to prevent France being condemned in infringement proceedings. The harmonisation of French law with European law was done in a minimalistic fashion, limited to the issue of access to the civil service (of which nursing staff are a part). It was only with the passing of the law of 5 January 1991 that there was a reform of the legal provision dealing with the general status of civil servants, which had provided that 'only French nationals may have the status of civil servant', and that nationals of EC Member States were permitted access only in respect of functions

---

15 1992 Report, p.278.

16 cf B.Stirn, *Le Conseil d'Etat et le droit communautaire, de l'application à l'élaboration*, *A.D.J.A.* 1993, p. 24.

17 *Les Petites Affiches*, 9.1.1995.

which were 'separable from the exercise of sovereignty, or did not involve direct or indirect participation in the exercise of the prerogatives of the State or other public bodies' (Article 5). However, the implementation of the reform to this provision has not yet been achieved. Moreover, Community law has in this context 'confused certain key elements of our law relating to the civil service'[18]. For example, contrary to the French law position that a subordinate agent may be accorded the status of civil servant, the European Court takes a more horizontal approach. It is only above a certain level of the administrative hierarchy that one reaches the zone of public power *(puissance publique)* which is reserved to nationals. The constitutional principle of equality between civil servants in respect of their career development, a second important principle of the French law relating to the civil service, can be undermined by this, as civil servants from EU Member States cannot accede to functions likely to be reserved to nationals. Moreover, in a case on 30 June 1988, the European Court, basing its decision on the principle of equality between the sexes, questioned the validity of most of the special recruitment procedures set out in a Decree of 15 October 1985. As for positive discrimination, serious problems are posed to the extent to which the way opened up by Community case-law requires France either to withdraw the preferential treatment granted to female personnel, which would reduce the level of protection, or grant the same advantages to male personnel, which would cause a certain economic inconvenience.

A *Public Service*

According to Professor Chapus, Administrative law in France is above all the law of the public service[19], a notion which is considered very important in the context of the issue of social cohesion. It is therefore not surprising that the weak references to the notion of public service found in Articles 77 and 90(2) of the Treaty, together with the policy of the Commission and Council, have given rise to a certain concern, rather late in the day perhaps, but nonetheless real, as to the compatibility of our system of public service with that of the Community. This reaction led to the 1993 proposal for a European Public Service Charter.

This problem needs to be clearly defined and delimited. On the one hand, the administrative public services are only affected to the extent that they act as economic agents. Furthermore, for the so-called

18 J-F Flauss, see n.17 *supra*.

19 *Droit Administratif Général*, Tome 1, 8ième ed., p. 5.

industrial and commercial public services, that is, those which have a productive or commercial function, a good part of their activity was already regarded in national law as being subject to private law, and in particular competition law. At issue then are the traditional prerogatives recognised in French law to enable the public services to carry out their mission (such as rights to a monopoly, and exclusive rights).

On the other hand, having largely confirmed the very restrictive position of the Commission and Council, the European Court, in two decisions which were carefully noted in France, the *Corbeau case* of 19 May 1993 and the *Almelo case* of 27 April 1994, made it possible for the notion of 'service of general economic interest'[20] to be given real content, and admitted that bodies having this mission had the right to 'assure its services in conditions of economic equilibrium', which justifies limiting competition in respect of profit-earning economic sectors.

It is not impossible that the two positions might come closer together to the extent that certain developing Community notions (such as 'universal service', continuing provision, uniform tariff practice, the use of objective criteria for changing services to be supplied, the need for a service to be provided in a uniform way throughout a territory) are not that far removed from traditional principles of French law (such as those of continuity, equality, variability, universality).

In presenting a report on these issues[21], Marceau Long, the Vice-President of the *Conseil d'Etat* clearly showed[22] that it was necessary for the notion of public service in France to be developed: Firstly by better distinguishing between types (in effect, public service is to be distinguished from monopoly, from the civil service and from public regulation); secondly in better marking out the distended field of public service; by elucidating and enriching the principles of public service, and finally by giving further consideration to the purpose and roles of the State and the public service. Two paths are currently being explored in France, neither of them exclusive. One relates to the interpretation of the treaties. Here it is sought to obtain confirmation of the recent tendencies of the Court of Justice; to put the brakes on the passing of restrictive general or sectoral directives; and to have approved of a document in which the role of public services as a necessary complement to the market is clearly affirmed. The other relates to the modification of the treaty. The French pre-occupation here

---

20 Art. 90(2) of the Treaty.

21 *Rapport Public du Conseil d'Etat, 1994, La Documentation Française.*

22 See his analysis in the *R.F.D.A. mai-juin* 1995, p. 497.

is to remove public services from their position of being regarded as a derogation from the market, and instead to give birth to a principle according to which the market is not the sole reference point. This debate has now commenced. It ought to be lively and fruitful - for although the French notion of public service strongly confronts the exigencies of Community law (and will thus necessarily emerge reformulated), Europe does not seem able itself to avoid 'the trial of the general interest'[23].

III INFLUENCE ON THE ADMINISTRATIVE COURTS' EXERCISE OF JUDICIAL CONTROL OVER THE ADMINISTRATION

Although less spectacular, European law exercises a far from negligeable influence on the way judicial control of the Administration operates. I will pick up on three of the many aspects which could be referred to: these illustrate the diversity of ways, modalities and incidences of the Europeanisation of Administrative law. The three examples concern administrative court procedure, judicial powers of control, and the way failings in the administrative justice system are corrected.

A Administrative Court Procedure

In essence, European law here provides the source for a simple readjustment of French procedure, by requiring greater openness to the public of court hearings in the specialist administrative tribunals, and by requiring greater respect of the principle whereby court procedure is to be contradictory in nature (i.e., both sides having to disclose to the other the grounds of fact and law on which their respective claims are based). In respect of the first point, the *Conseil d'Etat* can clearly been seen in its case-law to have changed its position, by express reference to the dispositions of Article 6(1) of the Convention. Although the court did not go as far (as had been suggested by the *Commissaire du Gouvernement*) as to reverse the principle by affirming that 'in the absence of contrary legislative disposition, administrative courts make their decisions in public'[24], the *Conseil d'Etat* did quash a decision of a Social Security Commission on the grounds that the latter had not sat in

---

23 *L'épreuve de l'intérdit général*, the title of a collective work published in January 1995 under the aegis of a working party on public utility services in Europe.

24 J-C Bonichot, *R.F.D.A.* 1995, p. 166.

public when determining a matter dealing with rights and obligations of a civil nature.[25]

On the second point there are two remaining problems in French law: the first is in respect of the discretion of the judge to raise issues on his own initiative, even if not raised by the parties (which, of course, makes it difficult for the parties to give a measured response). This matter is now regulated by a Decree of 22 January 1992 which inserted a new Article R. 153-1 into the Courts and Tribunals Code, and which requires the president of the court to inform the parties, before the hearing, where the judge thus exercises his discretion, and to give the parties time to make their comments. The second is to do with the possibility of the parties making a formal reply to the observations of the *Commissaire du Gouvernement*. Currently, French law does not grant a right for this to be done, although in practice it is tolerated in an informal way. It needs to be asked whether French law is in breach of its European obligations in the light of the case of *Borgès* v. *Belgium* (30.10.1991), in which the European Court held that the *Cour de Cassation* was wrong to forbid a reply to the observations of the *Avocat General* because prior notice of the reply had not been given.

B Judicial Review

European law has, in different ways, been at the heart of reforms in three areas; the subject-matter of judicial review, control techniques, and the extent of judicial powers.

Two categories of administrative act and decision have traditionally been excluded from judicial review: *actes de gouvernement* (on the one hand, acts of the executive concerning its relations with parliament and, on the other hand, the acts of the French government in its relations with international organisations and foreign countries), and measures known as measures of internal order (which according to R. Chapus refers to the internal life of the administration and the keeping of internal order, more particularly in the army, prisons and educational establishments). Although it is unlikely that the notion of *acte de gouvernement*, which has been closely defined by the *Conseil d'Etat*, will in the near future be much changed under the influence of European law, the latter should be credited with the recent and long overdue reform of the most disputed aspects of the notion of measures of internal

25 CE sec. 29.7.1994, *Département de l'indre*.

order as applied to detainees of penitentiary establishments[26] and military personnel[27]. True to its tradition, the *Conseil d'Etat* took care not to refer to the exigencies of Articles 6 and 13 of the European Convention on Human Rights as interpreted by the Strasbourg Court. There is no doubt that French law was ready for reform, a position which had the support of nearly all commentators. However, it is clear that the *Conseil d'Etat* could not hold to its hazardous position when at the very heart of the court authoritative voices had been for several years talking openly of reform[28], and *Commissaire du gouvernement* Patrick Frydman had expressly noted[29] that 'it is time to bring to an end a situation which in the light of the Convention is precarious in several respects, and which may well result in the future in a condemnation by the Strasbourg court'.

The control techniques used by the Administrative courts have also changed in several ways. Firstly, by a continuing reduction in the element of discretion allowed to the Administration. This has been brought about by increasing control being exercised by the Administrative courts in a certain number of areas where European law implied that judicial intervention where the Administration had been guilty of a manifest error in the assessment of the facts *(erreur manifeste d'appréciation)* should be replaced by normal judicial intervention, that is confined to an assessment of the correctness of the solution as applied to the facts *(la qualification juridique des faits),* or even an application of the doctrine of proportionality. In this area, the solutions adopted by European law have accompanied and sometimes encouraged the tendency of the French Administrative courts to tighten their control on administrative activity when civil liberties are at issue. In an audacious decision in 1994 the Administrative Tribunal of Strasbourg, on the basis of the well-argued observations of its *Commissaire du Gouvernement,* found against the State on the basis of a traditional German law principle, referred to by the Court of Justice as the principle of 'failure to observe legitimate confidence'[30]. It remains to be seen whether the *Conseil d'Etat* will permit the reception into French law of this

---

26 CE Ass. 17.2.1995, M.Marle, *A.J.D.A.* 1995, p.420, overruling the much-criticised case of *Calliol,* CE Ass. 27.1.1984.

27 CE Ass. 17.2.1995, M.Hardouin, *A.D.J.A.*, 1995, p. 421.

28 Rony Abraham, *R.F.D.A.* 1990, p.1058.

29 *R.F.D.A. mars-avril* 1995, p. 361.

30 TA Strasbourg, 8.12.1994. *Entreprise Freymuth c/ Ministre de l'Environnement, A.D.J.A. juillet-août* 1995.

enlargement of the principle of legal security which, on the facts, would lead to a broadening of administrative responsibility.

There is no doubt that it is due to Community law that French law has abandoned a long-held principle, not derived from legislative text, by which the powers of the Administrative courts were voluntarily limited. In 1992, in order to implement the Directive of 21 December 1989 relating to appeal procedures in respect of the awarding of public provision and works contracts, the Administrative courts were for the first time (if one excludes the power to make public collectivities liable to pay daily fines, *astreintes)* given power by legislation to grant injunctions against the Administration - for failure to abide by the rules relating to publicity and open competition in respect of public contracts subject to Community law. There was some reticence about the introduction of injunctions. However, although initially introduced only in respect of public contracts with a European element, the use of injunctions was extended one year later to cover public contracts more widely, and also to cover cases where public service functions are delegated. The use of injunctions was even more formally and generally entrenched in French law in a law of 8 February 1995 which reformed administrative procedure[31]. Thus Community law has contributed to the bringing down of a stronghold, and has opened the door to the rapid generalisation of the use of injunctions.

C *Correcting Failings in the Administrative-Justice System*

Finally, it is thanks to the Europeanisation of law that it has been possible to stigmatise and deal with (which was not possible under national law), one of the greatest weaknesses of French Administrative justice - its slowness. This was undoubtedly one of the greatest weaknesses of a system which otherwise had much merit. Its slowness was a permanent source of dissatisfaction for the parties, was regularly condemned by both commentators and practitioners, and by Parliament[32]. The important 1987 reform which created the Administrative Appeal Courts certainly reduced the blockage at the *Conseil d'Etat*, but did nothing to lessen the workload of the first instance courts. However, although in cases of emergency the Administrative courts could move swiftly, delays in other cases were causing injustice, and national law provided no solution.

---

31 D.Chabanol, '*Un printemps procedural pour la justice administrative?*' *A.J.D.A. mai* 1995, p. 398.

32 *Rapport du Sénateur Arthuis du 11.6.1992*, Doc. Sénat No. 400.

In recent years the European Court of Human Rights has found against France on several occasions because of the delay in court procedure; in 1978 France was unanimously condemned in respect of a case which lasted more than seven years and seven months[33]; also in 1992 for a case which lasted more than eight years[34]; a few days later, in the case of *X* v. *France* [35], there was another unanimous judgement against France in a case, involving a haemophiliac suffering from AIDS, which lasted more than two years, the interested party dying in the meantime. The Court called attention to the fact that 'what was at stake in the litigation was of extreme importance for the interested party, in the light of the incurable illness which he was suffering from, and which reduced his life expectancy'. The slowness to award compensation to haemophiliacs infected by the AIDS virus was again censured in a case of 24 April 1994[36], the court criticising the Administrative Tribunal for not having 'used its powers of injunction to press home the issue, even though it was aware of the case of *X* v. *France*, and was also aware of the state of health of Mr Vallée'.

There is no doubt that France only began to listen to its conscience in this area and take action to bring about a solution following the use of Article 6(l) of the European Convention and the resulting successive condemnations of France. From this point of view, the use of European law, and the threat of sanctions being imposed by the Strasbourg court, has acted as a constant and powerful invitation to continue to develop national law and practices. Although it is not as a direct result of the case-law of the Strasbourg court that we have seen recent reforms (such as the creation of two new Administrative Appeal Courts; new efforts to recruit more judges; consideration given to emergency procedures and the very important reform in February 1995 of administrative court procedure) the shadow of the Strasbourg court is constantly in the background of the reforms of the French Administrative justice system, and, indeed, has contributed to making the reform process dynamic.

IV CONCLUSION

The Europeanisation of Administrative law is vigorously taking place in the context of what R. Chapus has called the 'progressive privatisation

33 *H* v. *France*, 24.10.1978.

34 *Editions Périscope*, 26.3.1992.

35 31.3.1992.

36 *Vallée* v. *France*.

of the internal legal order'. The role of the Administrative judge has thereby been changed. Previously there to ensure subordination to national statute law, he is increasingly led to ensure respect for the hierarchy of norms set out in Article 55 of the Constitution, which places international sources above Parliamentary law, sometimes against the wishes of the legislator.

This process has contributed, sometimes quite actively, to the questioning of certain important taboos and archaic practices of Administrative law, such as: 'the unchallengeable nature of statute law once it has been promulgated; the position of the *Conseil d'Etat* as a sovereign court, but a servant not a judge of statute law; the concept of the separation of judicial and administrative functions in the name of which the judge refuses to grant injunctions against the Administration; the national preference given to French corporations and citizens'[37]. These matters are not trifling, and all this is being done with hesitance, with a certain reticence, or even resistance which is perfectly understandable, and which is leading to a serious dialogue between the judges.

These developments are far from over, and the hybrid life-forms to which they are giving rise should be viewed not as an agent of the erosion of French Administrative law, but as an element of new growth. How could the citizen not rejoice at the strengthening of the content of the doctrine of legality, the increase in judicial control of the Administration, greater judicial efficiency, the condemnation of the unacceptable slowness of the system?

The Europeanisation of French Administrative law is part of the long march towards the creation of a 'community of Administrative law'[38], but is it also the occasion for serious introspection on the interests and limitations of the solutions offered by internal law? From this point of view, in the words of Louis Dubouis 'Europeanisation appears therefore as more than just one of the factors of change of Administrative law, rather it becomes an instrument for the analysis of the very spirit of Administrative law'[39].

---

37 Louis Dubouis, *A.J.D.A, juin* 1995.

38 Jurgen Schwarze, *Droit Administratif Européen*, 1994, p.1506.

39 L.Dubouis, see n.37 *supra*.

10

TOWARDS A EUROPEAN CRIMINAL CODE?

Alberto Cadoppi

I

Some jurists might argue that a European Criminal Code would represent an important and useful achievement for the development of the criminal law and justice in Europe, irrespective of the political situation of the European Union or Community.

In my opinion, such an idea would be misleading. There might be areas of the criminal law in respect of which the jurist might suggest proper solutions quite independently from political issues. This is not one of those areas. The problem of a possible unification of criminal law in Europe, and consequently of the usefulness of a common European Criminal Code, is so deeply linked with the political development of Europe, to leave no room for a purely scholarly, juridical discussion about it[1]. In this paper I will not try, then, to argue either for or against a common European Criminal Code. As a jurist, I would not be in a proper position to give a suitable judgment on this matter.

The only way of reasoning from a purely juridical point of view about the question raised by the title of this paper seems to be the following: let us imagine that Europe becomes a *really unified Country*, say a *Federation of States*[2] comparable to Germany, Switzerland, Canada or the United States of America. In such a panorama, (i) would a common European Criminal Code be useful to fulfil the aims of the

---

1 In the Italian literature see A. Pagliaro, *'Limiti all'unificazione del diritto penale europeo'*, (1993) *Rivista trimestrale di diritto penale dell'economia* p.204.

2 See J.J. Hesse, ed., *Federalizing Europe?* (Oxford, 1995).

criminal law in that new political entity? (ii) in order to achieve the unification of European criminal law, would it be sufficient to have a common Criminal Code of substantive law, or would something else be needed? (iii) since in Europe two different legal traditions co-exist - i.e., the *civil law* and the *common law* traditions - would it be possible to frame a European Criminal Code that takes into account and harmonises them? (iv) even before a political unification of Europe, would it be useful for the European legal community to work on the project of drafting a Model Penal Code for Europe with a view to the future accomplishment of a European Criminal Code, or at least of a possible harmonisation of the criminal laws of the various European Countries?.

II

Let us start imagining, then, that Europe has become *one unified* State, say in the form of a Federation.

In such a situation, would it be more suitable to have a common, Federal Criminal Code or to have as many criminal codes as individual States, with some Federal criminal laws dealing with matters of Federal importance? In my opinion, in such a case a common, Federal Criminal Code should be preferred.

First of all, in a Country every person should be treated by the Criminal justice system in the same way, and it is impossible to treat people equally if the bulk of the criminal laws differ from one State to another[3].

Secondly, a unified Criminal justice system would be much more effective in fighting crime than would be many independent systems. This is especially true with regard to organised and economic crime, a field in which criminals operate today at international level. This supranational dimension of certain types of criminality will no doubt increase in the future, for reasons too obvious to be explained.

Moreover, a study of the most important federal systems in the Western world shows that where the States have kept their individual criminal codes and criminal justice systems, leaving only little space to a

---

3 See, in respect of sentencing, Council of Europe, 'Consistency in Sentencing: Recommendation to Member States and Explanatory Memorandum', 4 (1993) *Criminal Law Forum* 355.

The problem of cultural differences, which could involve the need of different laws for different European countries, will be considered below.

common, federal criminal law, serious problems have ensued[4]. The examples of the US and of Australia show clearly how difficult it is to deal with a criminal justice system in which every State has its own peculiar criminal law, and those different laws have to compete with the Federal criminal law[5]. In Australia, for example, there are noticeable differences between the criminal laws of the various States. There are common law States, and Code States: the common law States (Victoria, New South Wales, and South Australia) do not have any criminal code, and rely on the common law and on some statutes dealing with special offences; the Code States (Queensland, Tasmania, Western Australia and the Northern Territory) do have a criminal code, in some ways comparable to a Continental criminal code[6]. The criminal law is shaped differently in each State, but these differences become huge between common law States and Code States. For instance, the developments of English criminal law tend to creep into the criminal law of the common law States, while they find it hard to penetrate the criminal law of the Code States, where judges have to stick to the wording of the sections of the Code itself in deciding cases[7]. This puzzling shape of Australian criminal law required some intervention. The way they are currently dealing with it is the following: at a Federal level, the Criminal Law Officers Committee of the Standing Committee of Attorneys-General has been working for some years on the preparation of a Model Criminal Code for the Australian Commonwealth, which will in the first place be enacted at a Federal level, eventually becoming a common code for all the individual States as well[8]. It is not clear if at the level of the individual States lawyers and politicians agree with a plan which has been pursued so far mainly at a Federal stage. But undoubtedly

---

4 In January 1995 a Conference on this subject, organised by Professor Sergio Vinciguerra, has been held at the University of Genoa, and the *rapporteurs*, from various European countries, agreed on this conclusion.

5 Cf., for a discussion of some problems relating to the American system, W.R. LaFave and A.W. Scott, *Handbook on Criminal Law* (St. Paul, Minn. 1972) pp.112 ff.

6 See generally B. Fisse, *Howard's Criminal Law*, V ed. (Sydney 1990).

7 Cf. E. Colvin, 'Chapter Seven - Interpretation of Criminal Legislation and Codes', in J.A. Riordan, gen. ed., *The Laws of Australia*, B. Fisse, Title ed., *Criminal Law Principles*, R. Harding, coord., *The Criminal Laws* (Sydney 1993) p.131.

8 See G. Scott, 'A Model Criminal Code', (1992) 16 *Criminal Law Journal* pp.350-352; M. Goode, 'Codification of the Australian Criminal Law', (1992) 16 *Criminal Law Journal* pp.5-19.

Recently the general part of the Model Criminal Code has been turned into a Bill: Criminal Code Bill 1994 (The Parliament of the Commonwealth of Australia - Senate).

Australian criminal law would benefit from such a harmonisation of the different criminal laws now in force in the various States[9].

As a matter of fact, the Canadian example shows how a system in which the States have delegated practically their whole competence in the field of Criminal Law to the Federal Government operates more smoothly[10]. It is enough to think of how well the Canadian Supreme Court seems to work[11], having fewer problems than the Supreme Courts of Australia and of the United States because of the unity of the system.

Even in the UK, which is not a Federation, the coexistence of two different systems of criminal law - the English and the Scottish - does not seem to help in terms of fair and equal treatment of British subjects and in terms of effectiveness: difficult problems arising in the field of jurisdiction are just one example of how this separation of criminal justice systems can create trouble[12].

Finally, one should take into account that EC Law is creeping into national legal systems so extensively, that even without a common criminal code for Europe those systems are slowly harmonising. These interconnections will no doubt increase in the future, and they will eventually make national codes almost useless in face of a 'Europeanisation' of Law impossible to control[13]. In such a context the adoption of a common European criminal code would become not so much useful as unavoidable.

There are some possible advantages in the rejection of a completely unified criminal code for the Federation that should, of course, be taken into account. The most important one is linked with the cultural differences between the various European States; that could require different criminal laws for each of them. It is an indisputable

---

9 The problems created by this lack of uniformity of Australian criminal law are properly stressed by G. Scott, *loc. cit.*, p. 350.

10 Provinces can only create quasi-criminal offences: cf. E. Colvin, *Principles of Criminal Law*, II ed. (Canada 1991) pp.3-15.

11 See, e.g., my notes '*Colpevolezza e principi costituzionali: le recenti "coraggiose avventure" della Corte suprema canadese*', (1989) *Il Foro Italiano*, IV, c.250; '*Colpevolezza e principi costituzionali: la Corte suprema canadese "colpisce ancora"* ', (1992) *Il Foro Italiano*, IV, c.456.

12 See P.W. Ferguson, 'Jurisdiction and Criminal Law in Scotland and England', in R.F. Hunter, *Justice and Crime* (1993) p.117.

13 See H.G. Sevenster, 'Criminal Law and EC Law', (1992) *Common Market Law Review*, pp.29-70; and, about to be published, A. Bernardi, *Comunitarizzazione del diritto e codificazione penale*. It is not possible in this paper to deal with this question of the 'Europeanisation' of criminal law, that is becoming a reality particularly in respect of some special areas (protection of economic interests of the EC, organised crime, drug trafficking, etc.), and even more after Maastricht and Schengen.

truth that especially in the field of criminal law, moral and social attitudes have to be tuned to the law itself[14]. But I believe that in a unified Europe the main moral and social values would be very similar in the various States of the Federation[15]. This is true especially if one keeps in mind that the criminal law should only deal with the most serious and harmful behaviours, leaving to other fields of the legal system the task of preventing less serious and harmful actions and omissions. This way the new European criminal code would have the beneficial effect of reducing the scope of the criminal law to what should really pertain to it[16]: the principle according to which the criminal law should be the *extrema ratio* would thus be secured.

That the main values and principles that come into play in the field of the criminal law are very similar in Europe (at least within the EC) can even now be shown, if one looks at the different criminal laws in force in the European countries belonging to the EC from a comparative law perspective. The general parts of most European criminal laws - common law countries included[17] - are quite similar to one another, and even when they are not yet, they seem inclined to become more and more similar as time goes by. This is because most principles that stand behind the rules that give shape to the general part are shared by lawyers (and, probably, common people) in most European countries: this can be said about the principle of legality, the principle of culpability, the principle of proportionality, the principle of *extrema ratio*, the principle of lesser evil, the principle of respect for fundamental human rights and freedoms, etc. And even when the laws seem to be very different and seem to reflect opposite *Weltanschauungen* about the role of criminal law (an example that comes to my mind is related to impossible attempts, punishable in countries like Germany and UK, according to a traditional *subjective*

---

14 Among many others, one German author has shown, at the beginning of this century, the importance of the congruence between legal norms (and particularly criminal law ones) and the morality of the community: M.E. Mayer, *Rechtsnormen und Kulturnormen* (Breslau 1903).

15 See A. Pagliaro, see n.1 *supra*, pp.202-203.

16 The individual States could preserve legislative power in respect of the so-called 'administrative-penal law': they could create quasi-criminal offences like the German *Ordnungswidrigkeiten*, or the Italian *illeciti amministrativi*. The penalties should never amount to imprisonment.

Only in cases of exceptional public order emergency (terrorism, mafia outbursts, etc.) the individual States could face such an emergency with criminal legislation, which should have only temporary force.

17 I will come back later on to the specific point of the compatibility between common law and civil law traditions in the field of criminal law.

conception of criminal law, and not in Italy, according to a traditional *objective* conception of criminal law[18]), in the practice of the courtrooms they tend to converge[19].

From the point of view of the *special part* of criminal law, one can surely find criminal offences shaped differently in the various systems, and instances of behaviours that are considered criminal in one country and not in another. This is because it is in the special part that the interests protected by criminal law directly come into play.

These differences are traditionally thought to be greater in respect of values particularly linked with morality. Sexual and religious offences are well known examples. It is true indeed that in the history of European criminal law these kinds of offences have been treated in different ways in the various systems. Homosexuality is probably one of the most obvious examples. Homosexual acts, even when performed in private between consenting adults, were traditionally considered to be criminal in Britain, while in countries like Italy - whose criminal codes have always been framed upon the model of the French *code pénal* of 1810 - were very seldom criminalised. This example, though, shows at the same time that, even in respect of the protection of morals, the differences between the criminal laws of the various European States tend to grow thinner: as a matter of fact, while in Italy and related systems homosexual acts are still legal[20], in the UK and in other common law countries laws have been passed in the last decades in order to decriminalise what is usually referred to as 'sodomy', or

---

18 Beccaria put it this way: '...crimes are only to be measured by the injury done to the society. They err, therefore, who imagine that a crime is greater or less according to the intention of the person by whom it is committed...': C. Bonesana, Marquis Beccaria, *An Essay on Crimes and Punishments* (II American ed., Philadelphia 1819, rep. Stanford 1953) p.33.

According to the same tradition, in Italy attempts are *always* punished less than completed offences, while in some other systems (again, both in Germany and in England and Scotland) the judge has discretion not to diminish the penalty in certain cases of attempts.

19 For a comparative study focused on the differences between Italian and Anglo-American criminal laws in this respect see E.Grande, *Accordo criminoso e conspiracy* (Padova 1993) p.190 ff. On the specific point discussed in the text above see *Id.*, '*Dissociazione dei formanti e diritto penale: analisi di un chiasmo*', in P. Cendon, ed., *Scritti in onore di Rodolfo Sacco*, vol. II (Milano, 1994), pp.593 ff.

20 Even in the Continental legal tradition buggery has been criminalised in some countries. For example, it was a criminal offence in Germany until 1973, when a major reform of sexual criminal law was undertaken. It is now, according to §175 of the German *Strafgesetzbuch*, a criminal offence only if one of the parties involved is over 18, and the other is under that age.

'buggery'[21]. This way the differences in this area of criminal law are step by step disappearing. It is noteworthy that some years ago a Northern Ireland statute which proscribed sodomy as such was held to violate the European Convention on Human Rights by the European Court in Strasbourg[22]. This means that European law and its judicial institutions - at least in the area of the protection of human rights - already play an important part on the road towards the harmonisation of the various criminal law systems.

The slow but steady convergence of the different European criminal laws in the field of the protection of morals could be shown by means of other examples as well[23]. It is linked with a general cultural movement towards the secularisation of the (criminal) law that finds followers all over Europe and in the whole Western world. Seminal works like Hart's *Law, Liberty and Morality*[24] and more recently Feinberg's *The Moral Limits of the Criminal Law*[25], and their Continental counterparts[26] have shown the dangers of the so-called 'legal moralism'[27], and their *Weltanschauungen* seem to find fewer and fewer opponents among legal scholars.

In other traditionally difficult fields of the special part, as well, the comparative lawyer will find more similarities among the various European laws than before. There is a common trend, for example, toward giving recognition to some forms of euthanasia[28], even though

---

21 See, for the latest developments of the law on buggery in England, Card, Cross and Jones, *Criminal Law*, XIII ed. (London, Dublin, Edinburgh, 1995) pp.249-252.

22 See the decision *Dudgeon* v. *UK*, 22 Oct 1981, *série* A, No. 45.

23 One could mention abortion, an area in which until ten or twenty years ago laws in Europe were very different, and women had sometimes to travel abroad to undergo one in proper hospitals. Nowadays the differences between the laws have lessened, and - this is especially interesting - in some non-Catholic countries there are stricter laws than in some Catholic countries.

24 Oxford-New York, 1963.

25 In four volumes: *Harm to Others* (New York-Oxford, 1984); *Offense to Others* (New York-Oxford, 1985); *Harm to Self* (New York-Oxford, 1986); *Harmless Wrongdoing* (New York-Oxford, 1988).

26 In Italy see, e.g., G. Fiandaca, *Problematica dell'osceno e tutela del buon costume* (Padova, 1984).

27 The struggle against the confusion between criminal law and morals (or religion *tout court*) dates back to Beccaria and even before.

28 At least it is now commonly recognised than consensual homicide should be punished less severely than non-consensual homicide, while the laws have developed very differently in the various European countries. See generally on the problem of euthanasia, with some comparative law contributions, L. Stortoni, ed., *Vivere: diritto o dovere?* (Trento, 1992).

some legal systems[29] seem to be more courageous than others in finding new solutions for a problem the importance of which is felt all over Europe. While in more classical areas of criminal law (e.g., offences against the person, against property, and so on) there have always been striking similarities in the laws from all over Europe, since the times of the *ius commune*, an extremely important, common heritage sometimes overlooked by lawyers and especially by criminal lawyers. Finally, in more technical fields like economic crimes, the laws in various European countries are even more similar, for reasons too obvious to be discussed.

To sum up, the point I try to make here is that cultural/moral differences between European countries are not to be underestimated, but they do not seem to prevent a trend toward a harmonisation of the criminal laws, since from a comparative law perspective it is easy to show that the paths of the various criminal laws in Europe are, if not coincident, leading in the same direction, and running very close to one another. The problems and the faults of the criminal law are very often the same in different countries, and the solutions proposed by lawyers to solve and to mend them are usually very similar in the whole Western world[30].

The problem of cultural/moral differences is anyway linked with the political problem of a real unification of Europe: if European countries feel ready to frame a new common nation, it means that cultural/moral uniformity in the various States is sufficient to justify that unification. If Europe is prepared to become one unified nation, then, the individual European States should be content to give up their own criminal laws, and to frame a new criminal code in which common European values and interests would find equal protection and enforcement. According to the commonly accepted theory of 'positive general deterrence'[31], criminal law is a very important means to enforce values already shared by a community. A new, politically united European community should rely on a uniform criminal law, then, to

---

29 For example the Netherlands, where euthanasia has been recently allowed, subject to certain reqirements. See, in Italian, S. Vinciguerra and A. Ricci Ascoli, '*La giurisprudenza olandese in tema di eutanasia attiva*', (1995) *Diritto penale e processo*, p.1012.

30 From attending various international conferences and spending long periods of research abroad, with many chances of discussing topics related to the criminal law with a number of colleagues, these opportunities convinced me of what I briefly suggest in the text above, and about which I could give many more examples.

31 See J. Andenaes, *Punishment and Deterrence* (Ann Arbor, 1974).

secure and foster its commonly held values. In such an environment, nobody should fear a common criminal law.

Another reason usually given in cases like this in favour of the separation of the systems is that lawyers in each country are used to their own laws and it would be difficult for them to get used to a new different system. This point seems to be less serious than the previous one. Lawyers always tend to be conservative about their system even in face of the superior needs of society. In the UK the famous Criminal Code drafted by James Fitzjames Stephen and revised in 1879 by a commission of learned lawyers never came into force mainly because of this kind of laziness and the conservativeness of legal practitioners and judges. The same is probably one of the reasons why the English and the Scottish systems are still separated[32]. I do not believe that a possible unification of the criminal laws of a United Europe should be hindered by similar reasons[33].

III

Once the idea of framing a common criminal code for Europe has taken over, one should ask oneself if such a step would be enough to ensure a uniform implementation of the law in the various European States.

For this purpose, it is useful to consider a historical example.

Italy was divided into six different States before it was united in 1861: the Kingdom of Lombardo-Veneto, the Kingdom of Sardinia, the Duchy of Parma and Piacenza, the Duchy of Modena and Reggio, the so-called Papal States, and the Kingdom of the Two Sicilies. Each State had its own criminal code, its own code of criminal procedure, and

---

32 I do not want to say that there are no reasons in favour of a separated system of criminal law in Scotland. But my opinion is that the two systems are not so inherently different to be impossible to harmonise or even unify. The Scots pride for their own separated legal system has to be taken seriously, but nevertheless a unified criminal law and justice system would probably be more suitable to a unified country like the UK.

I dealt with Scottish criminal law in comparison with the Italian and with the English criminal laws with my colleague Prof. Alexander McCall Smith in the book *Introduzione allo Studio del Diritto Penale Scozzese* (Padova, 1995).

It is probably worth rememberng that Lord Bacon worked on the possible unification of the laws of England and Scotland: F. Bacon, 'A Preparation toward the Union of the Laws of England and Scotland', in *The Works of Francis Bacon, Baron Verulam*, vol. IV (ed. London, 1824) pp.287 ff., devoted in particular to criminal law.

33 Of course, the different legal backgrounds and mentalities of lawyers have to be taken into account: this question will be discussed below, when the so-called *cryptotypes* will be analysed.

its own judicial system. Some of them were similar (being framed on the French model), but others were very different. For example, the model for the criminal code of Tuscany (1853) had been the criminal code of Baden of 1847.

After the unification of Italy, the problem of the unification of the legal system arose, and especially in the field of criminal law it became evident that a common criminal code was needed. By 1861 the criminal code of the Kingdom of Sardinia (the King of Sardinia became, as is well known, the King of Italy) had been extended to most of Italy[34], together with the code of criminal procedure and the Judiciary Act. Only Tuscany kept its criminal code. The main reason for this refusal was that Tuscany was the only State in Italy (and one of the few in Europe) where the death penalty had been abolished, and accepting the criminal code of Sardinia would have implied the acceptance of the return of the death penalty, against the will of the Tuscans. But in 1864 the Tuscans decided to accept at least the code of criminal procedure and the Judiciary Act in force in the rest of Italy. They insisted though in refusing to abolish their substantive criminal code, even after 1865, when a new code of criminal procedure was enacted for the whole Country.

Only in 1889, when the new Italian criminal code - the renowned 'Zanardelli' Code - was enacted, after almost thirty years of hard work by eminent lawyers, had Italy a criminal code in force throughout the whole Country, including Tuscany.

How could a united Country like Italy have two different criminal codes (one for Tuscany and the other for the rest of the Country) for about thirty years, without terrible consequences for the criminal justice system?

The answer is that, even if the substantive criminal law was partly different in Tuscany and in the rest of Italy, the procedure was the same, and above all the judicial system was the same. And from the point of view of the social and political impact of a legal system, the procedure and the judicial system are probably more important than the substantive criminal law. This is so because a criminal justice system becomes better known to the people through its actors (judges, prosecutors, lawyers, etc.) and through the trial, and less through the technicalities of the substantive law. This is so also because two substantive criminal codes can differ, but in the end a wicked murderer

---

34 In Naples and Sicily the Codes were accepted but for some minor changes.

will be punished under both of them and most of the time with a similar punishment[35].

Another point should be stressed. If there are two different criminal codes but one code of criminal procedure and only one judicial system, and the highest court is the same for the whole country, it is likely that the differences between the two codes will in practice be reduced and almost cancelled. On the contrary, in a country where there is just one criminal code but two codes of criminal procedure or (this is even more important) two judicial systems, and there is more than one highest court, it is likely that in practice criminal law will be implemented in very different ways and take very different shapes according to the different interpretations given to it by the various courts[36].

This is exactly what happened in Italy after Unification. Even if between 1861 and 1890 there was only one criminal code in force in the whole Country (Tuscany excepted), there was more than one highest court. There was one *Cour de Cassation* in Turin, one in Florence, one in Rome[37], one in Naples, and one in Palermo. And it is interesting to notice that those five courts gave to the criminal code in force in the whole Country (Tuscany excepted) - and as well to the code of criminal procedure - very different interpretations, so that one could say that in Italy in practice there was not just one criminal code, but five[38]!

For this reason, when the new Italian criminal code was enacted in 1889, at the same time the five supreme courts were reduced to one, the *Corte di Cassazione* in Rome. From then, the criminal code began to be interpreted in the same way in the various regions of Italy.

---

35 The death penalty was very rarely carried out in practice even in the other Italian regions: see M. Da Passano, '*La pena di morte nel Regno d'Italia (1859-1889)*', in S. Vinciguerra, ed., *Diritto penale dell'Ottocento. I codici preunitari e il codice Zanardelli* (Padova, 1993) pp.579-651.

36 This is why, for example, Scottish and English criminal law tend to remain more diverse than Scottish and English private law: only in the field of criminal law the highest court for Scotland is a Scottish one (the High Court of Justiciary); in the field of private law the highest court for Scotland is the House of Lords. See on this point L. Farmer, '"The Genius of Our Law...": Criminal Law and the Scottish Legal Tradition', (1992) 55 *Modern Law Rev*. p.25, who argues that Scottish criminal law is less 'statutorised' than English criminal law in order to give more power of intervention to the High Court of Justiciary and to preserve as much as possible the 'Scottishness' of Scots criminal law.

37 This one since 1875.

38 Cf. '*Le discordanze delle Corti di Cassazione in materia penale*', (1889) 29 *Rivista penale*, pp.136 ff.

The aforementioned example should confirm that a single criminal code is not enough to ensure the practical uniformity of the criminal law in a country. For this purpose, it is at least of the same importance to have as well a single code of criminal procedure and even more important to have a uniform judicial system, with *only one Supreme Court* at the top of it.

If we want a unified criminal law for a unified Europe we must keep in mind that enacting a common European criminal code will not be enough. A uniform code of criminal procedure would also be needed and above all the judicial system should be the same and *one* Supreme Court should be at the top of it. This means that even the actors of the criminal prosecution and trial should have the same qualities in every European State. So, for example, judges and lawyers should be recruited in the same way in Italy, Spain, France, Germany, UK, etc. This would imply a major change in institutions and traditions sometimes very ancient. It would also affect the educational system. Universities and University teaching should become more compatible in the various States of Europe: this also, as we all know well, would be difficult to achieve.

IV

Another problem should now be considered. Within Europe - which represents a fairly small group of States quite similar to one another - two very different legal traditions coexist: those of the common law and civil law. Can they be reconciled in the framing of a common criminal code[39]?

This would in fact be a new experience in the field of legislative drafting. Looking at the history of the codification of criminal law, nonetheless, it is possible to derive some help in giving an answer to this question.

Considering the Continental codifying efforts it would be difficult to find any interesting example for our purpose. As a matter of fact, European codifiers never really worked together with common lawyers, nor used English codes as their model. This was obvious at the dawn of the age of codification, at the beginning of the last century, because then one would have looked in vain for an English code. The

---

39 The answers given to this question vary: for the negative, but almost thirty years ago, G. Bettiol, '*Sull'unificazione del diritto penale europeo*', in *Prospettive per un diritto penale europeo* (Padova, 1968) p.6; for the positive, A. Pagliaro, see n.1 *supra*, pp.200 ff. See also P. Nuvolone, '*Problematica dell'unificazione del diritto penale dei paesi europei*', *Trent'anni di diritto e procedura penale*, vol. II (Padova, 1969) p.1518.

only English influence on European codifiers (and especially on the framers of the French *Code pénal* of 1810) had been, at that stage, Jeremy Bentham's theory of codification. But that was mainly a philosophical impact, which did not bring to the attention of the Continental lawyer the forms and contents of the common law and its spirit. On the other hand, even more recent European codes did not seem to take advantage of the consideration of English criminal law.

If we look now at the history of codification in the *common law* world, we find that, at least in early times, criminal codes draftsmen derived some help from Continental models. One could think about Edward Livingston's Draft of a Criminal Code for Louisiana (1826), and Lord Macauley's Indian Penal Code (the draft of which dates back to 1838). Both these Codes (probably more than Stephen's Draft of a Criminal Code for England [1878] and Wright's Draft of a Criminal Code for Jamaica [published in 1877]) have something in common with Continental Codes and especially with the French *Code pénal* of 1810. Nevertheless, even in those codes the French flavour remains somewhat a distant hint, a sprinkle of French wine on a roast beef which is English in its taste.

In the fascinating history of the codification of criminal law in the common law world we find other instances much more interesting from our point of view.

First of all I can mention the Criminal Code for Malta of 1854. As is well known, Malta at that stage was a British colony. A commission was set up in the 1820s in order to draft a criminal code and a code of criminal procedure. It is interesting to notice that it was a mixed commission, formed by three British subjects (two of whom apparently Scots) and two Maltese lawyers. In those times, in Malta the written language was Italian, and the culture - at least the legal one - was mainly Italian. Malta's legal tradition was a tradition of civil law[40].

The mixed commission had some problems in carrying out its duties. The most eminent lawyer in the team was apparently a Maltese judge named Bonavita[41], and he had to struggle quite hard in particular with one of the British members of the commission, named Stoddart, who wanted to impose upon Malta legislative solutions derived from the common law tradition. Judge Bonavita left a manuscript in which he described the entire story of the compilation of the Criminal Code for

---

40 From this point of view it is improper to talk about the Maltese codification as a common law codification; anyway Malta was a British colony.

41 On his life and carreer see J.M. Ganado, 'Sir Ignazio Gavino Bonavita', 1 *The Law Journal (Malta)*, No.5, p.19.

Malta[42]. I had the good fortune to read that manuscript, where page after page Bonavita explains in detail the reasons for the struggles between him and Mr. Stoddart. The central point of the fight was the question of the official language of the code: Stoddart preferred, of course, the English language, and Bonavita the Italian one. In the end Bonavita won the battle, and the official language of the code - as well as generally the legal language - remained the Italian one[43]. But other reasons were more technical ones, linked with the formal and substantial differences between the English (or sometimes the Scottish) and the Italian legal traditions.

Later, partly because of the problems just mentioned, partly for other reasons, a new commission was formed, whose members were all Maltese. In 1842 they produced a Draft Criminal Code (together with one of Criminal Procedure), which was based on a previous Draft framed by the former mixed commission and on the Criminal Code for Naples of 1819. Interestingly enough, the Draft was sent to Scotland to be revised by an advocate of the Scots Bar named Andrew Jameson, who in 1844 published a *Report*[44], in which he scrutinised the whole Criminal Code[45], in order to check the compatibility of its legislative solutions with the British legal traditions. The result was that, even though the Scottish Advocate praised the work of the eminent Maltese lawyers with flattering compliments, he bitterly criticised most of the sections of the proposed Code as inconsistent with English, or more often Scottish legal practices and principles. It is impossible to mention in detail Jameson's criticisms to the Draft Code, but having carefully read the *Report*, the overall impression is one of scarce compatibility between the Maltese (i.e., the Italian) and the British legal traditions. One thing is so blatant that it has to be said: the Scottish lawyer showed

---

42 I.G. Bonavita, *Ricordi ossiano notizie de' fatti concernenti l'origine, il progresso e la terminazione della redazione delle Leggi Criminali promulgate per Malta nel 1854 e di alcune circostanze aventivi relazione che mi riguardano personalmente,* 1857.

On the history of the Criminal Code for Malta see also the comprehensive but unfinished research published by A. Ganado, 'The historical Development of the Criminal Code', 2 *The Law Journal (Malta),* No.4, p.211; No.5, p.258; No.6, p.355.

43 Only in this century things changed and slowly English became more used, while more recently Maltese became the official legal language.

44 *Report on the Proposed Code of Criminal Laws for the Island of Malta and its Dependencies* (Government Press, Malta).

45 Very few were the observations made on the Code of Criminal Procedure, which was mainly based on the Scottish Procedural Criminal Law, considered even by the Maltese judges more advanced than the Italian (Neapolitan) one.

a particular preference for precise definitions[46], while the sections drafted in Malta were most of the time quite loose and general. This is a difference that at least since the times of Blackstone has always divided the Continental and the British approach to statutory drafting, and which Stephen[47] was well aware of when he framed his Draft Criminal Code, deliberately avoiding choosing as a model the French *Code pénal*.

It must be added, though, that Jameson's *Report* was later carefully taken into account by the Maltese commission that prepared the final Draft Criminal Code, and the Criminal Code itself as it was enacted in 1854 contains most of the amendments proposed by the Scottish Advocate. This means that as a matter of fact the two legal traditions - the common law and the civil law one - were in the end successfully[48] brought together and harmonised in the Maltese Criminal Code[49].

In a country were the tradition is a civil law one and where the system is now highly influenced by the common law approach, the Criminal Code still in use, even though framed upon an Italian model, owes much to the common law. The practical result is nowadays quite interesting: in applying the sections of the code derived from Italian law, Maltese judges tend to follow the Italian interpretations of them, employing a civil law approach; in applying the sections of the Code influenced by the Law of England or Scotland, Maltese judges tend to follow the British interpretations of them, employing a common law approach. But the two approaches seem slowly to overlap[50].

Another interesting historical example of a code of mixed traditions is the Queensland Criminal Code of 1899[51]. This code was drafted in less than three years by Sir Samuel Walker Griffith, a

---

46 Even though he seems to think otherwise from a merely theoretical point of view: A. Jameson, see n.44 *supra*, pp.8-9.

47 See J.F. Stephen, *A History of the Criminal Law of England*, vol. III (London, 1883), pp. 347 ff.

48 The Criminal Code for Malta was praised by eminent contemporary lawyers (for example by Mittermaier in Germany and by Pessina in Italy) as a very fine piece of legislation.

49 Judge Bonavita - who did not take part in the final stages of the compilation and adoption of the Code - was never happy about the final form of the Criminal Code, especially because of the British practices introduced in it after Jameson's observations. But I think that his disappointment was more the product of personal pride than of impartial judgment of the Code of 1854.

50 I owe this information especially to Prof. Vincent De Gaetano, Judge of the Supreme Court of Malta.

51 On its history see especially R.S.O'Regan, 'Sir Samuel Griffith's Criminal Code', (1991) 7 *Australian Bar Rev.* pp.141 ff.

Welshman who moved to Australia when very young, and who later became Prime Minister of Queensland and the first Chief Justice of the Australian Supreme Court. His Code took as its first model the Draft Criminal Code for England of 1880, which was based upon Stephen's famous Draft Code. But Griffith was a man of great individuality and of refined legal and political culture, and he did not want to accept the English Code as such, a thing that had happened some time before in Canada and New Zealand, where Stephen's Code was adopted with minor alterations. He took into account other recent codifying experiences such as the Penal Code for the State of New York, inspired by the ideas of one of the greatest supporters of codification in the history of the common law world, David Dudley Field.

But another was the model that greatly inspired Griffith in his work. Let us listen to his voice on this point.

> 'In 1888 the Parliament of Italy enacted a Penal Code, the result of labours initiated in the year 1862 and continued by a series of Parliamentary Committees and Royal Commissions under the guidance of eminent lawyers. I have derived very great assistance from this Code, which is, I believe, considered to be, in many respects, the most complete and perfect Penal Code in existence. I have also derived much help from the masterly Ministerial explanation (*Relazione*) of Signor Zanardelli, who had charge of this Code during its passage through Parliament in 1888[52]'.

How was it that a Welsh *emigré* in a remote colony in Australia took as one of the major models for his Criminal Code the Italian Code of 1889? The main reason is probably that Griffith was very fluent in the Italian language (he later translated into English Dante's whole *Divine Comedy*!), so that it was easy for him to read and study the Italian Code and its *travaux preparatoires*. Another reason is that the Zanardelli Code had a good reputation all over the world and served as model for many other codes, especially in Continental Europe and South America.

---

52 S.W. Griffith, *Explanatory Letter to the Honourable Attorney-General*, 29 Oct 1897, in Id., *Draft of a Code of Criminal law, Prepared for the Government of Quuensland* (Brisbane, 1897) (C.A. 89-1897), p.VII. Very recently a new Criminal Code has been enacted in Queensland (Criminal Code Act 1994, Act No. 37 of 1995), after almost one hundred years. But it retains many of the provisions of the Griffith's Code. It has never come into force so far.

The Code drafted by Griffith was adopted almost without amendments as the Criminal Code for Queensland in 1899, and it can be considered a code based upon the English common and statutory law, as far as the description of most crimes is concerned; and a code based upon the Italian law as far as most principles and rules of responsibility are concerned: a code indebted both to the common law and to the civil law traditions.

Griffith's Code was welcomed by lawyers all over the world (even in England!) as a masterpiece of Codification[53], and was chosen with minor changes as the Model Criminal Code for the British colonies, overcoming the Indian Penal Code in that respect. It found its way to many countries all over the world, in Africa, in the Pacific, and even in Palestine (today Israel), and in Australia it became the model on which the other Code States framed their criminal laws[54].

One could venture to say, then, that the coexistence in it of the two traditions - the common law and the civil law - has been extremely successful. This deduction would probably be too superficial. In reality, even though the Code has no doubt been a great codifying effort and an exciting cultural adventure, probably without precedents in the history of codification, if confronted with its practical achievements, it gives the impression of being in scholarly terms a perfect work of art, but a disappointment in its judicial application. In a recent period of research spent in Australia, I had the chance of looking at the Queensland Criminal Code in action, and of discussing it with many lawyers and scholars. It seems that what creates the most difficult problems in the case-law are those sections of the Code which deal with the concepts of criminal liability and which were greatly derived from the Italian Code of 1889. Those concepts are foreign to the English legal tradition, and Australian courts find it very difficult to deal with them, not being able to make use of the developments and refinements of common law of England and of other jurisdictions[55]. A study of the Queensland

---

53 The present writer is about to publish some articles on the Griffith Code, where more references are to be found.

54 See the very interesting research published by R.S. O'Regan, 'The Migration of the Griffith Code', in R.S. O'Regan, *New Essays on the Australian Criminal Codes* (Sydney, 1988) pp.103 ff.

55 Just one example: 'thin skull' cases, easily resolvable applying the common law doctrine, prove to be more difficult in Queensland.

Other examples in E. Colvin, Ch. 7 & 8, in J.A. Riordan, ed., *The Laws of Australia*, B. Fisse, ed., 9. *Criminal Law Principles*, R. Harding, ed., *The Criminal Laws* (ed. R. Harding) (Melbourne, 1993) 131: Colvin is particularly critical in respect of the problems posed by the coexistence of the Griffith Code and its peculiar principles with the common law.

Criminal Code, then, could seem to reveal some inherent problems of compatibility between the common law and the civil law traditions, which come to light especially in the practical application of the law.

In my opinion, this conclusion is far too clear cut. It must be taken into account that Griffith no doubt derived some help from the Zanardelli Code, but more than once heavily amended the sections taken from that code and made them too hybrid and sometimes contradictory to be suitable to an easy interpretation. One must consider that most of the problems of applying the general principles of the Code derive from the developments made by common law in the last century. This is confirmed by the fact that in the first decades of the Code's existence, it did not create many of the problems that only recently arose, as long as the law developed in the common law jurisdictions in Australia.

The experience of the Queensland Criminal Code is not conclusive, then, in showing the incompatibility between common law and civil law approaches to criminal law and to its codification. It is useful though to show the importance of what comparative lawyers sometime call the 'cryptotypes'[56], that is to say of those schemes hidden behind the letter of the law and settled in the minds and in the mentalities of the jurists, deriving from their legal experience as it has been shaped in years and years of study and practical work. These cryptotypes are sometimes stronger than the letter of the law, and they are especially important in shaping the so-called 'law in action' as opposed to the 'law in the books'. This means, coming back to our present problem, that a common Criminal Code for Europe could be interpreted in a very different way, say, in England and in Italy, according to the cryptotypes of the English and Italian judge respectively.

This historical overview has shown, then, at least two things:

(i) it is not impossible to conceive the drafting of a common criminal code for Europe notwithstanding the two legal traditions coexisting in it. But the commissioners who take part in that adventure have to give up their (national and

---

The example of the 'thin skull', though, seems to prove that in some areas of the criminal law the presence of general principles such as the ones provided by the Griffith Code can lead to decisions more in line with recent developments of criminal law theory.

That a Criminal Code like Griffith's is very useful in assuring the survival of important criminal law principles has been argued some time ago by C. Howard, 'The Protection of Principle Under a Criminal Code', (1962) 25 *Modern Law Rev.* pp.189 ff.

56 See R. Sacco, *Introduzione al diritto comparato*, IV ed. (Torino, 1990) p.155. The notion of *cryptotyps* was borrowed by Prof. Sacco from B.L. Whorf, *Language Thought and Reality* (Cambridge Mass., 1956).

individual) pride and work humbly for achieving the goal of a common codification;

(ii) in framing the code the commissioners have to take into account the different cryptotypes settled in the minds of common and of civil lawyers, and must draft the sections as precisely as possible especially in the fields where the two different traditions might affect the law in action in the future. In any case, since it is impossible and sometimes inappropriate, in a code, to define everything with absolute precision[57], different interpretations of the law in different jurisdictions will be inevitable. But this problem could be solved by establishing a common European High Court whose precedents should be binding on inferior courts all over Europe[58]. This way slowly the law will take a uniform shape everywhere, and slowly the cryptotypes themselves will harmonise.

This second observation is linked with what has already been said about the importance of unifying not only the substantive criminal code but also the code of criminal procedure and the judicial system.

V

If Europe becomes a Federation of States comparable to today's Germany, the United States of America, Australia or Canada, a common Criminal Code should then not only be desirable, but probably, with some precautions, feasible.

This assumption is not only supported by what has just been said, but also by the fact that what has proven to have been difficult, even though not impossible, in the last century, will be much easier now. This is because the differences between common law and civil law systems are becoming smaller and smaller, as time goes by. This point has already been made clear by comparative lawyers, who have shown that the two families are slowly getting closer to one another. If one looks at the criminal laws, say, of England and Italy[59], one will find that many of the traditional differences between them are no longer to be

57 On this problem see A. Cadoppi, ed., *Omnis definitio in iure periculosa? Il problema delle definizioni legali nel diritto penale* (Padova, 1995) with essays by criminal lawyers from various European countries.

58 In this respect the common law tradition seems to work better than the civil law tradition, where, as it is well known, precedents are not binding.

59 Recently in Italy a textbook devoted to the comparison of the English and the Italian criminal law (in the area of the general part) has been published: S. Vinciguerra, *Introduzione allo studio del diritto penale inglese. I principi* (Padova, 1992).

found nowadays, when the basic principles tend to be the same everywhere (e.g. the principle of legality[60], of culpability[61] and so on[62]), and the values reflected by the descriptions of the offences tend to be more and more uniform[63]. These similarities become even more striking if one compares the criminal law of Italy with the criminal law of Canada, because both Italy and Canada have a Bill of Rights that affects dramatically the shaping of the criminal law itself[64]. This leads to the conclusion that English criminal law could be even more similar to the Italian (or the German, or the Spanish, or the French) one, had England also adopted a Bill of Rights[65].

Finally, it must be added that the traditionally most striking difference between English (as well as Scottish) and Continental criminal law, the absence of a criminal code both in England and Scotland[66], is now less dramatic than before, at least after the major efforts of codification of English criminal law recently carried out in

---

60 It is true that the principle *nullum crimen nulla poena sine lege* has very different backgrounds in common law countries and in civil law countries, but in recent times the differences are gradually fading away. While in England (and generally in the common law world) the statutory law is growing and common law crimes are fewer and fewer, in Italy the judiciary seems slowly to be more inclined to play a creative role in shaping the 'law in action'. This tends to mitigate the differences between English and Italian criminal law in this respect. This is true even if one compares Scottish criminal law with Italian criminal law, notwithstanding the peculiar reluctance of the Scottish criminal law system to accept the *nullum crimen* principle: see my *'La genesi delle fattispecie penali. Una comparazione tra civil law* e *common law'*, in G. Fiandaca, ed., *Diritto penale in transizione* (Padova, 1996).

61 The issue cannot be discussed in detail here. For references see my *'Mens rea'*, 7 *Digesto delle discipline penalistiche,* IV ed. (Torino, 1992) p.618.

62 See also what has been said before, Ch. 1.

63 See A. Pagliaro, see n.1 *supra*, pp.200 ff. More generally, at a European level, see A. Bernardi, ' *"Principi di diritto" e diritto penale europeo'*, *Annali Università di Ferrara* (1988) p.75; G. Grasso, *Comunità europee e diritto penale* (Milano, 1989) p.89.

64 See A. Cadoppi, 'Recent Developments in Italian Constitutional-Criminal Law', (1990) 28 *Alberta Law Rev*. pp.427 ff.

65 From this point of view, the European Convention on Human Rights and its principles are a first step towards the harmonisation of the criminal laws in the various European countries. Some decisions of the European Court of Human Rights have already contributed to this end (see what has been said earlier about the criminalisation of buggery). In a future unified Europe a common, more detailed Bill of Rights should be framed, and the Supreme Court (or a separated Constitutional Court) should deal as well with problems of the conformity of the European Criminal Code and Laws with such a Bill of Rights.

66 G. Bettiol, see n.39 *supra*, p.6, particularly underlined the importance of this difference.

England[67]. The existence of an English Draft Criminal Code[68] will make the future codification of European criminal law much easier.

Can something be done at this stage in order to be ready to cope with the need for this criminal code when the time comes?

Perhaps it could be worth setting up a commission of experts in the field of comparative criminal law whose task should be that of drafting a European Model Penal Code[69]. This commission could probably obtain grants from the EC, and from National research institutions. Each Country of the Union should be represented by a small team. Those teams should work almost full time on the project.

In six or seven years a final Draft European Model Penal Code could be ready. It could be a good starting point for the adoption of the European Criminal Code when the time is mature for it. And anyway, even if such a time never came[70], that joint effort of jurists from many European countries could serve as a model for the compilation of other

---

67 On these developments of English criminal law (and of the criminal law of other common law jurisdictions), see, in Italy, my *'Dalla judge-made law al Criminal Code'*, (1992) *Rivista italiana di diritto e procedura penale*, pp. 923 ff.

68 Law Comm. No. 177, *A Criminal Code for England and Wales* (London, 1989).

In Scotland there is no such draft code nor do Scottish lawyers seem to be in favour of a codification of the criminal law: C.G.B. Nicholson, 'Codification of Scots Law: A Way Ahead, or a Blind Alley?', (1987) *Statute Law Rev.* pp.183 ff. Nevertheless, even north of the Tweed some scholars seem to be more inclined to the adoption of a criminal code and something is about to be done for that purpose (I owe this information to A. McCall Smith). Finally, in a future European Federation the main reasons for the refusal of a codification of Scots criminal law would probably be less forceful than now.

69 The task of drafting a Model Penal Code for Europe was considered in the early Seventies by the Council of Europe, but without any result: see H. Sevenster, *loc.cit.*, p.38; C.J. Enschedé, *Een uniform Europees Strafrecht* (Arnhem,1990).

70 As it has been said before, a real political union (which, is my view, implies a cultural, moral, social, and up to a certain point economical homogeneity) of Europe should be achieved before one could even think of adopting a common criminal code. This time could well never come, and a political (as well as cultural, moral, social, etc.) diversity among the European nations could even be the best solution for the future! In this respect, I deliberately do not venture to express any opinion in this paper on such a political matter, which goes beyond my competence as a (comparative) criminal lawyer.

One thing however has to be stressed. With so many different languages a thorough unification of Europe seems to be Utopian. If a real unification of Europe is what we want (but I would not be so sure about it...), we must choose one (not more) official language, and that language should become perfectly known by all Europeans. Until that day, a proper unity of Europe will never be reached. This is applicable to legal matters as well, because without a common language it would be impossible to have a common law, since the interconnections between law and language are so strong that the same law translated in more than one language will be interpreted in different ways and will end up as being more than just one law.

criminal codes to be adopted in various European countries, in which case at least an harmonisation of European criminal law[71] would possibly be realised step by step by each country.

The experience of the Model Penal Code of the American Law Institute is too well known to be described here. It is useful, though, to meditate about it and about other similar efforts (I think of the recent Model Criminal Code for the Australian Commonwealth, for example[72]), in order to achieve something similar in our old, small and sometimes too fragmented Europe.

In this respect, it is noteworthy that in recent years most European countries have been drafting or enacting new criminal codes, sometimes very different from one another: as is well known, in France a new criminal code was enacted in 1992 and came into force in 1994; in Spain a new criminal code has just been adopted[73]; in Portugal the code has recently been thoroughly revised[74]; in Italy a draft code[75] has

---

71 Many authors have stressed the importance of a basic harmonisation of the different European criminal laws, even the ones who strongly oppose a total unification of them: see e.g. J. Pradel, *Droit pénal comparé* (Paris, 1995).

72 See Criminal Code Bill 1994 (The Parliament of the Commonwealth of Australia - The Senate), and the annexed *Explanatory Memorandum*. On the Australian Model Criminal Code see the authors cited at n.9 *supra*. Another Standard Penal Code (*codigo penal tipo*) was framed in Latin America between 1963 and 1979 (the project is unfinished yet, but the general part was completed in 1971): see H. Dahl, 'The Influence and Application of the Standard Penal Code for Latin America', (1990) 17 *Am.J.Crim.Law* pp.235 ff. But one can find instances of Model Penal Codes way back in the history of the criminal law: Colonial criminal codes have been framed following various Model Penal Codes, the first being Wright's Draft Code for Jamaica (drafted in the early 1870s, published in 1877): the second (not very fortunate) H.L. Stephen's Code, drafted for the Colonial Office in 1901 (on these two codes see M.L. Friedland, 'R.S. Wright's Model Criminal Code', 1981) 1 *Oxford Journ. Legal Studies* pp.307 ff.); the third A. Erhardt's Model Penal Code (drafted in 1925: see H.F. Morris, 'A History of the Adoption of Codes of Criminal Law and Procedure in British Colonial Africa, 1876-1935', (1974) *Journ. African Law*, p.15) Other codes (or draft codes) have been very influential in the history of the codification of the criminal law, even though they were not originally framed as Model Criminal Codes: one could mention, in respect of common law countries, Macauley's Indian Penal Code (1837, adopted in 1860); J.F. Stephen's Draft Code (drafted in 1878, and revised by a Royal Commission in 1879), and Griffith's Queensland Criminal Code (drafted in 1897 and adopted in 1899) In respect of civil law countries the French *Code pénal* of 1810, the Italian Zanardelli Code of 1889; and more recently the German *Strafgesetzbuch* as modified in 1975. Those codes can probably be considered as '*de facto* Model Penal Codes'. It is because of them as well that many criminal law principles and institutions are similar or at least comparable in various countries throughout the world.

73 See *Ley Organica del Codigo Penal*, 8 Nov 1995.

74 See *Decreto-Ley* No. 48, 1995 (15 Mar 1995).

recently been submitted to lawyers for comments (1992), and a Bill concerning the general part is about to be examined by the Senate[76]; and in the UK Reports have been drafted by the Law Commission in order to implement step by step the Draft Code of 1989[77].

Without a common guideline like a Model Penal Code for Europe, our criminal laws are running the risk of separating more and more instead of harmonising.

75 *Schema di delega legislativa per l'emanazione di un nuovo codice penale, Documenti giustizia* (No.3, 1992). It was drafted by a commission of professors of criminal law (A. Pagliaro, F. Bricola, F. Mantovani, T. Padovani, A.R.Latagliata, A. Fiorella) appointed by Professor G. Vassalli, then Minister of Justice.

76 *Senato della Repubblica, XII legislatura: Disegno di legge* No. 2038, *Libro primo del codice penale* (August 2, 1995).

77 See various Consultation Papers and Reports under the common title *Legislating the Criminal Code* (London, HMSO, 1993-1995).

11

MONEY LAUNDERING AND THE CONFISCATION OF THE PROCEEDS OF CRIME

A Comparative View on Different Models of the Control of Money Laundering and Confiscation

Prof. Dr. Hans-Jörg Albrecht

I. INTRODUCTION: THE EMERGENCE OF MONEY LAUNDERING AND CONFISCATION POLICIES

Anti-money laundering and confiscation measures rank high on the policy agendas of European countries. Pressures arising out of widely voiced demands to prevent organised crime from profiting from various types of crimes, especially drug trafficking, have led in many EC countries to legislation facilitating seizure, freezing and forfeiture of crime proceeds and have pushed also non-EC countries to follow these policies[1]. The Council of Europe's Convention on Money Laundering guidelines issued by the European Commission obliges Member States to enact legislation forbidding money laundering and to establish systems of control in order to enhance the potential of identifying, freezing and confiscating proceeds of crime. Moreover, the 1988 UN Convention against Trafficking in Illicit Drugs emphasizes the need to crack down on illegal profits and to establish severe legal restrictions on money laundering. In the last years all Member States of the European

---

1 See Levi, M.: 'Incriminating Disclosures: An Evaluation of Money Laundering Regulation in England and Wales' (1995) 3 *European Journal of Crime, Criminal Law and Criminal Justice*, pp. 202-217, at p. 205.

Union have taken action against money laundering and have intensified their efforts to confiscate and forfeit the proceeds of crime.

Money laundering and confiscation legislation must be analysed within a broader scope of policy making which aims at the control of the flow of money, especially in the context of banking transactions. Policing financial transactions is not an end in itself but is linked to a wide range of policy goals among which forfeiture of illegal gains (as a middle range goal) as well as deterrence of organised crime play major roles. When looking at the rather short history of money laundering and confiscation legislation illegal profit from drug trafficking has certainly been a core issue[2]. The interest in strengthening control over the flow of money and the interest in confiscation of crime proceeds arose primarily within a drug trafficking context and related drug problems at the beginning of the eighties[3] but has since been extended to the profits generated by criminal enterprises and criminal organisations at large[4]. Organised crime has become an important rhetoric in the debates on money laundering and criminal profits (with the United States of America, Germany, The Netherlands and Italy representing those countries where the concept of organised crime has been used extensively in criminal justice debates throughout the eighties while other European countries do not seem to have had the topic of organised crime on the political and research agenda that explicitly). First, legislative bodies have been very active in adjusting the legal framework to the needs as expressed by advocates of confiscation and forfeiture. Confiscation and forfeiture of criminal proceeds now seem to represent the most powerful weapons available in the fight against drug trafficking and other types of organised crime[5]. It is even argued that the traditional responses to crime such as imprisonment and fines alone are ineffective, the better alternative being to follow the money trail[6].

---

2 Meyer, J. et al.(Eds): *Gewinnabschöpfung bei Betäubungsmitteldelikten. Eine rechtsvergleichende und kriminologische Untersuchung*. Wiesbaden 1989.

3 See Pachmann, Ch.: *Gigantisches illegales und internationales Finanznetz. Kriminalistik* (1985), pp. 182-189, at p. 184.

4 See Gilmore, W.C.: 'International Efforts to Combat Money Laundering' (1992) *Commonwealth Law Bulletin*, pp. 1129-1142.

5 Tullis, L.: *Handbook of Research on the Illicit Drug Trade. Socioeconomic and Political Consequences*. (New York et al 1991), p.133, quoting voices assuming that asset-forfeiture policies are the ultimate solution to international drug trafficking.

6 Savona, E.U.: 'The Organized Crime/Drug Connection: National and International Perspectives', in: Traver, H.H., Gaylord, M.S.(Eds.): *Drugs, Law and the*

Within just one decade most of the European countries have amended both basic criminal codes and procedural laws with the intent to facilitate seizure and forfeiture of ill-gotten gains[7]. Although, the debate on efficient ways to reduce drug supply has been centered around the topics of freezing and seizure of crime assets as well as confiscation laws, these issues are but a part of a general criminal law based strategy encompassing other means as well. A second issue related to illegal profits concerns money laundering and statutes requiring financial business and banks as well as commerce to channel information relevant to identify possible money laundering activities to criminal justice agencies.

Both, confiscation and anti-money laundering policies have contributed to change criminal law and criminal procedure significantly. Policies designed to prevent organised crime from profiting from various types of crimes, especially drug trafficking, are backed up by commitments to uniform legislation and joint efforts in law enforcement as expressed in international treaties and supra-national directives[8]. Among these international efforts, the Council of Europe Convention on Money Laundering has to be mentioned which goes far beyond the traditional activities of the Council of Europe in the field of crime and criminal law insofar as the Convention is open to countries outside of Europe and the obligations concern creation of uniform criminal law. Then, the European Commission has issued precise guidelines obliging Member States to enact legislation to forbid money laundering and establish systems of control monitoring banks and other financial institutions[9]. Moreover, with the 1988 UN Convention against Trafficking in Illicit Drugs a most important international instrument has been set up which emphasizes the need of forfeiture of drug proceeds as well as the need to establish severe legal restrictions on money laundering and the efficient mutual help in law enforcement and judicial affairs based upon uniform policies towards drug offences and money laundering as well as upon a restrictive approach to bank secrecy and related issues (see Article 3 and Article 5 paragraph 3 of the Convention 1988). It seems as if the recommendations issued by the Financial Action Task Force in 1988 have also been rather efficient. They contain

---

State. (New Brunswick, London 1992), pp.119-133, at p.131; Pieth, M.: *Gewinnabschöpfung bei Betäubungsmitteldelikten. Strafverteidiger* (1990), pp. 558ff.

7 Meyer, J. et al. (Eds.): *Gewinnabschöpfung bei Betäubungsmitteldelikten. Eine rechtsvergleichende und kriminologische Untersuchung.* (Wiesbaden 1989).

8 Pieth, M., 1990, see fn.6 *supra*, p.559; Levi, M., 1995, see fn.1 *supra*, pp. 205.

9 See Pieth, M., 1990, see fn.6 *supra*, pp. 559 with an outline of the history of anti-money laundering activities.

minimum standards on supervision and control of financial systems as well as money laundering which should be complied with (in order to prevent a country being deemed to be a money laundering place with the consequence of becoming isolated by the major industrial nations, see in this respect recommendations 21 and 22). In the last years, most EC countries have taken action against money laundering in terms of administrative and criminal legislation and have intensified their efforts to confiscate and forfeit the proceeds of crime[10].

II. THE RATIONALES UNDERLYING MONEY LAUNDERING AND CONFISCATION POLICIES

The most important rationale underlying the search for illegal profits points first of all to prevention by means of reducing opportunities and increasing deterrence and incapacitation[11]. It is argued that organised crime can be hit most effectively by confiscating assets derived from criminal activities and preventing the proceeds of crime from being re-invested, as profits and financial gains are deemed to represent major incentives to commit crimes[12]. Besides prevention and deterrence which are to be pursued through strengthening confiscation statutes, another goal concerns backing up the principle of 'crime does not pay". This means that ill-gotten profits have to be removed and unjust enrichment has to be avoided in order to reinstate legitimate distribution of property within a society.

Thus, confiscation measures and anti-money laundering may work in the field of drug trafficking through several mechanisms. The first of these mechanisms aims at reducing the supply of drugs. Drug traffickers are to be discouraged by reducing opportunities to profit from drug markets and deterred by the risk of losing those assets acquired in the past. The second mechanism concerns demand for drugs. Confiscation policies should contribute to increasing prices by way of increasing risks for distributors of drugs (or perceptions of risk), which may be regarded as representing a significant determinant of the retail

---

10 See Gilmore, W.C., 1992, see fn.4 *supra*, pp. 1130.

11 Levi, M., 1995, see fn.1 *supra*, p. 203.

12 See e.g. Home Office: *Tackling Drug Abuse: A Summary of the Government's Strategy*. (London 1988), p.7, 20; Kaiser, G., 1989, see fn.20 *infra*, pp. 685-704; ONCDP: *National Drug Control Strategy April 1995*. (Washington 1995) p. 28; Ministry of the Exterior et. al: *Drugs Policy in the Netherlands. Continuity and Change.* (Rijswijk 1995), p. 54.

price of controlled drugs. Lessened demand will then in turn have an impact on trafficking as supply and demand are intertwined. Finally, by way of confiscation policies and re-allocation of ill-gotten gains the message is supported that crime doesn't pay which in turn may contribute to (positive) general prevention in terms of respect for the law. Moreover, the last message may be transformed into a general response to criticism raised by the main stream debate on organised crime. The debate on organised crime has turned from a crime specific discussion into a general criticism of contemporary society highlighting the vulnerability of the social fabric caused by large parts of the population voicing demand for various vices provided by organised crime groups as well as corrupt officials protecting criminal organisations and facilitating criminal business in various fields. Behind that criticism stands the firm belief that social values have been subject to fast erosion and must be reinstated in order to make society immune against organised crime groups. Moreover, the question of what is done with crime proceeds as well as proceeds stemming from legal but immoral vices like prostitution etc. has triggered responses claiming undermining of legitimate business by illegal or dirty money and urging the need for protective measures in favour of legitimate economy and commerce. In this respect, shaming of conventional members of society might prove to be useful in terms of producing effects of positive general prevention, at least within the banking system[13].

A side effect of anti-money laundering and forfeiture policies may also be increased revenues for the public sector, especially for law enforcement, which in turn may result in increased efforts to maximise the outcome of confiscation activities. This rationale is emphasized especially in the USA where forfeited proceeds are divided among those agencies making the 'bust'[14]. Asset sharing might indeed create additional incentives to increase law enforcement activities. But on the other hand, a bias in law enforcement might be encouraged simultaneously if law enforcement concentrates on those cases most

---

13 See Levi, M. (1995), see fn.1 *supra*, p. 204 who actually accredits shaming effects a rather limited potential.

14 Tullis, L.: *Handbook of Research on the Illicit Drug Traffic. Socioeconomic and Political Consequences*. (New York et al. 1991), p.133; see also *Annual Report of the Attorney General of the United States 1992. US Department of Justice 1993*, p.45, according to the information provided in this report a total of 230 million US dollars was shared with law enforcement agencies that participated in joint investigations. Asset sharing is extended to foreign law enforcement agencies (US $12 million were transferred in 1992).

likely to result in further confiscation while other types of crimes (especially street crime) are neglected.

Although the importance of tracing and seizing criminal profits is accepted virtually everywhere and the approach is qualified to represent the most promising way not only to combat drug trafficking but also various types of organised, economic or environmental crimes, the question of the conditions under which money laundering should be made a criminal offence and confiscation should be allowed is, nevertheless, answered differently. But before describing and analysing different models of confiscation as well as money laundering offences implemented in Europe and North America, another topic must be dealt with, a topic which concerns the very basis of confiscation, that is the criminal profits, their extent and their flow.

Recent and current legislative attempts to combat drug trafficking and other types of organised crime by means of forfeiture, confiscation and money laundering statutes are based upon several assumptions which deserve careful inspection and analysis as these assumptions are turned into far-reaching consequences for criminal law and criminal procedure shifting the focus from justice to efficiency. We may suppose that these assumptions are grossly exaggerating the nature and the size of crime proceeds as well as the benefits which may be drawn from anti-money laundering and confiscation policies.

Basic assumptions on the profits of drug trafficking which can easily be applied to other crime fields also, may be outlined as follows:

- Drug trafficking generates enormous profits.

- Large profits are one of the most important incentives to engage in drug trafficking and, furthermore, incentives for organising criminal enterprises.

- Large profits are concentrated in the hand of organised criminals.

- Profits are to a large extent either re-invested, be it in drug supplying activities, be it in other illicit activities, or transferred to legal markets.

- Re-investment of criminal profits creates potential dangers as criminal organisations thus may corrupt and undermine legitimate businesses, the political system and finally the social fabric at large.

It follows then that ill-gotten profits have to be cut down in order to

- reduce supply of drugs (and other illicit goods and services),
- eliminate a source of continuing criminal enterprises,
- protect legal markets and societies from being penetrated by organised criminals,
- and to prevent the underworld becoming part of the upper world.

III. DOES CRIME PAY? THE NATURE AND EXTENT OF ILLEGAL PROFITS

It is evident that criminal justice systems rely on the goal that crime shouldn't pay as all modern criminal codes provide statutes authorising criminal courts to seize and forfeit property owned by an offender found guilty or property deemed to create dangers. Historically, forfeiture (or confiscation) of property has been used widely as punishment, especially in the case of certain (political) felonies (e.g. high treason, espionage). Rights of inheritance over the property were removed in order to maximise the punitive impact. This meant that an offender and his family were deprived of all assets and property which went to the Crown or to the local ruler. The incapacitative and political nature of this type of confiscation is for example still well recognised in the French doctrine where confiscation of this type is equated with *la mort civile*[15]. With the emergence of modern criminal law and its emphasis on individual guilt, retribution, rehabilitation and reintegration, confiscation lost its very basis, although in times of political unrest or times of dictatorship confiscation sometimes was reinstated in European countries and used as a weapon against political dissidents or political criminals[16]. Basically, three traditional approaches to confiscation exist which differ with respect to the relationship between the criminal

---

15 Robert, J.-H.: *Droit Pénal General*. (Paris 1988), p.404.

16 See e.g. Jeandidier, W.: *Droit Pénal General.* (Paris 1988), pp. 378-379; Robert, J.-H., 1989, see fn.15 *supra*, pp. 403-404; Meyer, J.: '*Gewinnabschöpfung durch Vermögensstrafe?*', (1990) 23 *Zeitschrift für Rechtspolitik*, pp. 85-89, at p.87.

offence and the confiscated object. These three approaches concern: Confiscation of the *instrumentum sceleris*, e.g the weapon used in committing a crime, confiscation of the *objectum sceleris*, e.g the drugs which were trafficked (in the common law systems the term *forfeiture* is used regularly for taking property which relates directly to crime), and finally confiscation of the *productum sceleris*, which is the profits that are drawn from committing a crime (here, the term *confiscation* applies). With respect to the handling of proceeds coming from theft offences like receiving stolen goods have been introduced as a measure to respond to black markets where stolen items are sold and bought.

Although criminology was throughout the sixties and seventies preoccupied with research on penal sanctions and their potential for reducing recidivism and the crime rate at large, penalties and measures like confiscation, forfeiture and pecuniary sanctions in general didn't fall within the scope of evaluation studies[17]. It was prison and the rehabilitative or deterrent properties of imprisonment which had been issues of criminological concern. Besides the lack of interest as demonstrated by evaluation research, criminology also neglected the topic of crime profits actually derived from various types of crimes. Scientific attention was rather drawn to the damages caused by crime and the costs incurred on society and individual victims.

A. Criminal Proceeds and Crime Theories

Although, it seems evident that financial motives are actively involved in various property and other crimes, criminology certainly did not consider financial gains as playing a significant role in the emergence of crime in terms of theory. Even in the field of crime, phenomena such as organised crime where the pursuit of economic gains is evident the role and function of illegal profits have not been studied systematically[18]. Most mainstream criminological theories on crime causation do not refer to variables highlighting illegal profits or the motive of profiting from crime. It is essentially economic crime theories which have been on the criminological agenda since the sixties that point to a cost-benefit

---

17 Albrecht, H.-J.: '*Landesbericht Deutschland*'. in: Meyer, J. et al. (Eds.): *Gewinnaschöpfung bei Betäubungsmitteldelikten. Eine rechtsvergleichende und kriminologische Untersuchung.* (Wiesbaden 1989), pp. 25-84.

18 See the summarising analysis in Albrecht, H.-J. (1989), see fn.17 *supra*, pp. 25; Dessecker, A.: *Gewinnabschöpfung im Strafrecht und in der Strafrechtspraxis* (Max-Planck Institut: Freiburg, 1992).

calculation (and hence also to profits associated with various behavioural options) in explaining criminal behaviour[19]. Findings based on this type of criminological research should be at the centre of discussion but are rarely addressed in the political and legal debates on the potential of confiscation and money laundering policies[20].

In economic crime theories, illegal profits represent the benefits necessary to create incentives which then in turn lead to decision-making where potential benefits are calculated against the potential losses (in terms of punishment risks and punishment severity). Economic theories of crime and punishment suggest that potential gains should be outweighed by perceived costs of behaviour. Traditionally, costs in this sense have been conceived as the risk of being apprehended and the severity of criminal penalties. Taking away the profits stemming from criminal behavior does not increase costs within the framework of economic theory but at most diminishes benefits at a rate dependent on perceptions of the risk of apprehension.

Economic theory then has been used in the evaluation of law enforcement activities and their impact on drug markets[21]. But here, the focus is put on the effects certain law enforcement strategies may have on retail prices of illicit drugs and whether resources invested in drug law enforcement are followed by reasonable benefits in terms of less demand for drugs or less drug consumption. The reason for putting the question this way lies in assumptions regarding the relationships between law enforcement risks in terms of interceptions of drugs, apprehension and punishment of drug traffickers, the retail price of drugs and the demand of drugs. The demand for a certain type of drug, according to these assumptions, is dependent on elasticity of the demand which in turn might be influenced by the price of this type of drug on the streets[22]. But economic studies on the relationship between street prices of illicit drugs and different law enforcement strategies pointed to

---

19 Becker, G.S.: '*Kriminalität und Strafe. Ein ökonomischer Ansatz*' in: Becker, G.S.(Ed.): *Der ökonomische Ansatz zur Erklärung menschlichen Verhaltens.* (Tübingen 1982), pp. 39-96.

20 Dessecker, A. see n.18 *supra*, (1992), pp. 80; Kaiser, G.: '*Gewinnabschöpfung als kriminologisches Problem und kriminalpolitische Aufgabe*' in: Jescheck, H.-H., Vogler, T.(Eds.): *Festschrift für Herbert Tröndle zum 70. Geburtstag.* (Berlin 1989), pp.685-704.

21 Reuter, P.: 'Can The Borders Be Sealed?' in: Weishaupt, R.(Ed.): *Drugs, Crime and the Criminal Justice System.* (Nunn Hall, Cincinnati 1990), pp.13-26.

22 Albrecht, H.-J.: '*Voraussetzungen und Konsequenzen einer Entkriminalisierung im Drogenbereich*'. in: *Institut für Konfliktforschung* (Ed.): *Entkriminalisierung im Drogenbereich?* (Köln 1991), pp.1-38; Kaiser, G. (1989) see fn.20 *supra*, pp.685-704.

rather modest effects which can be attributed to forfeiture of traffickers' assets and conveyances, increased punishments as well as to forfeiture of the illicit drugs themselves[23]. For the English heroin market it was calculated that rather optimistic confiscation rates of crime proceeds would result in negligible increases in the retail price of drugs on the street[24]. Moreover, it was shown that the effects of changes in traditional law enforcement strategies, e.g. tougher prison sentences, were even more efficient in driving retail prices up.

On the level of individual decision-making, economic reasoning supposes that opportunities to profit from crime actually exist. Opportunities to make profits clearly emerge with black markets. Therefore, it seems unlikely that penalties or penal measures aimed at eliminating crime incentives might have a significant impact as long as the source for building up motivations, that is the black market in drugs, continues to exist. Recent research in Germany on the deterrent properties of confiscation and forfeiture lends support to this conclusion[25]. It could be shown that, on the one hand, profits represent major incentives for criminal behavior, but, on the other hand, the risk of confiscation of the crime proceeds has only marginal effects on the decision to commit a criminal offence[26]. It was concluded from this study that elimination of incentives in terms of profits could indeed serve as an eminent tool in prevention. But such elimination of incentives obviously cannot be pursued by policies of confiscation as these do not affect the existence of a black market and the potential profits and therefore do not help in preventing cost-benefit calculations. Confiscation represents just a threat in terms of increased costs or in terms of reduced benefits and thus is dependent on perceptions of the risk of apprehension. Economic studies which put the focus on the effects of confiscation on drug markets and drug trafficking thus lead to similar findings as did most research on the effects of increasing the costs in terms of punishment for other types of criminal behaviour.

---

23 Reuter, P. (1990) see fn.21 *supra*, pp.13-26.

24 Wagstaff, A., Maynard, A.: *Economic Aspects of the Illicit Drug Market and Drug Enforcement Policies in the United Kingdom.* (London 1988), pp.98, at pp.117.

25 Smettan, J.: *Kriminelle Bereicherung in Abhängigkeit von Gewinnen, Risiken, Strafen und Moral.* (Freiburg 1992).

26 Smettan, J. (1992) see fn.25 *supra*, p.210.

B. Estimates on the size of the proceeds from illegal drug markets

Global estimates on the proceeds from drug trafficking receive paramount attention as can be shown through a review of literature on the proceeds of drug trafficking and confiscation. Currently, figures produced by the Financial Action Task Force are among those that are regularly cited in publications internationally.

The Financial Action Task Force created at the recommendation of the seven major industrialised nations and the President of the European Communities at the 1989 Paris Economic Summit[27] has estimated the sales of cocaine, heroin, and cannabis amounts to approximately 122 billion Dollars per year in the US and in Europe. Furthermore, it was estimated that as much as two-thirds of this sum (circa US $80 billion) could be available for money laundering and (re-) investment[28]. Upper estimates of the overall worldwide flow of drug money go as far as US $500 billion, even US $800 billion per year[29], while the Financial Action Task Force put the gross receipts from illegal drugs at $300 billion[30]. The basis of these estimates is not clear nor are these global estimates very helpful[31]. Global estimates rather are useless as a basis for assessments of confiscation policies as confiscation usually is directed towards individuals. Therefore, it makes a significant difference whether $500 billion are distributed among a group of 1000 individuals or among a group of 1 million individuals. A rational policy of confiscation must be based on the hypothesis that significant amounts of drug money are accumulated by individuals or organisations. The use of such global estimates of drug trafficking prevails, and provokes the question whether the reason for doing so lies in an attempt to strengthen the mere belief in the eminent dangers associated with organised crime. Actually, a review of the context of drug-related figures on total revenue

---

27 See Pieth, M. (1990) see fn.6 *supra*, p. 559.

28 *Financial Action Task Force on Money Laundering: Report*. (Paris, February 1990); see also Gilmore, W.C. (1992) see fn.4 *supra*, p. 1130.

29 Storbeck, J.: *Internationale Dimension der Rauschgiftbekämpfung - Perspektiven. Bewährungshilfe* (1990), pp. 266-278, at p.267; Rüter, C.F.: *'Die strafrechtliche Drogenbekämpfung in den Niederlanden'*,. (1988) 100 *Zeitschrift für die Gesamte Strafrechtswissenschaft*, pp. 385, at p. 390.

30 *Financial Action Task Force on Money Laundering: Report*. (Paris, February 1990).

31 Van Duyne, P.: *'Geldwäscherei. Umfangschätzung in Nebelschwaden'*, *Kriminologisches Bulletin* 1995.

reveals that neither analytical nor theoretical purposes prevail, but that such global estimates are cited to demonstrate the financial potential of criminal groups and the danger thus created for the social fabric[32]. With the reference made to huge and uncontrolled sums of money fears are associated that the Mafia will take over honest and respectable businesses[33], undermine the system of values, corrupt the political system[34] and finally will establish a society modelled according to the rules of organised crime.

Regularly, research on the profits of drug trafficking and their distribution is based on several assumptions which concern:

- the number of drug users,
- drug using patterns in terms of the amount of drugs consumed per user in a given period of time,
- the number of traffickers and distributors of drugs,
- the structure of the drug distribution system,
- the quality (purity) of drugs and 'cutting' practices along the distribution chain,
- the price of controlled drugs (at various points of the distribution chain),
- the (internal) costs of drug trafficking and drug distribution (transportation, bribing, costs of living, losses in terms of drugs which are intercepted by police and customs etc.).

---

32 See e.g. Pieth, M. (1990) see fn.6 *supra*, pp.558-562, at p.558 stating that there is no consensus on the turnover in illicit drug markets on the one hand but that on the other hand the turnover is as large as in the crude oil market.

33 See e.g. Keyser-Ringnalda, F.: 'European Integration with regard to the Confiscation of the Proceeds of Crime' (1992) 17 *European Law Review*, pp.499-515, at p.499.

34 See e.g. Wilhelms, U.: '*Politische und polizeiliche Dimensionen der organisierten Kriminalität*' (1993) *Der Kriminalist*, pp.233-236, at p.235; Pieth, M. (1990) see fn.6 *supra*, pp.558-562, at p.558.

The Financial Action Task Force has used rather problematic assumptions in making estimates of the size of drug proceeds. These are based first of all upon the estimate that approximately 10% of illicit drugs are intercepted by police and customs, a somewhat problematic guess which obviously can be traced back to the year 1935[35] and has since developed a history of its own; furthermore, the estimates rely heavily on retail prices of illicit drugs and, moreover, although considerable variation can be observed with respect to prices as well as the size of drug supply, 'the high end' of both ranges are used to calculate the total revenue of drug distribution. Finally, another guess concerns costs of drug trafficking which are set at 10% of the gross receipts.

All these estimates must be questioned as they do not refer to a reliable body of research, nor can it be expected that such estimates are stable over a certain period of time. In a study of drug trafficking and the proceeds of drug trafficking carried out recently in the Federal Republic of Germany, it was sought to make estimates of the proceeds generated by heroin. In this study, which relied heavily on Anglo-American research on the structure of heroin markets, it was calculated that one kilo of heroin generates on the retail level of the heroin market approximately 560.000 DM (circa US $330,000), the overall net profit of heroin trafficking is set at approximately 1.5 billion DM (circa US $900 million)[36]. This calculation is based upon the assumptions that the number of heroin users is approximately 70,000 in the FRG (with a total consumption of 700 kilos of pure heroin per year), that the retail price of heroin averages around 350 DM, that the purity of heroin is cut down to 6-11%, that the distribution system can be broken down into 5-6 levels (importers, wholesalers, weightdealer, streetdealer, 'jugglers'[37]). But each of these assumptions is questionable, subject to considerable variation over time and space and may be replaced by plausible figures leading to completely different estimates. The 1992 figures from a major metropolitain area in Germany demonstrate for example that the retail value of one kilo of heroin is approximately 80,000 DM (US $47,000)[38]. If this information replaces the figure used in the study referred to

---

35 Korf, D., de Kort, M.: *Drugshandel en Drugsbestrijding*. (Amsterdam, Criminologisch Instituut Bonger 1990).

36 Dessecker, A., Smettan, R.: '*Gewinnabschöpfung bei Betäubungsmitteldelikten. Kriminologische Untersuchung*' in: Meyer, J. et al. (Eds.): *Gewinnabschöpfung bei Betäubungsmitteln*. (Wiesbaden 1989), pp.539-681, at p.559.

37 See Moore, M.K.: Buy and Bust. *The Effective Regulation of an Illicit Market in Heroin*. (Lexington, Toronto 1977), p. 100.

38 *Lagebericht Rauschgift. Frankfurt am Main 1992*, (Frankfurt 1993), p.25.

above, then, all other estimates being equal, the net profits of heroin trafficking in the FRG are reduced to approximately 30% of the original estimate. The net profits from heroin trafficking then do not amount to 1.5 billion DM but to some 450 million DM[39].

Much less is known about the cannabis market and profits derived from trafficking in cannabis in the FRG. A virtually completely unknown phenomenon concerns the cocaine market. While some information is available on the prices of cocaine and traffickers at the front end of the distribution chain, low level distribution is still a dark field. Thus, any guesses on consumption rates or profits made along the distribution chain for cocaine lack any reliable basis.

The study on the revenue of drug traffickers in the FRG at large and the distribution of these proceeds over the various groups and individuals engaged in the illicit drug market is still at an early stage which should preclude their use for descriptive, policy or evaluative purposes[40].

When assessing the value of such analyses of drug markets one should keep in mind that the very basis consists of mere estimates. These estimates, moreover, should be regarded as being highly unstable. The studies carried out so far have revealed that obviously we cannot expect enormous amounts of money to be concentrated in the hands of a few organised criminals or a few large scale criminal organisations[41]. For the Federal Republic of Germany it might be concluded on the basis of police accounts of trafficking in various illicit drugs that the drug market is dominated by organised drug traffickers but is also highly competitive[42]. Profits most likely are widely dispersed among a rather large number of groups of drug offenders[43]. These groups actually are organised as 'division of labour', hierachies etc. can be observed down the chain from import to the retail level although there is virtually no

---

39 In 1985 the net profits derived from tafficking in heroin, cocaine and cannabis were estimated to range around 1 billion DM, see Pachmann, C.: '*Gigantisches illegales und internationales Finanznetz*'. *Kriminalistik* 1985, pp. 182, at p.182.

40 Such estimates sometimes are contrasted with information on the value of forfeited assets in order to assess the efficiency of forfeiture regulations, see Dessecker, A. *op. cit.*, 1991, pp.174, where it is calculated that the confiscation rates of profits from drug trafficking in the USA range between 0.4% and 4.6%.

41 See Dessecker, A. see n.18 *supra*, (1992).

42 See e.g Kriminalpolizeiamt Schleswig-Holstein (Ed.): *Jahresbericht 1992 zur Rauschgiftkriminalität in Schleswig-Holstein.* (Kiel 1993), p.62; *Lagebericht Rauschgift 1992. Frankfurt am Main.* (Frankfurt 1993), p.6.

43 Moore, M.K. (1977) see fn.37 *supra*, p.109.

empirical evidence that large scale criminal enterprises dominate heroin, cocaine or cannabis trafficking. Most probably, many of these groups of traffickers are rather unstable and do not manage to continue traffic over extended periods of time. However, groups which go out of the market are obviously easily replaced. On the lowest level of the distribution system it seems clear that the amounts of money collected by retail sellers are rather low while most of the value is received through consumption of part of the drugs and a considerable amount of drug money is spent on daily living expenses[44]. These findings are backed up by research in Scandinavia, where it is also concluded that belief that the income of the average drug offender is exceptionally high is without empirical foundation[45].

Although criminological research cannot provide empirical or theoretical knowledge which would support the assumptions outlined above and the strong policy emphasis which is placed on criminal proceeds and confiscation of those proceeds, international reform of criminal law currently nevertheless is driven by these hypotheses.

IV. THE INTERNATIONAL FRAMEWORK OF ANTI-MONEY LAUNDERING AND CONFISCATION POLICIES

In the analysis of current policies on confiscation of the proceeds of crime the international framework which has been built up during the eighties has to be taken into account[46]. The first major effort on the international level became visible with the 1988 UN Convention Against Illicit Traffic in Narcotic Drugs and Psychotropic Substances[47]. Article 5, paragraph 1 of the said Convention reads thus: Each party shall adopt measures as may be necessary to enable confiscation of (a) proceeds

---

44 Johnson, B.D., Kaplan, M.A., Schmeidler, J.: 'Days with Drug Distribution: Which Drugs? How many Transactions? With what Returns?' in: Weisheit, R.(Ed.): *Drugs, Crime and the Criminal Justice System*. (Nunn Hall, Cincinnati 1990), pp.193-214 found in a study on 201 heroin users active in drug distribution had an average annual economic return from drug distribution of about US $1.000 in cash and US $2,000 in drugs (p.206); Dessecker, A. *op. cit.*, 1991, p.378; Levi, M. 1995, see fn.1 *supra*, p. 204.

45 Laitinen, A.: 'Finnish Drug Control: Change and Accommodation' in: Traver, H.H., Gaylord, M.S.(Eds.): *Drugs, Law and the State* (New Brunswick, London 1992), pp.65-78, at p.73; pointing also to the finding that little evidence exists with respect to major organised drug trafficking. Empirical evidence suggests some low-level organisations with offenders from poor social backgrounds.

46 See for summaries Keyser-Ringnalda, F. (1992) see fn.33 *supra*, pp.499-515; Commonwealth Secretariat: *Basic Documents on International Efforts to Combat Money Laundering*. (London 1991); Pieth, M. (1990) see fn.6 *supra*, pp.558.

47 The FRG has ratified the UN Convention of 1988, 19 January 1989.

derived from offences established in accordance with article 3 para. 1, or property the value of which corresponds to that of such proceeds; to ensure the effectiveness of confiscation procedures paragraph 2 of Article 5 and to enable international cooperation in confiscation matters either by giving effect to a confiscation order of a requesting party or by issuing on request its own confiscation orders. Broad attention is paid to mutual assistance in identifying, searching and seizing suspicous property. Then, Article 3 paragraph 1(b)(i) and (ii), and (c)(i) oblige treaty members to enact legislation making various money laundering activities criminal offences precisely broken down into transfer activities (Art. 3 paragraph 1(b)(i)), disguise activities (Article 3 paragraph 1(b)(ii)) but also purchase, possession and use of assets knowing the illicit origin of those assets (Article 3, paragraph 1(c)(i)).

For Europe the 1990 Council of Europe 'Convention on Laundering, Search, Seizure and Confiscation of the Proceeds of Crime' of September 1990 is of particular significance. This Convention is the joint product of an initiative taken by the Council of Europe and the European Community. While this Convention takes into consideration the UN Convention of 1988, its scope is much broader and not restricted to drug trafficking[48] but is extended to other serious criminal offences likely to be committed within a context of criminal enterprises. Moreover, the Convention does not carry the title 'European Convention' as other nations which have participated in preparing the draft (e.g. the USA, Canada, Australia) are encouraged to join the Convention. The main purpose of the Convention is to facilitate identification, seizure and confiscation of proceeds of those types of crime generating large profits. Parties to the Convention therefore are obliged to enact legislation enabling freezing and seizure as well as final confiscation of crime proceeds. Money laundering must be made a criminal offence and assistance with respect to confiscation matters of any kind has to be granted to requesting parties of the Convention. Thus, the Convention of the Council of Europe carries much stricter obligations as all those points are specified which are not allowed to justify refusal of requests of mutual assistance.

Another European treaty which makes reference to drug trafficking and confiscation concerns the 'Schengen Agreement' and the 'Schengen Convention' of 1985/1990 which have been signed so far by

---

48 Council of Europe: *Explanatory Report on the Convention on Laundering, Search, Seizure and Confiscation of the Proceeds from Crime*. (Strasbourg 1991).

several EC countries (including the FRG). The most important aim of the Schengen Agreement concerns harmonisation of criminal law in EC countries (especially in the field of drug laws and laws on firearms) and establishing a general framework for police cooperation in Europe as well as laying the groundwork for a system of unified European police. Article 71 of the Schengen Treaty obliges parties to make all types of trafficking in narcotics a criminal offence; Aricle 72 expresses the need to establish measures designed to seize and confiscate proceeds from drug trafficking.

The EC directive on money-laundering[49] obliges EC countries to enact legislation which complies with certain guidelines on money laundering, and more importantly, to establish a system of control over banks, financial institutions and commerce with identification, documentation and reporting duties[50].

Summarising the international framework established so far with respect to drug trafficking, confiscation of the proceeds of drug trafficking and related issues we may state that the international (and European) community has adopted an approach to illicit drugs which is essentially based upon criminal law and doesn't take into account alternative drug policies[51]. Although most European countries have either already signed the international conventions or will do so in the future, sceptical voices are still heard and probably consensus on vital points will not be that easy to achieve below the abstract level of international treaties[52].

In comparative analysis of forfeiture and money laundering control systems several models must be included with quite considerable differences in terms of legal regulations as well as implementation. Among these models which have received considerable attention in policy debates are the US statutes on forfeiture, on the one hand, and the English Drug Trafficking Act of 1986 (and the Criminal Justice Act 1993), on the other hand. German police and the Ministries of the Interior advocated these systems strongly as these jurisdictions were among the first to introduce forfeiture legislation which put the

---

49 Council Directive of 10 June 1991 on the prevention of the use of the financial system for the purpose of money laundering.

50 See in this respect the German draft law on tracing proceeds from serious crimes (*Geldwäschegesetz*) of 2 July 1993 (*Bundesratsdrucksache* 456/93).

51 See e.g. Albrecht, H.-J., van Kalmthout, A. (Eds.): *Drug Policies in Western Europe*. (Freiburg 1989).

52 Rüter, C.F.: '*Harmonie trotz Dissonanz. Gedanken zur Erhaltung eines funktionsfähigen Strafrechts im grenzenlosen Europa*', (1993) *Zeitschrift für die Gesamte Strafrechtswissenschaft*, pp. 30-47.

emphasis on those issues which were perceived to create severe obstacles in the attempt to combat drug trafficking through tough confiscation policies. These issues concern the problem of whether the net profits of criminal offences or the gross receipts or proceeds of crime should be the object of confiscation and the problem of evidence which according to German forfeiture statutes must be provided to prove links between assets and a criminal offence beyond a reasonable doubt. Both, the US model and the British model of confiscation were assessed to provide efficient responses to the problems experienced with German forfeiture statutes. It is especially the reversal of the burden of proof which has been focussed upon during the debates. The 1988 Vienna Convention in this respect adopted soft regulation demanding parties to the treaty to consider whether it would be possible to introduce reversal of the burden of proof in case of forfeiture of suspect assets (see Article 5 paragraph 7 convention 1988).

V. DIFFERENT MODELS OF MONETARY STRATEGIES IN CRIMINAL LEGISLATION

A. The US model of confiscation: penal and civil forfeiture

The United States of America was among the first countries to boost confiscation legislation in order to intensify law enforcement in the field of drug trafficking and organised crime. Although, in 1981 a report of the US Comptroller General stated that asset forfeiture was rarely used, some years later the picture had changed completely. Confiscation has become the major tool in the 'war on drugs'.

The Federal law of thc US differentiates between two approaches to confiscation of criminal proceeds: civil forfeiture (*in rem*) and criminal forfeiture (*in personam*).

Criminal forfeiture finds its legal basis in the Comprehensive Drug Abuse Act, (21 USA §853) as well as in the RICO statute (as amended by the Comprehensive Forfeiture Act of 1984 and the Anti-Drug Abuse Act 1986). According to the Comprehensive Drug Abuse Act forfeiture shall be ordered in case of drug offences which carry a minimum penalty of one year imprisonment or more, The RICO statute provides for criminal forfeiture in case of racketeering activities (organised crime). Objects of criminal forfeiture may be all proceeds from drug offences as well as interests stemming from such proceeds, all those assets which in any matter or part were used in committing the offence, and finally all rights, interests etc. affording a source of control over a continuing criminal enterprise. Criminal (and civil) forfeiture authority has been extended drastically through the introduction of the offence of money laundering which carries not only severe penalties in terms of imprisonment and fines but may result also in civil and criminal forfeiture (18 USC §§981, 982)[53], as a money laundering offence can be established whenever a person engages in virtually any type of commercial transaction, transportation or transmission of funds with the proceeds of crimes such as fraud, theft, gambling, arson, counterfeiting, bribing, drug trafficking, racketeering, environmental crimes etc. (18 USC §§1956, 1957). Although most of these offences do not carry a confiscation provision of their own, with the money laundering offence they are (at least partially) eligible for confiscation orders. Forfeiture is mandatory if the jury arrived at a verdict of guilt and a (separate) verdict of forfeiture[54].

Civil forfeiture is based on an *in rem* procedure. The procedure is initiated against certain property (including real estate) which was involved in a crime, for example. Crime involvement of property in turn may lead to a finding of 'guilt'. In a civil *in rem* procedure only probable cause that the property was involved in illicit activities must be established. This brings about a reversal of the burden of proof for the owner of the property who may not be involved at all in the offence itself. The government needs to establish only probable cause that the property was involved in illicit activities, such as, for instance, drug trafficking. Unlike criminal forfeiture procedures, no charge has to be brought against the owner of the property. In order to stop civil forfeiture of 'contaminated' property the owner must establish an 'innocent owner defense' (see e.g. 21 USC §881a(6), 18 USC §981). Through the 'relation back doctrine' transfers subsequent to the criminal offence do not invalidate the government's title on the forfeited property. Until now no uniform application of the innocent owner defence exists. But, in general it is not easy to establish such defences[55].

Forfeiture laws have resulted in the USA in large amounts of ill-gotten gains which, on the Federal level, are deposited in the Assets Forfeiture Fund (28 USC §524), which was created to fund law

---

53 Rudnick, A.G.: 'Cleaning-up', (1992) 7 *Criminal Justice*, pp. 2-5, at pp. 50-51.

54 But the court may set aside the verdict if the verdict is, to the opinion of the court, not justified on the basis of evidence presented during the trial or reduce the amount which shall be forfeited if otherwise punishment would be grossly disproportional.

55 Zeldin, M.F., Moscowitz, J.W.: 'Innocent Third Parties In Federal Forfeiture Proceedings', (1993) 8 *Criminal Justice*, pp. 11-16, at pp. 61-63.

enforcement activities, preferrably activities which result in further forfeiture action. In 1992 the amount deposited totalled approximately $531 million[56].

The problems, currently discussed concern among others the problem of third parties who easily get involved in confiscation procedures (*in rem*) and thus might be punished without having committed a crime[57]. What is required to establish an innocent owner defence is specified in the different civil forfeiture statutes. The requirements differ; the Narcotics Violation forfeiture statute, for example, provides that the owner must have been without knowledge or consent (21 USC §881(a)(6)), the money laundering forfeiture statute requires that the owner was without knowledge (18 USC §981), while according to other statutes it must be established that the owner was without knowledge, consent or wilful blindness (21 USC §881 (a)(4)(c)). Although defences exist and international treaties take up the problem of innocent third parties and try to implement certain safeguards, the language of the statutes as well as judicial interpretation to be found in some recent decisions[58] lend support to the impression that the threat of forfeiture increasingly is used to force the private sector or parts of it into joining drug law enforcement. By making innocent owner defences dependent on the owner doing everything reasonable to preclude the proscribed use of property, informal systems of control are activated by means of the threat of punishment. As any business through which illegal proceeds may pass is at risk, preventive procedures have to be developed, aimed at identification and exclusion of individuals or organisations from commercial transactions etc.

Critical voices then are raised against the obvious trend to create a 'drug exception to the law'[59] as forfeiture policies concentrate on drug trafficking.

Another point of concern is the proportionality of both civil and criminal forfeiture. Although, draconian forfeiture policy is

---

56 Office of the Attorney General: *1992 Annual Report of the Attorney General of the United States*. (Washington 1993).

57 Sagor, E.G.: 'Innocent Owner and Other Defenses to Forfeiture Under the Drugs Laws, Money Laundering, and RICO', in: Lichtenberger, J.(Ed.): *Readings in White-Collar Crime*. (Westport, London 1991), pp. 35-51.

58 See Zeldin, M.F., Moscowitz, J.W.: 'Innocent Third Parties in Federal Forfeiture Proceedings', (1993) *Criminal Justice*, pp. 11-15, at pp. 61-63.

59 Wisotsky, S.: Crackdown: 'The Emerging "Drug Exception" to the Bill of Rights'. (1987) 38 *Hastings Law Journal*, pp. 889-926.

recommended officially to be used against large scale drug traffickers, in practice minor drug offenders seem to be affected considerably, too[60].

B. *The English System of Forfeiture*

The English system of forfeiture in the past was similar to that of German criminal law. Under Section 43 of the powers of the Criminal Courts Act 1973 any property which was in the possession of an offender at the time of apprehension and, furthermore, was used or intended to be used in the commission of any offence, could be forfeited[61]. These powers underwent significant changes in 1987 when the Drug Trafficking Offences Act 1986 came into force. Although, initially the 1986 Act was restricted to drug trafficking offences, it has since been extended to other types of crime in order to cover all profits generated in the context of organised crime.

Confiscation of proceeds of drug trafficking may take place only at the level of crown courts. Magistrates are not empowered to use confiscation provisions. The reason for restricting confiscation orders to higher level courts is to concentrate this measure on serious drug offences and to spare small scale offenders. But at this level the court is obliged to make use of confiscation[62]. The law leaves no discretion if certain conditions are fulfilled. In every case where the defendant has been found guilty of a drug trafficking offence, the court has to initiate special proceedings after the finding of guilt and before sentencing. Drug offences which trigger such proceedings concern: production of controlled substances, possession of controlled drugs with the intent to sell, import and export of controlled drugs, conspiracy and attempt to commit these drug trafficking offences. In this in-between procedure the court has to deal with three questions. The court has to inquire: (a) whether the defendant has benefited from drug trafficking, (b) how much the defendant received from drug trafficking and, (c) what amount actually should be confiscated.

The first question has a firm basis in the law itself, which says that those offenders benefiting from drug trafficking, who have at any time (whether before or after the commencement of the statute) received

60 King, R.: 'The Unwinnable War on Drugs. Why the ABA should pull out', (1992) *Criminal Justice*, pp.10-15, pp. 49-52, at p. 15.

61 Zander, M.: *Confiscation and Forfeiture Law. English and American Comparisons*. (The Police Foundation. London 1989).

62 In Scotland courts have discretion with respect to confiscation orders. This holds true also for the extension of confiscation to other offences by the 1988 Act in England and Wales.

any payment or other reward in connection with drug trafficking carried out by him or another can be cited. Thus, not only those offences which have been dealt with in the finding of guilt may be included but any other drug offence (independent from whether such offences have been the subject of criminal proceedings). The English legislator made use of the term 'proceeds of drug trafficking'. This means that not only the net profits may be subject to confiscation but everything which was derived from drug trafficking (the court must not take into account deductions in terms of expenses etc.).

If the court has found that the offender has benefited from drug trafficking, then, the second decision concerns the value of these proceeds.

Here, the drug trafficking law of 1986 has brought considerable changes. As many of the problems of forfeiting crime proceeds are perceived to be rooted in the difficulties of proving beyond reasonable doubt that any assets are derived from drug offences, the amendment has lowered the burden of proof. If the court is convinced that the offender did actually profit from drug trafficking, then, the law empowers the court to base the decision on certain (rebuttable) assumptions on the origins of the assets.

- The court may assume that those assets which are owned by the offender at the time of the finding of guilt have been purchased by means derived from drug trafficking.

- The court may assume that all those assets which have been acquired during a period of six years preceeding commencement of actual criminal proceedings are also the proceeds of drug trafficking (it does not matter whether the offender still owns these assets at the time of the finding of guilt);

- The court may assume that the source of means covering all expenses made during those last six years was drug trafficking;

- The court may assume that the offender received full property in those assets.

As these assumptions are but rebuttable assumptions on the origins of assets, the offender may provide evidence proving that all or part of the assets were not acquired by drug proceeds.

The third question the court has to answer concerns the fixing of the amount which should be confiscated. Basically, the court should order confiscation of the value of all those assets which the court is convinced or has assumed were proceeds of drug trafficking. But as not all of these proceeds actually may be recovered, the court shall order confiscation of an amount which is 'realisable'. The realisable amount corresponds to the value of the actual assets and property of the defendant (minus certain financial obligations as, for example, fines, compensation orders, obligations which have priority in the case of bankruptcy, plus the value of all the gifts the defendant made during the last six years).

In order to freeze assets likely to be forfeited and to ensure confiscation, the public prosecutor may apply for civil restraints and charging orders.

Although the confiscation order is not understood to be a criminal penalty, it is handled for the purpose of collection like a criminal fine. The criminal court therefore has to fix all those conditions which would be determined if the defendant was sentenced to a criminal fine (payment by instalments etc.). This means first of all determination of a term of substitute imprisonment in case of confiscation default. The maximum term of substitute imprisonment amounts to ten years if confiscation of an amount of one million pounds or more can not be collected (Section 6).

Although the English system of forfeiture has operated now for some seven years, assessment of the performance of confiscation orders is difficult. While it is estimated that up to the end of 1991 some £35 million have been ordered to be confiscated and that at any time approximately £27 million are under restraint[63], these data alone are not sufficient for evaluation purposes. Recent criminal justice data demonstrates that obviously one of the problems experienced up to now lies in the enforcement of confiscation orders. The amount of money actually realised represents only a small proportion of the value of confiscation orders. While 37.9 million have been ordered to be confiscated in 1989 alone, just £1.1 million have been collected during

63 Vallance, P.F.: *Money Laundering: The Situation in the United Kingdom*. (The Money Laundering Conference, Strasbourg 28-30 Sept 1992).

the two-year period 1989/1990 (a proportion of 14% at best)[64]. With respect to the question whether strategic goals have been reached in terms of confiscating significant parts of drug trafficking proceeds at large and discouraging drug supply, research came up with the finding that confiscation orders probably do not affect those who make large profits from drug trafficking[65], but rather the small-scale retail market. Two thirds of the confiscation orders concern amounts of less than £1000 throughout the eighties and at the beginning of the nineties[66]. It is concluded from interviews with traffickers that they are generally not subject to confiscation orders[67]. This assessment is consistent with the findings from an English study that confiscation policies have a marginal impact only on drug trafficking[68].

C. *The French Response to Profits from Drug Trafficking*

French drug laws allowed for the forfeiture of the drugs themselves as well as the instruments used to produce drugs and the profits which could be linked to a specific drug offence.

Considerable changes with respect to forfeiture occured with the Law No. 87-1157, which came into force beginning of 1988. Criminal courts were empowered to order confiscation (*confiscation generale*) of the total property of an offender found guilty of drug trafficking (especially import, export, production of controlled drugs)[69]. This type of general confiscation was not new to French criminal law but until then had been confined to certain types of political criminal offences such as treason (Section 38 FCC). Section 629, paragraph 5

---

64 The Home Office Working Group on Confiscation: *Report on the Drug Trafficking Offences Act 1986*. (London 1991), p.8.

65 Green, P.: *Drug Couriers. The Howard League for Penal Reform*, (London 1991), p.19.

66 Home Office: *Criminal Statistics. England and Wales 1991*, p. 166; in 1991 26% of those offenders who were eligible for confiscation orders received such an order (1005 out of 3883). 72% of the confiscation orders concerned amounts of less than 1000 Pounds, while the average amount confiscated was appr. £5,500 ($8,500 US). 12 orders amounted to more than £100,000.

67 Green, P. (1991) see fn.65 *supra*, p. 19.

68 Wagstaff, A., Maynard, A. (1988) see fn.24 *supra*, p. 123, where it is estimated that under the assumption of a 10% risk of assets valued at £500,000 seized on arrest the retail price of heroin would increase in the order of 3.6-5.2% (p.123).

69 Detzkies, J.: *'Landesbericht Frankreich'*, In: Meyer, J. et al.(Eds.): *Gewinnabschöpfung bei Betäubungsmitteldelikten*. (Wiesbaden 1989), pp. 103-156.

(Code of Public Health) says now that in cases of drug trafficking the criminal court may order confiscation of all or part of the property of the offender. The confiscation order is at the discretion of the criminal court and represents a 'complementary penalty'. As it is clear that the general confiscation order is punitive in nature, critics point to the problem that general confiscation does not match with the personal character of punishment and violates the principle of individual guilt.

D. The German Reform of Forfeiture Law

The German Parliament when discussing amendment of criminal forfeiture and confiscation could refer to various drafts prepared by state governments (as criminal law and drugs laws fall under federal legislative competence, the single states (*Länder*) are not empowered to set up legislation in these fields) and by political parties favouring different approaches to the problem of ill-gotten profits[70]. In 1992 the Federal Parliament voted a bill which introduced two penalties which are supposed to become efficient tools in combatting organised crime through facilitating forfeiture of ill-gotten gains[71]. These two new penalties or measures combine some of the features of the French model and the technique of reversal of the burden of proof as was outlined for the Anglo-American systems. Additionally, the principle of net-profits was abolished and substituted by the principle of crime proceeds. These newly introduced penal sanctions concern:

- the penalty of confiscation of property (*Vermögensstrafe*, §43a GCC),
- extended forfeiture of crime proceeds (*erweiterter Verfall*, §73d GCC).

§43a GCC authorises criminal courts to sentence an offender to the penalty of confiscation of property if

---

70 See for a summary of these drafts Dreher/Tröndle: *Strafgesetzbuch. Kommentar*. 46th Edition, (München 1993), §§43a, 73d.

71 Law Against Drug Trafficking and other Types of Organised Crime, July 15th 1992, *BGB*l. I, p.1302.

- a criminal statute provides for this penalty[72]
- the offender is sentenced to a term of imprisonment exceeding two years.

If these requirements are fulfilled the criminal court may order confiscation of an amount of money, of which the upper limit is set by the value of all of the offender's assets and property. The total value of the offender's property may be estimated by the court. No difference is made between ill-gotten gains and property stemming from illegal sources, on the one hand, and those parts of the property which come from legal sources, on the other. Together with the penalty of confiscation, the court has to determine a period of substitute imprisonment if the amount of money confiscated cannot be collected. Substitute imprisonment may (according to §43a GCC) range between one month and two years).

The penalty of confiscation is subject to the general principles of sentencing (§46 GCC) which require that the penalties meted out have to match with individual guilt as expressed in the offence which was committed. It follows that a prison sentence to which the penalty of confiscation is added may not exceed the size of punishment that is deserved in terms of individual guilt. So, if a penalty of confiscation is imposed, repercussions on the length of prison sentences have to be taken into account.

With the penalty of confiscation all those problems of forfeiture which were embedded in the requirement of ascertaining the criminal origins of proceeds just faded away. It is no longer required to establish links between certain pieces of property and some specified criminal offence.

With 'extended forfeiture' the court is authorised to order, independent from individual guilt, forfeiture of assets or property if an offence provides for this measure and if the assumption is justified that these assets or property were proceeds of criminal offences. Extended forfeiture is mandatory. Other than the penalty of confiscation, extended

---

72 Offences which provide for this new penalty concern §150 (forgery), §181c (trafficking in human beings and certain prostitution offences), §244 III (theft committed by gangs), §260 III (receiving of stolen property committed by gangs), §261 VII (money laundering), §285b I (certain types of illegal gambling), §30c BtMG (various drug trafficking offences); in general, it was sought to cover those types of offences which are part of organised crime activities.

forfeiture is still based upon a link between a criminal offence and the assets of the offender. But with extended forfeiture the burden of proof is reduced, as proof beyond a reasonable doubt is not required with respect to the criminal offence from which it is assumed that the property or assets originated (although it is not yet clear upon which facts the assumption of a link may be based and how convincing such facts must be in order to justify the assumption of such links).

Throughout the parliamentary debates on the penalty of confiscation and extended forfeiture, constitutional concerns were raised[73]. It has been argued that the penalty of confiscation as well as extended forfeiture violates the constitutional right of property (as guaranteed by Article 14 of the German Constitution) and, moreover, that both of these penal sanctions do not comply with the rule of law, as the principle of individual guilt is violated. The violation of the principle of guilt through extended forfeiture seems rather obvious as the reversal of the burden of proof is not consistent with the doctrine that criminal punishment may be imposed only if an offender has been found guilty after a criminal trial where certain procedural safeguards with respect to establishing that a crime has been committed have been given due regard. Although advocates of extended forfeiture argue that forfeiture does not represent a criminal penalty but must be considered a criminal measure which might be imposed without a finding of guilt, this argument could be accepted only if extended forfeiture was restricted to the elimination of unjust enrichment in terms of the net profits of crime. But as forfeiture now is extended to the proceeds of crime, criminal courts are authorised to forfeit property of the offender. Extended forfeiture must then be considered to represent a criminal penalty as it encroaches upon the rights of the offender (like other pecuniary penalties). But in this case the principle of presumption of innocence applies and precludes such punishment being meted out without proper proof of a criminal offence from which the proceeds originated.

With respect to the penalty of confiscation the problem arises whether the discretionary power may be used without violating the principle of guilt as its size is dependent also on the extent of the property of the offender and thus not related to the seriousness of the offence. Moreover, in the case of default the amount of money confiscated must be converted into a period of imprisonment (between

---

73 Ostendorf, H.: '*Organisierte Kriminalität. Eine doppelte Herausforderung für die Justiz*'. *Kriminalistik* 1991, pp.509-514; '*Deutscher Richterbund*', in : *Deutsche Richterzeitung* 1990, p.106; '*Deutscher Anwaltsverein*': *Anwaltsblatt* 1990, pp.247; Meyer, J. (1990), see fn.16 *supra*.

one month and two years), but no conversion rate can be imagined which could be related to the concept of guilt[74]. Finally, as was outlined above, the penalty of confiscation must be imposed beside a prison sentence of more than two years and thus must be converted also into periods of imprisonment as the sum of both may not exceed individual guilt. So, in case of large fortunes there might be the choice between an offender 'buying his way out' of prison, on the one hand, and excessive punishment, on the other hand[75].

As both extended forfeiture and the penalty of confiscation may affect the property of an individual which does not stem from criminal offences, the question must be asked whether the constitutional right to property might be in conflict with the new legislation. Although the constitutional court has ruled that pecuniary sanctions do not *per se* infringe upon the right to property (as for instance fines create an obligation to pay a certain amount of money)[76], the constitutional court has ruled that this opinion is not valid if a pecuniary penalty fundamentally affects the offenders' financial circumstances. As the penalty of confiscation may amount to the total value of assets and property of an offender, there is no doubt that the constitutional right of property grants full protection. Confiscation penalties and extended forfeiture then can be considered to comply with the constitution only if it can be established that these sanctions are appropriate, indispensable and proportional instruments in an attempt to reach legitimate goals. It goes without saying that the state pursues acceptable and legitimate goals and interests with the introduction of extended forfeiture and the penalty of confiscation in terms of deterrence and general prevention. Although, these sanctions may be deemed to be indispensable as German criminal law does not provide for pecuniary or other sanctions

---

74 Obviously, the eminent goal of the penalty of confiscation concerns incapacitation.

75 See also Köhler, M., Beck, W.: '*Gerechte Geldstrafe statt konfiskatorischer Vermögenssanktionen*'. (1991) *JZ*, pp. 797-804; Krey, V., Dierlamm, A.: '*Gewinnabschöpfung und Geldwäsche - Kritische Stellungnahme zu den matteriell-rechtlichen Vorschriften des Entwurfs eines Gesetzes zur Bekämpfung des illegalen Rauschgifthandels und anderer Erscheinungsformen der organisierten Kriminalität*' (1992) *JR*, pp. 353-360.

76 *Bundesverfassungsgerichtsentscheidungen* (Constitutional Court Decisions) 68, pp. 287.

which authorise confiscation of 'suspicious' assets[77], no scientific basis exists to suggest their appropriatness. As was outlined above, criminological theory and research does not support the assumption that drug traffickers might be deterred and drug markets might be eliminated by means of confiscation policies. Finally, serious doubts must be expressed with respect to the proportionality of both sanctions. Proportionality of punishment is established through the guilt of the offender and the seriousness of the offence. But the impact of both sanctions, extended forfeiture and the penalty of confiscation extends to more than the offence for which the offender was found guilty. Then, appropriateness in terms of significant preventive effects alone might establish proportionality. As such appropriateness neither can be proven today, nor can be reasonably expected to be established in the future, extended forfeiture and the penalty of confiscation are exposed to the charge of infringing on rights in an unproportional and unappropriate manner.

VI. MONEY LAUNDERING LEGISLATION AND THE IMPLEMENTATION OF MONEY LAUNDERING OFFENCE STATUTES

A. An Overview of Offence Characteristics and Related Issues

From the end of the eighties onwards, the focus of criminal policy turned to money laundering and related issues as it was found to be rather difficult to implement confiscation policies without basic knowledge of the flow of crime proceeds which essentially requires basic knowledge of the national and international flow of money which in turn must be based on access to the system of money transfers. The outcome of these debates was the creation of money laundering offence statutes which are described in some detail below along with the objective and subjective elements which make up the offence as well as monitoring and reporting systems designed to channel information from money handling systems to criminal justice agencies.

Among the objective elements of the money laundering offences as they were constructed through legislative bodies throughout Europe, the most important element deals with the object of money laundering itself as this element essentially determines the range of

---

77 Nevertheless, it could be argued that alternative options exists with respect to the prohibitive approach to drug problems, see Pieth, M. (1990) see fn.6 *supra*, pp. 558-562.

behaviour potentially falling under the offence statute. It goes without saying that first of all money and other items which are the direct proceeds of crime fall under the scope of money laundering offence statutes. But, then the question has to be asked what money or assets should be included. As chains of transfers of crime proceeds should also fall under money laundering offence statutes, the problem arises how to limit in some way the criminalising effect money laundering statutes may have, and to avoid contamination of too large a share of cash or other items which at some point in their transactional history might have been the object of some criminal offence. Together with incrimination of mere negligent money laundering and the extension of the range of offences being eligible as a pre-condition for money laundering, this could turn out to be a perfect way to extend penal control over large segments of commerce and the economy, on the one hand, as well as every day individual financial and other transactions, on the other[78]. Such a type of open and unprecise offence statute would not comply with constitutional principles either, for example, the principle of the rule of law demanding exact and precise offence statutes. Moreover, such offence statutes are likely to display considerable side effects and to interfere in other systems, especially in the economic system. The crucial question here does not concern so much 'who did it?', a question ordinarily arising with respect to ordinary crimes, but rather concerns the question 'did a crime actually occur?'[79]. So, we may even say that the legislative process is to be continued in the field of enforcement of criminal law. So far, elements of symbolic legislation might be hidden in money laundering offence statutes, which are likely to create serious obstacles for positive general prevention and the moralising functions of criminal law. General rrevention in this sense requires clearly defined behaviour in criminal law if criminal law should serve as a credible moral message. Although, on an abstract level this does not seem to be that difficult in the field of money laundering as all assets or money stemming from crime should be included, separation of dirty money from clean money in everyday practice is not easy at all. Thus, the most important function of criminal law, that is individuating behaviour which is not tolerated under any conditions, is not fulfilled.

---

78 See Levi, M. (1995) see fn.1 *supra*, p. 203 pointing out that the range of behaviour which can be classified as money laundering can include minor exchange of money into foreign currency up to cocaine cartels investing millions of dollars.

79 Albrecht, H.-J., Heine, G., Meinberg, V.: '*Umweltschutz durch Strafrecht?*' (1984) 96 *Zeitschrift für die Gesamte Strafrechtswissenschaft* pp. 943-998.

In order to individuate minor cases Austria has set the value of criminal proceeds which may trigger the money laundering offence at 100,000 Austrian Schillings (some £7000 sterling) which seems to represent a viable way to restrict the scope of the money laundering offence while excluding (especially in the field of mere possession or acquiring assets or money with a criminal background) small scale and/or every day behaviour.

A second objective element in the construction of the money laundering offence concerns the activities or behaviours which may fall under the term of laundering. Here, we observe that money laundering offences regularly involve handling crime proceeds in a very wide sense covering (a) transactions, (b) concealing activities, and, (c) possession and acquiring crime proceeds.

A third element refers to the so-called predicate offences which may invoke the money laundering offence. While policy debates on money laundering originally have been centered around drug trafficking offences, the nineties have seen in some jurisdictions a considerable extension of predicate offences. In 1994 France amended the money laundering law to include criminal proceeds from all criminal offences in order to comply with obligations under the Council of Europe Convention on Money Laundering of 1991 [80]. In Germany the range of predicate offences has been widened, too, but, tax offences and some property and economic crimes are still excluded. The Criminal Justice Act 1993 has extended the range of crimes from drug trafficking and terrorist acts and includes now major theft and fraud, forgery, robbery and other crimes. So, today we find extremely different money laundering statutes throughout Europe, from those strictly bound to drug trafficking offences (e.g., Luxembourg) to those attempting to hit at all those offences likely to be committed within an organised crime context, and finally to those including virtually all criminal offences (eg. Belgium). However, the trend seems to be towards including all criminal offences.

A fourth objective element in constructing the money laundering offence concerns the causal relationship between the predicate offence and the object of money laundering. The causal relationship is an especially crucial point because forfeiture and confiscation statutes actually have been amended in order to avoid the problem of establishing a causal relationship (which is beyond reasonable doubt) between a particular crime and its proceeds.

---

80 *Le Courrier de la Chancellerie. Mensuel d'Information du Ministere de la Justice*, No. 27, Paris 1994, p. 1.

Obviously, requiring a causal relationship creates a major problem as it is difficult to link money or other assets to a specific predicate offence. The German money laundering offence statute actually demands proof that (a) a (predicate) criminal offence has been committed, and, (b) the assets in question are the proceeds of the proven predicate offence.

With respect to subjective elements we find maximum variation insofar as money laundering legislation varies between intent and negligence. So, for example, in France and Austria the money laundering offence can only be established if intent can be proven. In Germany gross negligence is sufficient. Additional intent to obstruct the course of justice in terms of creating obstacles to seizure and forfeiture of criminal proceeds is required by the Swiss money laundering statute.

The penalties provided for money laundering in European criminal legislation differ enormously. While the English law threatens a maximum prison sentence of fourteen years, Italian criminal legislation has introduced a maximum penalty of twenty years for certain money laundering offences[81]. But most other European countries have set the range of penalties for money laundering from two to five years imprisonment and/or a fine[82].

B. *The Implementation of money laundering offence statutes*

1. *The framework of implementing offence statutes*

The analysis of anti-money laundering measures has to focus on the process of implementation of anti-money laundering policies and the problems which are encountered when enforcing criminal law in this field. With respect to implementation of money laundering statutes it can be assumed that similar problems as those known from analysis of implementation of other types of modern criminal law such as environmental criminal law enforcement will show up although the type of actors and type of activities involved will differ. This assumption is based upon the central role of information and information exchange for implementing criminal laws. Money laundering occurs within a system (of financial institutions, banks, building societies, commerce) which is not easily penetrated by law enforcement although having access to this system is a crucial point for implementation. In case of traditional crime,

81 Art. 11 Italian Law on Narcotic Substances; Art. 648 Italian Criminal Code.

82 Austria: §165 Criminal Code, up to two years imprisonment.

initiation of criminal investigations are dependent on a victim reporting the crime. Moreover, successful investigation is primarily dependent on the victim's capability to give a clear account of what has happened and, more important still, some information on the suspect which then can be used in tracing down the offender. Therefore, the victim's role in social control has been compared to that of a 'gate-keeper' of the criminal justice system. However, money-laundering is essentially a victimless crime. It follows that someone else has to take care of collecting and passing on intelligence. The functions normally fulfilled by the victim in the case of ordinary crimes have to be taken up either by the private sector which is engaged in financial transactions or by administrative authorities which have routine access to information on financial transactions. Success or failure of anti-money laundering laws is essentially dependent on whether relevant information can be provided for law enforcement purposes.

Two options are available for criminal justice agencies in attempting to cope with the deficit caused by the lack of a reporting victim. The first option consists of criminal justice agencies becoming proactive and acquiring themselves the particular knowledge and the access necessary to produce and to use meaningful information with the ultimate goal of initiating criminal investigations, preparing solid charges and finally reaching a judicial verdict. This option has been used extensively in the field of drug offences where proactive policing has become a major mechanism in controlling drug markets and drug scenes. The second option would consist of criminal justice agencies creating 'artificial victims' or creating private law enforcement staff thus making use of the knowledge and intelligence on money laundering available in other systems which usually would not be ready to invoke criminal law and do not stick to the goal of law enforcement. This option is for instance in use in the field of various environmental offences where particular administrative agencies are responsible for implementing administrative environmental law. The creation of 'artificial' victims supposes that persons or institutions can be made interested in reporting suspicious cases or suspects as personal victims of other crimes are interested in crime reporting. This in turn means that persons or institutions relevant for money laundering can somehow be persuaded that they are victimised by money laundering. Although, it might be that the culture of the financial systems includes an image of honesty and trust, confidentiality and respect for customers' privacy have always been central values in the finacial system, too. The second way therefore seems preferrable: making banks and their employees 'deputies' of police.

With respect to the latter option, attention should be drawn to the fact that hitherto primarily independent organisations have to be brought into systematic co-operation towards a common goal. Although, in the case of anti-money laundering measures the overall goal might be the same in terms of contributing to a clean and honest monetary system, independence in terms of organisation creates a solid basis for conflicts. These conflicts arise out of the simple fact that independent organisations will (or will have to) operate this overall goal quite differently, which in turn leads to differences in how the roles in responding to deviant acts are defined by those independent organisations[83]. Within the monetary system the values of confidentiality and mutual trust seems to be of particular importance, with regard to their relationship towards clients who from the perspective of money laundering and law enforcement must be viewed first of all as potential law-breakers.

The consequence of the structural problems of implementing criminal laws has been to set up money laundering regulations which are thought to come to terms with the problem of intelligence and reporting in case of money laundering. As victims are not available, those who have been targeted as major actors in the efforts of policing crime money and its flow are the banks and other financial institutions (plus those commercial companies whose transactions involve large amounts of money, for instance car dealers, jewellers, etc.).

2. Controlling suspicious money and dubious transactions

i. Reporting and Recording Duties

In implementing the EC-directive of 1991 and following the money trail as demanded by the general policy on organised crime, European countries have enacted legislation aiming at strict control of monetary transactions and requiring the private sector to record transactions and to report suspicious cases. The body of money laundering regulations may be broken down into rules on the content of identification, recording and reporting duties, the sanctions provided for non-compliance with these duties and the consequences linked to reporting, in terms of delays for

---

83 Albrecht, H.-J.: 'Particular Difficulties in Enforcing the Law Arising out of Basic Conflicts between the Different Agencies regarding the best-suited Reactions upon Highly Sensitive Kinds of Crime', in: Council of Europe (Ed.): *Interactions Within the Criminal Justice System.* (Strasbourg 1987), pp. 45-90.

financial transactions, civil and criminal liability *vis-à-vis* the transferring subject.

In Austria, money laundering regulations came into force on 1 January 1994. Since then, banks and other financial institutions have to identify customers who open accounts or transfer money (if the amount to be transferred exceeds 200,000 Austrian Schillings or £11,700 sterling). Although, the EC Directive is precisely defining the lower limit of sums requiring identification (Article 3 paragraph 2: 15,000 ECU) some variation in this respect may be observed in Europe (with amounts ranging from 50,000 FF or 6,200 EP in France, 8,300 EP in Italy, 20,000 DM or 8,300 EP in Germany, 500,000 FL or 11,400 EP in Luxembourg).

In implementing the EC Directive, obligations on banks (and other financial institutions) to report suspicious cases have been created. Although, all regulations refer to 'suspicion' as the basic trigger of reporting duties, it is clear that clarification on what *suspicion* means in the context of financial transactions has not had high priority in drafting money laundering regulations. Besides the rather unsophisticated type of money laundering - with the unknown customer putting a bag with £1 million in cash on the counter and demanding immediate transfer representing the most popular example[84] - legislators and experts in police etc. have not contributed much to facilitate the operation of 'suspicion' of money laundering. Although, concrete rules would be most important in order to ensure that money laundering regulations carry a clear and understandable message (in terms of what the financial system is expected to do), legislative bodies have argued that the statute should be unprecise and rather abstract to avoid learning and adaptation on the side of potential money launderers[85].

A crucial question concerns the period of time which is made available for law enforcement agencies to check on the transaction and eventually apply for a court order to stop transactions altogether and to freeze the money involved. The balance between law enforcement interests, on the one hand, and commercial interests, on the other hand, has led to rather short though varying legally prescribed delays. In case of suspicion of money laundering, Austrian banks and other financial institutions are required to report the case and all information relevant for investigation (the latter on demand of the receiving authority). Transactions have to be postponed until the day following the report. If

---

84 See e.g. Fülbier, A., Aepfelbach, R.R. (1993) see fn.92 *infra*, pp. 56-57.

85 This argument has been stressed by the German legislator, see Fülbier, A.. Aepfelbach, R.R. (1993) see fn.92 *infra*, p. 55.

the reporting bank is not notified by the competent authority that further postponing is required then transactions can be carried through. A similar rule has been adopted in the German system of money laundering control. Banks, building societies and other financial institutions are required to delay transactions until the end of the day following the report (with a maximum of 48 hours). Moreover, banks can proceed with transactions if they define transactions as being urgent matters. In France, the reporting party may with the report notify a time period within which the transaction must be carried through. TRACFIN then may oppose this formally which leaves them with 12 hours beyond the date set during which a court order must be obtained.

Failure to comply with reporting and documentation obligations in European countries may lead to a variety of responses from mere internal or disciplinary measures (France, Luxembourg, Switzerland) up to administrative sanctions or even criminal punishment. For some systems criminal penalties apply only if, on the side of those individuals obliged to report a suspicious transaction, a money laundering offence can be established (for example, France, Luxembourg). The German and Austrian money laundering regulations provide for administrative sanctions, such as administrative fines in cases of mere non-reporting (by banks), in England and Wales a criminal fine and imprisonment of up to two years may be meted out (§5 paragraph 2, Money Laundering Regulations).

The consequences of reporting a 'false positive' can result in economic and other costs for those who are reported. In order to protect such people restrictions on civil and criminal liability in case of false reports have been introduced. The economic costs of delay partially are placed on the suspects themselves leaving them the burden of false reporting (as in Germany), partially the State is made liable for damages (see, for example, the French regulation).

ii. Information processing and evaluation: who is reponsible for making choices?

Various approaches have been used in European countries in responding to the question how to organise processing and evaluation of reports on potential money laundering cases.

In Germany, the reporting agencies or institutions themselves have to screen cases for suspicion as is the case in France, England and Wales, Austria and Switzerland. Those cases which the reporting agency believe to be potential money laundering cases then have to be channeled to the regular police or to the public prosecutor's office for further decision-making on criminal investigations. In France a new agency (TRACFIN) has been created which is located in the Ministry of Finance. TRACFIN decides upon further reporting to the public prosecutor. In Italy, it is also the treasury which is responsible for evaluation of money laundering cases, but banks and financial institutions are not required to screen transactions for suspect cases (all transactions with sums any amount deemed to be suspicious have to be reported). This type of screening procedure seems to be preferrable from the view of bank-customer relationships. From the law enforcement point of view this approach to control places a heavy burden on public control agencies. In Austria a new department has been established which is responsible for screening and evaluating the reports made by banks etc. The department is located within the Ministry of the Interior and is empowered to demand additional information as well as to order that a transaction must be postponed (in case of an urgent suspicion that the transaction serves to launder money) and finally to initiate criminal proceedings through reporting a case to the public prosecutor's office.

The scope of use of information collected on the basis of money laundering regulations has been a widely debated issue. Again, wide variation can be observed with systems restricting the use of information to the prosecution of money laundering (for example, Luxembourg, Austria) to others allowing investigation and prosecution of various crimes (excluding or including tax offences).

C. *Evaluating the impact of money laundering controls*

There has up to now not been much research addressing the issue of evaluation although cost benefit analyses are important in view of the demands and costs placed on the private sector with money laundering regulations. The most important question which arises concerns the identification of the goals of anti-money laundering policies[86]. The ultimate goal of anti-money laundering efforts surely is to eliminate the financial basis of organised crime. But as such a goal does not seem to be well-suited for evaluative purposes - as it is hard to imagine such a goal being operational - it is necessary to find other criteria which can be measured properly. An approach to evaluation may be based on short-range as well as on middle-range criteria. Short-range criteria are found in the immediate goals of criminal laws, that is: reporting of

---

86 See also Levi, M. (1995) see fn.1 *supra*, p. 204.

offences (or suspicious cases) to law enforcement agencies; initiation of criminal investigations and proceedings, and finally conviction and sentencing. In this respect the emphasis is on the question whether and to what extent the legal and organisational framework actually allows successful (criminal) prosecution of money laundering. Middle-range criteria should be found in overall estimates on amounts of crime money which actually may be laundered in a given jurisdiction which may then be compared with different possible techniques of money-laundering. From here, answers to the question may be found whether it is plausible to assume that anti-money laundering measures can be circumvented and by what means this might be done. Although anti-money laundering policies are primarly concerned with banks and financial transactions, it should be stressed that money laundering may be organised through using other commercial devices as well. Besides these goals, potential side effects have to be considered in evaluation, too. Implementation of criminal laws produces, as does any law enforcement activity, side effects. Among such side effects, the amount of money first considered to be of suspicious or criminal origins but which then turned out to be either of legitimate origin, or at least not that suspicious that further criminal investigation can be initiated has to be taken into account.

When reviewing evidence on implementation of money laundering laws we find in Germany preliminary data on suspicious case processing which are available for the year 1993. Approximately 1000 reports have been passed from banks and other organisations to the competent authorities with a total sum of 555 million DM (circa £240 million). Out of these 555 million DM, 25 million DM have been seized by the criminal courts although they have not been finally confiscated[87]. The most often noted reasons to report a case are (a) suspicious behaviour of a client, (b) the size of transactions, and, (c) particulars of the transactions involved (e.g., a large number of small amounts being transferred)[88]. From the perspective of law enforcement a series of problems are observed which are linked to serious deficits in implementing money laundering regulations. First of all, it is noted that public prosecutors' decision-making is not based on a uniform understanding of the law as some public prosecutors require for the initiation of criminal investigation a double reasonable suspicion

---

87 See Zachert, H.-L.: *Erfahrungen mit der Geldwäsche in Deutschland. Bundeskriminalamt*, (Wiesbaden 1994), p. 5.

88 See Zachert, H.-L. (1994) see fn.87 *supra*, p. 5.

referring to the predicate offence, on the one hand, and to the money laundering activity, on the other; others are satisfied with the suspicion of money laundering. Sometimes, bank officials obviously also adopt the view that reasonable suspicion of both activities must be present. The duty to report is made dependent on the suspicion that a predicate offence as listed in the money laundering offence statute has been committed. A major problem seems to be located in the legal requirement to establish a causal relationship between the predicate offence and the assets in question as well as the knowledge the money laundering suspect must have had of the predicate offence. Police then suspect that banks sometimes turn down the transaction demands of potential (but obviously suspect) clients in order to avoid reporting duties[89].

In Austria, from August 1994 up to March 1995 a total of 177 cases involving suspicious transactions have been reported to the competent authority. These 177 cases include a sum of 17 billion Austrian Schillings (approximately £1 billion)[90]. Out of these, eighteen cases have been reported to the public prosecutor's office (to be investigated further and finally prosecuted) with 400 million Austrian Schillings (or approximately £25 million) having been seized by criminal courts. Most of the dubious or suspicious transactions are related to the eastern countries of transition with countries of the former Soviet Union coming up with a share of some 40% of all reports[91].

In England research has focussed more extensively on the outcome of money laundering regulation. In recent years up to 14,000 transaction reports are made annually (1994). But, just four out of every 1,000 reports seem to generate criminal investigations or to have had a certain impact on already existing investigations[92]. Reporting patterns seem to be consistent with the assumption of 'aggressive compliance'[93] and a view which sees the principal benefit of money laundering reporting regulations not in the field of proactive policing but in producing information which can be used for post-arrest

89 Zachert, H.-L. (1994) see fn.87 *supra*, p. 10.

90 See Fehervary, J.: '*Transnationale Kriminalität. Erkenntnisse aus Österreich*'. Paper presented at the Colloquium on Transnational Crime, Budapest, August 1995.

91 Fehervary, J. (1995), see fn.90 *supra*.

92 Levi, M. (1995) see fn.1 *supra*, p. 214; see also Fülbier, A., Aepfelbach, R.R.: *Das Geldwäschegesetz*. 3rd ed., (Köln 1993), pp. 281-282 with completely differing figures: according to them 10% of the reports lead to successful investigations, but no sources are made available.

93 Levi, M.: '*Pecunia non olet*: Cleansing the Money Launderers From the Temple', *Crime, Law and Social Change* (1991), pp. 217-302, at p. 251.

investigations[94]. Inter-company transactions seem to have been neglected as objects of control[95].

Summarising the evidence available so far we find that from a law enforcement point of view money laundering regulations and the money laundering offence statute are rated rather negatively. Moreover, the number of cases out of all those reported to be potential money laundering cases make up a proportion of well below 1%[96]. This holds true also for the proportion of money finally seized. With the latter, a crucial point comes up as obviously large sums of money fall into the system of control with potentially serious economic consequences. The basic demand put forward by law enforcement perspectives points toward the goal of making the financial system immune against criminal transactions as well as criminal money. Ultimately, this could be done if the economic perspective and functions could be replaced by law enforcement perspectives and functions.

VII. CONCLUSIONS

a. International efforts to follow the 'money trail' in crime policies have created a network of demands and obligations which back each other up on various policy levels. The most important justifications are drug trafficking and organised crime. But, basically the efforts point to the attempt to keep separate honest business, on the one hand, and black markets as well as the underworld, on the other hand, by way of setting new standards and a revised set of values in the upper world, especially in the financial system.

b. Confiscation, forfeiture and money laundering have triggered basic changes in criminal law thinking and practice. Forfeiture and confiscation point to developments which emphasize efficiency in law enforcement and deviate from basic traditional concepts of criminal law. The focus shifts from punishment based on individual responsibility and guilt to incapacitative and preventive measures based upon affiliation, be it to black markets, be it to criminal groups. This is also linked to

---

94 Levi, M. (1991) see fn.93 *supra*, p. 254.

95 Levi, M. (1995) see fn.1 *supra*, p. 214.

96 A somewhat higher proportion is reported from France where between February 1991 and the beginning of 1993 ca. 800 cases have been reported to TRACFIN out of which 25 cases have been prosecuted successfully, see Fülbier, A., Aepfelbach, R.R. (1993) see fn.92 *supra*, p. 275.

important changes in the goals pursued by criminal punishment. Here, the focus shifts from rehabilitation and retribution to incapacitation, deterrence and prevention.

c. Criminological research and theory do not support assumptions suggesting that through current confiscation policies problems of drug trafficking or drug problems in general may be influenced other than marginally.

d. Economic crime theories and economic research on drug markets rather support the view that these markets cannot be eliminated by means of criminal law as prohibitive policies (including criminal law) should be conceived as the major causes of black markets (creating those conditions in terms of incentives which at the same time should be overcome through criminal law). Thus, confiscation policies suffer from serious internal inconsistencies.

e. Evaluation of the effects of the new legislation on forfeiture will be rather difficult as outcomes will be dependent on the size of drug trafficking proceeds which cannot be identified without accepting large error margins. However, internationally, estimates on the rate of confiscated proceeds do not amount to more than marginal taxes on illicit goods and services (which indeed are modest compared with ordinary taxing).

f. Money laundering regulations represent more of a police type of criminal law: maintaining order in the monetary system and in society at large becomes the primary concern.

g. With money laundering regulations, new demands for information become visible which fit into concepts of crime as networks.

h. Private policing seems to be an essential element of money laundering enforcement because of structural problems of implementing criminal law without personal victims.

i. Large amounts of money reported and large number of potential money laundering (or suspicious) cases have been the visible and surface outcome of money laundering regulations. On the other hand, it seems clear that only negligible parts of these sums will be seized and confiscated.

j. Most probably money laundering regulations have had two other effects: a) setting firm limits to all unsophisticated forms of money laundering (and tax evasion) thus creating some pressure to rationalise in black markets and b) dislocation of money laundering.

12

THE EUROPEANISATION OF ENVIRONMENTAL LAW

John Gibson

I INTRODUCTION

Environmental law as a subject is a relatively recent phenomenon - environmental *laws*, on the other hand, have a much longer history and are derived from a variety of sources. The common law of England and Wales has for a very long time protected private interests in the environment. Statute has also given protection to selected public interests, and for a shorter period international law has reflected global concerns about the common heritage of mankind. But for the last twenty years, European Community law has made an increasingly important contribution to environmental protection.

In this paper, I shall be examining that contribution, not as a European lawyer, but as a British environmental lawyer encountering European law and forced to ask some basic questions about its role - questions which could equally be asked in any European Union Member State, but which might receive different answers.

Those questions can be broadly framed as follows:

First, what effect has European law had on national environmental legislation?
Second, how has European law affected the way environmental law is enforced?
And third, how has it affected environmental liability?

II EUROPEAN BASIS OF ENVIRONMENTAL LAW

A The Treaty of Rome

The European Community has enacted environmental laws since the late 1960s, and there are now over 200 pieces of such legislation, but it is only since the Single European Act of 1986 that there has been an explicit consitutional basis for Community action in the field of the environment. Before then, Community environmental legislation was justified either on the basis of the harmonisation of industrial standards within the Common Market[1] or was attributed to the Community's residual powers to do anything necessary to achieve one of its basic objectives[2] - in this case raising the standard of living. This ambiguous constitutional basis for environmental action was accepted by the European Court of Justice, but the situation was regularised in 1987 when the Single European Act[3] added a new title to the Treaty of Rome,[4] providing specifically for Community legislation on the environment, and those provisions were further extended by the Maastricht Treaty[5] in 1993.

B Directives

The principal mechanism that the Community employs to legislate for the environment is almost always the directive, and it is rare for European regulations to be used for this purpose. Directives are preferred for environmental legislation because they can specify the scientific standards or quality objectives that must achieved, but they leave it to the Member State to devise the legal and administrative measures necessary to meet those targets. In theory, this flexibility should enable the Member State to adopt a mechanism that is appropriate to its own political and administrative system. It also means, of course, that the use of directives rather than directly applicable regulations is much less likely to lead to consistency between

---

1 Treaty of Rome, Art. 100.

2 *Ibid*, Art. 235.

3 Art. 25.

4 Title VII.

5 Art G(38) of the Maastricht Treaty inserted a new Title XVI 'Environment' into the Treaty of Rome.

the environmental laws of different Member States - it is an *indirect* form of Europeanisation.

1. Advantages of directives

i. Stimulate reform

Every European government is in principle in favour of a better environment, but not all are equally prepared to accept the costs involved or agreed about the best way to achieve it. One of the most obvious consequences of European environmental action, therefore, is to persuade (if not coerce) Member States to legislate in matters that they would have preferred to leave alone (for example, the introduction of environmental impact assessment in the United Kingdom) or to legislate when they would have preferred to rely on non-statutory measures or voluntary co-operation (for example, the conservation of natural habitats in the United Kingdom). It also leads to the imposition of expensive technical requirements (for example, the treatment of sewage prior to disposal, instead of the British Government's favoured reliance on untreated discharges through long outfall pipes into the sea). On the other hand, it is facile to represent European legislation as something imposed on Member States by an alien European power, when they are themselves participants in the institutions that produce these laws; and in fairness to the British Government it has in recent years played a more positive role in the Environment Council than its traditional rearguard action against reform.

ii. Overcome conceptual barriers

A more subtle benefit of European legislation is that it can oblige governments to transcend conceptual boundaries that may have no logical justification but which are entrenched in national legal systems and in the psychology that perpetuates them. The United Kingdom, for example, has very different traditions in the way it regulates its land and sea environments. On land, we have a highly-developed planning system that is based on local decision-making and public consultation. At sea, such regulation as exists is normally conducted by national rather than local government and is often veiled from public scrutiny. The dividing line between the terrestrial and the marine regimes is usually located on the seashore, and is defined by the position of the tide. Unfortunately, environmentally damaging developments occur on both land and sea; they may also cross the tidal boundary or may have impacts on either side of it. Yet the British Government has always resisted the extension of land-based controls to marine areas. European legislation, however, has now forced it to make concessions, since the Directives on Environmental Impact Assessment[6] and the Conservation of Natural Habitats[7] apply to the marine environment as well as on land. Environmental impact assessment is a procedure which requires the environmental consequences of a proposed development to be identified and considered before permission for that development is given. The principal mechanism through which it has been implemented on land in the United Kingdom is the planning system. However, the Government has been somewhat grudging, and rather than give local planning authorities jurisdiction in the sea, it has been given instead to bodies that are already involved in marine areas in some other capacity. This has led to organisations with questionable environmental credentials, such as the Department of Trade and Industry, the Ministry of Agriculture, the Department of Transport and the Crown Estate Commissioners being given responsibility for environmental decisions, but it does at least involve greater consultation and publicity than would otherwise have occurred. Moreover, in June 1995, following a complaint to the European Commission by Friends of the Earth (Wales) and the Friends of Cardigan Bay,[8] the Government was forced to concede that it must provide a statutory procedure for the environmental assessment of offshore oil and gas development.[9]

The Habitats Directive also requires Member States to give legal protection to a network of important terrestrial and marine sites for nature conservation purposes. Although Britain has possessed its own national legislation for designating marine nature reserves since 1981, only two have been created due to a failure of domestic political will. Now the European initiative has galvanised the British Government into identifying a large number of marine sites for prospective designation under the directive.

---

6 Council Directive 85/337/EEC of 27 June 1985 on the assessment of the effects of certain public and private projects on the environment, *OJ* L175, 5.7.85, p. 40.

7 Council Directive 92/43/EEC of 21 May 1992 on the conservation of natural habitats and of wild fauna and flora, *OJ* L206, 22.7.92, p. 7.

8 See ENDS Report 245, June 1995, p. 29.

9 HC Debs, Vol 261, 7 June 1995, Written Answers, col 238.

2. *Disadvantages of directives*

i. *Cause delay*

On the debit side, however, there are a number of disadvantages in relying on European directives as the legal source of environmental protection. One obvious chacteristic of a directive is that it is a very slow way of dealing with an environmental problem, since it requires two legislative stages instead of one - the European legislation must be followed by national legislation, neither of which is likely to happen quickly. It took, for example, five years of negotiation to agree the 1985 Directive on Environmental Assessment,[10] which itself allowed a further three years for implementation by Member States, making a total of eight years before any practical benefit for the environment could be achieved. The introduction by the Maastricht Treaty of qualified majority voting[11] in the Council of Ministers for environmental legislation may assist the adoption process, but the fact remains that most States fail to meet the deadlines for implementing directives, and even when they are implemented the national legislation is frequently found to be defective. The situation is further complicated in the United Kingdom, because it is often necessary to produce separate implementing measures for Scotland and Northern Ireland, and these usually appear significantly later than the equivalent English legislation. In this respect, the complexities are less than those faced by European States with a federal structure, but the introduction of devolution in the United Kingdom may make the situation worse.

ii. *Discourage interim measures*

Another consequence of the delays inherent in the use of directives is the excuse or justification that they provide for a State failing to take any interim legal measures on its own initiative. Indeed, it can be very much to the disadvantage of a State if it does act unilaterally in advance of European legislation, as the United Kingdom has found to its cost. In 1990, Britain passed the Environmental Protection Act, which contained major reforms of the system for licensing the disposal of waste on land. In 1991, a European Directive on Waste[12] was agreed, which proved to

---

[10] See n. 6 *supra*.

[11] See Arts. 130s and 189c of the Treaty of Rome, inserted by the Maastricht Treaty.

[12] Council Directive 91/156/EEC of 18 March 1991 amending Directive 75/442/EEC on waste, *OJ* L78, 26.3.91, p. 32.

be incompatible in some important respects with the British Act, in particular with the concept of 'waste' itself. In its frantic efforts to produce regulations that would reconcile the European and British legislation, the United Kingdom missed the deadline for compliance with the directive by a full year, and delayed the introduction of its own much needed reforms. The United Kingdom also pioneered in its 1990 Environmental Protection Act the integration of pollution control over industries that discharge to air, water and land; the European Community has now followed suit with a directive on integrated pollution prevention and control,[13] and it is to be hoped that the problems of the Waste Directive will not be repeated again.

iii. Undemocratic

The normal method by which European directives are implemented in the United Kingdom is not parliamentary legislation but ministerial regulations made under the European Communities Act 1972,[14] which empowers ministers to make whatever regulations are necessary to implement a Community obligation. Although this has the advantage that it bypasses the limitations of the parliamentary timetable, it also seriously limits democratic involvement in the legislative process. The regulations must be laid before both Houses of Parliament, and may be debated there, but the power of Parliament is either to approve or reject them in their entirety, and they cannot be amended. In practice, this means that their passage is normally a formality. Despite highly critical debates in both Houses of Parliament in 1994 over the regulations to implement the Habitats Directive, they were approved without a vote.[15] This procedure therefore effectively confers very substantial power on the Government department and its draftsmen who prepare the regulations.

iv. Restricted to Community obligations

Another complication is that regulations under the European Communities Act can *only* be used to implement a European obligation, and cannot contain additional provisions not required by European law,

---

13 Council Directive 96/61/EC of 24 September 1996 concerning integrated pollution prevention and control, *OJ* L257, 10.10.96, p.26.

14 s. 2(2).

15 HC Debs, Vol 247, 19 July 1994, cols 239-261; HL Debs, Vol 558, 17 October 1994, cols 85-116.

however desirable or sensible they might be. For example, the list of developments that are subject to environmental impact assessment under the Environmental Assessment Directive was recognised to be too restrictive, but the Government could not legally add extra categories to the relevant British regulations made in 1988,[16] and it was necessary to pass separate parliamentary legislation[17] three years later to achieve the same result.

v. Produce uncertainty

The problems of implementation are not attributable solely to the attitude of Governments, but also result from legal difficulties inherent in the process of transposition, which vary according to the nature of the obligations that a directive is seeking to impose. An environmental directive which prescribes scientific standards for pollution control, for example on the quality of drinking water, should not in principle be too difficult to translate into national legislation. There may well be practical problems of achieving, monitoring and enforcing those scientific standards, but they are primarily issues of administration rather than law. Much greater difficulty, however, arises from the increasing tendency for European legislation to intervene in the procedural aspects of environmental protection, and to seek to control how regulatory decisions are made. This is particularly evident in the areas of nature conservation and the control of land-use, where it is not possible to specify objective criteria, but instead judgments must be made about the acceptability of environmental impacts.

For example, under the 1979 Directive on the Conservation of Wild Birds,[18] Member States must classify the 'most suitable territories'[19] as special protection areas for the conservation of particular species of birds. The directive does not explain how the 'suitability' of sites is to be determined or whether economic and social considerations can be weighed against the interests of birds when they are selected. Although it may well be thought desirable that complex questions of this kind should not be prejudged by rigid European legislation, but should be determined according to the merits of each case, the consequence has inevitably been legal conflict and administrative uncertainty.

---

16 Town and Country Planning (Assessment of Environmental Effects) Regulations 1988, SI 1988/1199.

17 Planning and Compensation Act 1991, s. 48.

18 Council Directive 79/409/EEC of 2 April 1979 on the conservation of wild birds, *OJ* L103, 2.4.79, p. 1.

19 *Ibid*, Art. 4(1).

vi. Increase the power of the executive

In the past, the British traditions of legislative drafting have concentrated on the literal and precise meaning of words, in contrast to the more purposive approach to statutory interpretation elsewhere in Europe. More recently, legislative draftsmen have come to realise that they risk misinterpreting European directives if they translate their provisions too precisely into British legal language. In consequence, we now find that British regulations implementing European legislation attempt to avoid the problem by copying the wording of directives and leaving undefined expressions which the directives themselves do not explain. While this may have the desired effect of rendering the national legislation immune from challenge on the grounds of inconsistency with the European provision that it purports to implement, it also tends to defeat the purpose of using a directive rather than a European regulation, and it does nothing to assist those who have to apply the law in practice. Thus, the 1994 Waste Management Licensing Regulations,[20] which implement the 1991 Directive on Waste[21] are particularly difficult to understand. It is obviously of basic practical importance to know whether a substance qualifies as 'waste' and whether a licence is needed for dealing with it. The Directive defines waste in the broadest terms as any substance which the producer or person in possession discards,[22] and this wording is transposed without explanation into the British regulations.[23] The concept of 'discarding' is therefore crucial, but it is not defined; there will inevitably be problems of interpretation in relation to substances that are recycled, since one person's waste may become another person's raw material, and it is vital to identify the point at which it ceases to have the legal character of waste. The regulations identify a number of exemptions from licensing,[24] but qualify them with the proviso that they will not apply if they would conflict with the objectives of the directive,[25] which means that they cannot safely be relied on. The Government has published explanatory guidance[26] which is four times as long as the regulations themselves, but it has no legal status, and avoids committing itself on

20 SI 1994/1056.

21 See n. 12 *supra*.

22 Art. 1(a).

23 Reg. 1(3).

24 Sch. 3.

25 Reg. 17(4).

26 Department of the Environment Circular 11/94.

the legal issues. In theory, it will, of course, be for the courts to resolve ambiguities in the legislation, and this will doubtless happen in the fullness of time as people are prosecuted for breaking the regulations. But the reality is that most people will have to rely on the interpretation adopted by the Environment Agency whose job it is to issue licences for waste disposal. The practical effect, therefore, of ambiguity in the law is to enhance the effective power of unelected officials.

III THE ENFORCEMENT OF EUROPEAN ENVIRONMENTAL LAW

I turn now to the second question: how has the European dimension affected the way environmental law is enforced?

It is no accident that the growth of Community involvement in environmental protection has coincided with the rise of the environmental movement, and green campaigners have welcomed European law as providing an additional weapon in their armoury. Its attraction is that it offers access to a potentially sympathetic authority above that of national governments, which is not constrained by the traditional jurisprudence that often impedes their efforts at national level.

A Complaint to the European Commission

The European Commission operates a complaints procedure whereby anyone may report a suspected breach of a provision of Community law. If the Commission considers that the complaint is justified, it has the power under Article 169 of the Treaty of Rome to issue a letter of formal notice to the defaulting State, followed, if necessary, by a reasoned opinion and finally an application to the European Court. Not surprisingly, the complaints procedure is increasingly popular, and a third of all complaints (about 500 a year) concern environmental matters.[27] At the same time, the Commission is overloaded as a result, and it can take four years for a complaint to be resolved by the European Court.

The United Kingdom has been prosecuted and convicted twice for breach of environmental directives: once in 1992[28] for improper implentation of the Drinking Water Directive[29] and again in 1993[30] for

---

[27] See Ludwig Krämer, *Focus on European Environmental Law* (1997) ch. 10.

[28] *EC Commission* v. *United Kingdom* (Case C-337/89) [1992] I ECR 6103.

[29] Council Directive 80/778/EEC of 15 July 1980 relating to the quality of water intended for human consumption, *OJ* L229, 30.8.80, p. 11.

failing to meet the quality standards of the Bathing Water Directive[31] at Blackpool and Southport beaches. The judgments were, of course, declaratory and not enforceable as such, and it is still the case that the United Kingdom has not fully complied with them. Although there is provision under the Maastricht Treaty[32] for the possibility of fines for defying the Court, political embarassment remains the normal sanction. So, although the complaints procedure has a useful symbolic function, it cannot be regarded as sufficient by itself to police the environmental policies of national governments.

B Action in the national courts

The alternative remedy is, of course, to take action in the national courts of Member States. There has been considerable interest among environmental lawyers at the prospect that unimplemented or inadequately implemented environmental directives might be enforced by British courts on the basis of the European law doctrines of direct effect, sympathetic interpretation or the principles in the *Francovich* case.[33] The reality, however, has proved somewhat disappointing. No environmental directive has yet been held by the European Court to have direct effect, and the Court ruled in 1994 that a provision of the 1975 Framework Directive on Waste[34] was not sufficiently precise or unconditional to qualify.[35] There is an obvious problem that environmental directives commonly require some unspecified regulatory procedure to be established by a Member State, or a discretionary decision to be made, which is likely to defeat the test of unconditionality and precision. Moreover, while public health legislation, like the Drinking Water Directive,[36] which is clearly for the protection of people, might logically be capable of conferring rights on citizens, it is more difficult to claim the same human benefit for other laws that protect the natural environment itself or the wild creatures and plants that inhabit it; if they have rights, they can hardly claim them in the courts.

---

30 *EC Commission* v. *United Kingdom* (Case C-56/90) [1993] I ECR 4109.

31 Council Directive 76/160/EEC of 8 December 1975 concerning the quality of bathing water, *OJ* L31, 5.2.76, p. 1.

32 See Art. 143(2) of the Treaty of Rome, inserted by the Maastricht Treaty.

33 *Francovich* v. *Italy* (Case C-6/90) [1991] I ECR 5357.

34 Council Directive 75/442/EEC of 15 July 1975 on waste, *OJ* L194, 25.7.75, p. 39.

35 *Comitato de Cordinamento per la Difesa dela Cava* v. *Regione Lombardia* (Case C-236/92) [1994] I ECR 483.

36 See n. 29 *supra*.

Nevertheless, there have been several reported cases in British courts in which the Directive on Environmental Impact Assessment[37] was alleged to have direct effect. In October 1990, in *Twyford Parish Council* v. *Secretary of State for Transport*,[38] the English High Court held that it did. Five months later, in *Kincardine and Deeside District Council* v. *Forestry Commission*,[39] the Scottish Court of Session, without referring to the English decision, held that it did not. These cases strictly turned on different provisions of the directive, but in neither instance did it ultimately matter, because the applicants failed on other grounds. Both cases decided that developments for which permission was sought before the directive was due to be implemented, but not obtained until afterwards, were not subject to its provisions. The Scottish case also held that the Directive on the Conservation of Wild Birds does not have direct effect. In 1993, in *Wychavon District Council* v. *Secretary of State for the Environment*,[40] the High Court in England again denied that the Environmental Assessment Directive was directly effective, and refused to treat the directive as in force at a time when the Government ought to have implemented it but had not yet done so.

Apart from these cases, however, on other reported occasions when the Government has been challenged in the High Court for allegedly breaking European environmental law, the legal basis for the action has not been provided by the European legislation itself. Instead, the cases have been brought under the traditional British public law procedure for the judicial review of administrative action. An important example is the recent unsuccessful claim by the pressure group, Friends of the Earth, that measures so far taken by the Department of the Environment are inadequate to comply with the judgment of the European Court, when Britain was convicted for breach of the Drinking Water Directive.[41] That claim was rejected by the High Court in March 1994 and again by the Court of Appeal in May 1995.[42] In judicial review cases of this kind it is not necessary to show that the directive has direct effect, but rather that the applicants have *locus standi* or a sufficient interest to bring the proceedings. In the past, establishing *locus standi*

---

37 See n. 6 *supra*.

38 [1992] *Journal of Environmental Law* 273.

39 [1992] *Journal of Environmental Law* 289.

40 [1994] *Journal of Environmental Law* 351. This case was followed in *R* v. *North Yorkshire County Council, ex parte Brown* [1997] Env LR 391.

41 See n. 29 *supra*.

42 *R.* v. *Secretary of State for the Environment, ex parte Friends of the Earth*, *TLR*, 4 April 1994 and 8 June 1995.

has been difficult for environmental organisations compared with individuals, but several recent cases have accepted the standing of major non-governmental organisations. Thus, for example, in 1993, Greenpeace was allowed to challenge (albeit unsuccessfully) the grant of temporary licences for radioactive discharges from the THORP nuclear fuel reprocessing plant at Sellafield.[43]

One reason why judicial review is attractive to pressure groups is the general absence of third-party rights to appeal against administrative decisions on their merits. Most environmental licensing procedures afford an opportunity for an aggrieved applicant to appeal against the refusal or qualification of a licence, but they give no such right to the public to challenge the merits of a grant. Their only recourse is to the courts, where the justification for a decision is not reviewable unless it is wholly unreasonable, and procedural illegality must be shown instead. Environmental organisations have become experienced at this rather disingenuous process, in which real objections on grounds of policy have to be disguised as complaints about errors of law.

Perhaps the most significant judicial review case recently before the courts on a European environmental matter was brought by the Royal Society for the Protection of Birds to challenge a decision of the Secretary of State for the Environment, who had omitted an area of intertidal mudflats (called the Lappel Bank) from a special protection area in the Medway Estuary designated under the Directive on the Conservation of Wild Birds. The Lappel Bank was due to be reclaimed from the sea for port development, and the case disputed the right of the Government to take economic factors into account when deciding the boundaries of a special protection area. The European Court had already held, in a case against Germany,[44] that Member States may not reduce the size of an existing special protection area for economic reasons. It had also held, in a ruling against Spain,[45] that States must designate sites that are of major conservation importance. But as the precise point in the British case had not previously been decided by the European Court, and was certainly debatable, the House of Lords referred it to the Court in February 1995 for a ruling under Article 177 of the Treaty of Rome.[46] It took, of course, a considerable time before the European Court was able to make a decision, and it was then too late to prevent the Lappel Bank being developed. Nevertheless, the

---

43 *R.* v. *Inspectorate of Pollution, ex parte Greenpeace (No. 2)* [1994] 4 All ER 329.

44 *EC Commission* v. *Germany* (Case C-57/89) [1991] I ECR 883.

45 *EC Commission* v. *Spain* (Case C-355/90) [1993] I ECR 4221.

46 [1995] *Journal of Environmental Law* 262.

European Court adopted a purposive approach to the interpretation of the Birds Directive, and held that the Government had acted unlawfully in taking account of factors other than nature conservation.[47] This case will be of major significance in relation to many other special protection areas. Indeed, in Cardiff, the Government similarly excluded Cardiff Bay from the Severn Estuary Special Protection Area in order that the Cardiff Bay Barrage could be built and the Bay developed as an inland lake. In 1994, the Government negotiated a compromise with the European Commission that the Barrage would be acceptable if compensatory measures were taken to provide an alternative habitat for the birds,[48] but the decision of the European Court may now show that to have been legally wrong.

Another recent environmental case[49] which attempted to extend the influence of European law challenged the Government's failure to apply what is called the 'precautionary principle' in decisions affecting the environment. The precautionary principle states that preventative action should be taken where there is a risk of environmental harm, even though there may not be scientific proof that it will result. This principle was incorporated in the Treaty of Rome by the Maastricht Treaty as part of the basis for Community policy on the environment.[50] The applicant in the case claimed that the Department of Trade and Industry should have followed the precautionary principle and prohibited the laying of high voltage electricity cables near houses because of a possible link between radiation and leukemia. However, in October 1994, the High Court dismissed the case, concluding that the Treaty applied to Community and not national policy.

The only environmental case in which the Government has been held by a British Court to have breached European environmental law is the decision in *R.* v. *Secretary of State for the Environment, ex parte Kingston upon Hull City Council*[51] in January 1996. Here the High Court ruled that the Secretary of State for the Environment had acted unlawfully in taking the cost of treating sewage into account when

---

47 *R.* v. *Secretary of State for the Environment, ex parte Royal Society for the Protection of Birds*, (Case C-44/95) [1997] *Journal of Environmental Law* 139.

48 *The Daily Telegraph*, 15 April 1994, p. 24.

49 *R.* v. *Secretary of State for Trade and Industry, ex parte Duddridge* [1995] Env LR 151.

50 See Art. 130r(2) of the Treaty of Rome, inserted by the Maastricht Treaty.

51 [1996] Env LR 248.

defining the limits of estuaries for the purposes of the Urban Waste Water Directive.[52]

Accordingly, although there has been a significant number of environmental cases in the British courts involving European law, the parties bringing them have achieved very limited success. That is perhaps not surprising, since these are inevitably test cases which seek to probe the frontiers of environmental law. But in most cases, the reason for failure is the wide scope of administrative discretion. Although the European influence is emphasised by the regular citation of decisions of the European Court, little if any use is made of decisions about similar issues in the national courts of other Member States. Only the European Court seems to be regarded as relevant because its decisions are legally binding. Indeed, Commonwealth cases are more likely to be used as analogies than national European decisions, and this distinction is doubtless compounded by language differences. In short, the impact of European jurisprudence on the enforcement of environmental law in the United Kingdom may be more apparent than real.

IV CIVIL LIABILITY FOR ENVIRONMENTAL DAMAGE

So far I have been concentrating on environmental regulation - that is, the control by public authorities of activities potentially harmful to the environment - because that is the area with which the European Community has principally concerned itself. If environmental regulation were completely effective there would be no need for any other kind of environmental law. In reality, regulation will always fail to prevent some pollution or other environmentally harmful consequence, and some form of legal liability will be necessary to deal with it. At present, with the exception of a few statutory remedies in special cases (such as oil pollution from ships), civil liability in the United Kingdom for environmental harm remains firmly based on the traditional principles of the common law - the torts of nuisance, negligence and trespass. Environmental liability still rests uncomfortably on precedents established during the industrial revolution and the public health movement in the nineteenth century. To sue successfully, one needs to prove damage to one's property or person - damage to the wider environment is simply not actionable at common law. But, within those limitations, civil actions for compensation for

---

52 Coucil Directive 91/271/EEC of 21 May 1991 concerning urban waste water treatment, *OJ* L135, 30.6.91, p. 40.

environmental harm can be surprisingly successful, often more so than a criminal prosecution.

European environmental law is frequently cited in these cases, not as a legal source of liability, but rather to demonstrate a failure to meet an appropriate standard. In *Gibbons* v. *South West Water*[53] in 1992 and *Cambridge Water* v. *Eastern Counties Leather*[54] in 1993, compensation for the pollution of drinking water supplies was claimed under the common law, but it was evidence of that pollution that they failed to meet the requirements of the Drinking Water Directive. In 1994, the owner of a commercial pleasure beach at Croyde Bay in Devon received compensation from South West Water in an out-of-court settlement because his beach was denied the European Blue Flag award (signifying compliance with the Bathing Waters Directive) due to pollution from a sewage outfall.[55] In 1995, a shellfish farmer received compensation from the same company because a sewage outfall contaminated the Taw estuary to such an extent that he was banned from harvesting his shellfish under the Shellfish Hygiene Directive.[56] South West Water now faces a negligence claim from windsurfers who became ill after immersion in the sea near other sewage outfalls.

Although these cases are distinguished by the citation of European legislation, the European dimension is not contributing here to the development of a different form of civil liability. But that may change in the future because of moves within Europe towards the introduction of strict liability for hazardous industrial operations. In 1993, the Council of Europe Convention on Civil Liability for Damage Resulting from Activities Dangerous to the Environment was agreed, although it is not in force, and the United Kingdom does not intend to ratify it. One of its provisions would allow common interest groups to initiate some proceedings.[57] In 1993, the European Commission also issued a green paper on *Remedying Environmental Damage*,[58] which favoured a strict liability regime coupled with a compensation fund. The subject is highly controversial, with profound economic implications, and the British Government is cautious in its response, prefering the present mixture of fault-based and selective strict liability. Nevertheless, the

---

53 [1993] Env LR 244.

54 [1994] 2 AC 264.

55 *The Times*, 10 May 1994, p.33.

56 Council Directive 91/492/EEC of 15 July 1991 laying down the health conditions for the production and the placing on the market of live bivalve molluscs, *OJ* L268, 24.9.91, p. 1. See *The Independent*, 1 February 1995, p. 7.

57 Art. 18.

58 COM (93) 47 final.

need for a modern system of apportioning environmental liability will not go away, and the seeds of change have probably been sown.

V CONCLUSION

In conclusion, then, how should one summarise the answers to my original three questions? It is clear that European *policy* has exerted a massive influence on national environmental law - it has in most cases been the catalyst for reform - but the influence of European *law* itself has actually been less than might perhaps have been expected. The implementation of directives has forced the abandonment of some outmoded traditional concepts, but has also been characterised by delay, textual obscurity and centralisation of power. The enforcement of European environmental law against the State by complaint to the Commission is reasonably successful but is also selective and symbolic. Enforcement in the national courts, on the other hand, seems unable to exploit European procedures in environmental matters, and relies instead on judicial review where actions repeatedly founder on the rock of administrative discretion. Finally, in the field of civil liability, European law has so far contributed little, but it is also in this area that the opportunity for developing its influence may lie.

13

A REPLY TO PROFESSOR ZIMMERMANN

David J. Ibbetson

Relish the opportunity or resent the intrusion, we cannot ignore the fact that European law is here to stay. The real question, as Professor Zimmermann argues, is how the legal scientist should respond to it. There is something obviously unsatisfactory about the fiercely regulatory nature of modern European law. Without a grasp of the sense behind a mass of specific rules argument by analogy becomes arbitrary, agreement on the correct resolution of a legal problem impossible. The courts of the European Union have, it is true, developed a wholly workable conceptual jurisprudence in certain areas, but this is not yet the case in the main areas of private law where piecemeal regulations supplement the positive law of national jurisdictions. Legal scientists can sit back and await the growth of a new European jurisprudence; or they can contribute to the process of that growth.

Professor Zimmermann argues forcibly that it is the duty of the legal scientist to help the formation of this jurisprudence; those who believe in the desirability of a rational and coherent legal order will not disagree with him. He argues no less forcibly that this jurisprudence should be built on historical foundations; again, those who believe in our legal culture and do not wish to abandon it in a sense of cynical self-destructiveness will not want to disagree with him. It is true that this may necessitate some change in the relationship between the legal practitioner and the academic lawyer or legal historian, but the uncodified nature of English law has meant that legal practitioners have never completely cast themselves adrift from the historical roots of the modern law; in this respect at least, English law is in a slightly healthier state than its continental counterparts.

There is, however, a difficulty in discovering the historical foundations on which to build this new jurisprudence. The *ius commune* of mediaeval and early-modern Europe is on the face of it the best candidate, based on the intellectually sophisticated groundwork laid down by the Roman lawyers. In nearly all of Europe there was some sort of reception of Roman law in the mediaeval or early modern period, even if the form which that reception took varied considerably from place to place. In nearly all of Europe, the mediaeval and early modern commentaries on Roman law which we group together under the title of the *ius commune* had some part to play in the formation of the national laws of individual States. In nearly all of Europe the *ius commune* provided a conceptual vocabulary which could be used and understood by lawyers versed in the law of their own States.

But there is a genuine problem in seeing England as part of this tradition. Admittedly, this must not be exaggerated. On the one hand, the historically-minded English lawyer is in danger of rejecting it too easily without reflection, for it has been a major facet of English legal ideology since the middle of the fifteenth century that English law is different from (and better than) that found in continental Europe[1]. Nonetheless, the Europhiliac keen to maximise the common ground beween England and the continent must not accept the thesis of relative uniformity of tradition without subjecting it to a full critical examination. Both of these extremes must be avoided; but it is none too easy to pick a path between them.

In an attempt to do this we should first identify a number of points at which the English tradition moved in parallel with the continental - crudely speaking, where English law was influenced by Roman or Romano-canonical law - and then indicate some salient differences between England and the continent.

We must first disabuse ourselves of the idea that English lawyers would normally have no knowledge at all of the main outlines of Roman law[2]. Judges and lawyers in the twelfth and early thirteenth

---

1 This is most visible in Sir John Fortescue's *De Laudibus Legum Anglie*. See H. D. Hazeltine, General Preface, to S. B. Chrimes, *Sir John Fortescue* (Cambridge, 1942), xix-xxiv, xxvii-xxx, xl-xlviii. Fortescue's work is not the earliest example of such an anglocentric ideology: F. W. Maitland, 'Wyclif on English Law and Roman Law' (1896) 12 *LQR* 76.

2 See for example, J. L. Barton, *Roman Law in England* (*Ius Romanum Medii Aevi*, V.13) (Milan, 1971); C. Donahue, Jr., '*Ius Commune*, Canon Law, and Common Law in England' (1992) 66 *Tulane Law Review* 1745; Zimmermann, '*Der europäische Charakter des englischen Rechts - Historische Verbindungen zwischen civil law und common law*' (1993) 1 *Zeitschrift für Europäisches Privatrecht* 4

centuries, at the infancy of the Common law, were not insulated from the excitement which the rediscovery of Roman law generated in England; it was only in the second half of the thirteenth century that an 'English' legal profession came into its own, applying a body of law recognisably distinct from that studied in the universities or cathedrals[3]. There is sufficient citation of civilian maxims through the fourteenth and fifteenth centuries for us to suspect that at least some English lawyers had some rudimentary knowledge of Roman law ideas[4]. The same is true of the sixteenth century lawyer, though all too frequently a maxim which looks suspiciously Roman might in fact have been taken from a mediaeval English text. But this is not always the case: in 1584, for example, we find a serjeant-at-law arguing before Common law judges adopting a definition from the canonist *Summa Angelica* and treating it as an accurate statement of English law; what is more, a lawyer sitting in the wings of the court taking notes accurately recognised it as such[5]. A seventeenth-century student in Arts in an English university might be advised to skim the Institutes of Justinian since that was all that a scholar needed[6], though his eighteenth-century counterpart learning Law might conversely be advised to take the Institutes more seriously as the foundations of his legal education[7]. In the second half of the eighteenth century Blackstone's Commentaries are replete with illustrative examples expressly culled from the Institutes. When examinations were introduced for those intending to practise as barristers in the middle of the nineteenth century, Roman law was laid down as a compulsory paper, surviving as such until the late 1960s. And those studying Law at the universities, before the middle of the present century, could expect to have studied Roman law as a component of their course. None of this points necessarily in the direction of any sophistication of knowledge or understanding, but it does suggest that a rudimentary knowledge of Roman law would have been widespread.

---

3 P. G. Stein, *The Teaching of Roman Law in England around 1200* (Selden Society, Supplementary Series, vol.8) (London, 1990), xxii-xxvii, xxxviii-xliii; R. V. Turner, *The English Judiciary in the Age of Glanvill and Bracton*, 226-239; P. Brand, *The Origins of the English Legal Profession* (Oxford, 1992), 50-69.

4 D. J. Seipp, 'The Reception of Canon Law and Civil Law in the Common Law Courts before 1600' (1993) 13 *Oxford Journal of Legal Studies* 388.

5 *Boughton* v. *Bishop of Coventry and Lichfield*, BL MS Add 35943 f.8v. The quotation is taken from the *Summa Angelica, sub verb Scandalum*.

6 R. Holdsworth, 'Directions to a Student in the University', in H. F. Fletcher, *The Intellectual Development of John Milton* (Illinois, 1961), 2.646.

7 P. Birks and G. McLeod, *Justinian's Institutes* (London, 1987), 22.

Professor Zimmermann points to the continental (Roman) influence on such legal writers as Bracton and Blackstone. Bracton's Treatise, indeed, is characterised by a wide-ranging though ragged use of Roman law, and can without too much difficulty be seen as an offshoot of the continental mainstream of legal literature; but although manuscripts of the work were widely copied in the late-thirteenth and early-fourteenth centuries its influence waned rapidly after that. The ferment of legal writing in England around 1600 produced only one book aiming to frame English law in Roman terms, John Cowell's *Institutiones Iuris Anglicani*; and this was a pathetic failure[8]. In the long term Blackstone was more influential than Bracton, though his Roman law is both less broad and less deep than that found in the earlier work. Generally speaking, we may say that is not uncommon to find stray references to the Roman law in English treatises, but that it is unusual to find a thoroughgoing analysis of an area of English law expressed in terms that are more than superficially Roman[9]. Charles Gale's *Treatise on the Law of Easements*, incorporating the Digest's treatment of prædial servitudes into the English law of easements, is both the best and the best-known example[10]. More commonly, though, the English writers betray remarkably little awareness of or interest in what is going on elsewhere in Europe or in the Roman foundations of the law. Those writers who did bring out and apply foreign learning, as too the few judges who did so, were undoubtedly agents of a sporadic reception; but this reception was indeed sporadic and we cannot properly deduce from these spikes of Romanism or Europeanism that there was any wider reception going on concealed from our eyes.

Just as there were some individuals who operated as conduits along which Roman law might have flowed into England, so too there were particular courts which were firmly part of the European *ius commune* tradition; the most important of these were the ecclesiastical courts and the Court of Admiralty[11]. Here the procedure was avowedly

---

8 This is not to deny that other writers did make some use of Roman parallels. In a positive sense, for example, Francis Bacon pointed to common foundations of legal principles in his *Maxims of the Law*; rather less positively, a writer like William Fulbecke was more concerned to contrast the Common law, the Civil law and the Canon law.

9 cf M. H. Hoeflich, 'John Austin and Joseph Story' (1985) 29 *American Journal of Legal History* 36, 38-56.

10 A. W. B. Simpson, 'The Rule in *Wheeldon* v. *Burrows* and the Code Civile' (1967) 83 *LQR* 240. For Roman law in the English law of easements at this time, see A. D. E. Lewis, '"What Marcellus says is against you": Roman law and Common law' in Lewis and Ibbetson (eds.) *The Roman Law Tradition* (Cambridge, 1994), 199.

11 J. H. Baker, *An Introduction to English Legal History*, 142-143, 146-152.

Romano-canonical, and the law was the Civil law rather than the Common law. An advocate in an ecclesiastical court might cite the Decretals or the case-law of the Roman Rota[12]; an advocate in the Admiralty might cite the Digest or commentaries of the *ius commune*[13]; both would have degrees in Civil law and be members of Doctors Commons. Even more than the Common law judges and treatise writers who had a smattering of Roman law, these courts could have channelled sophisticated *ius commune* ideas into English practice. No doubt, in patches they did so; but we must not ignore their marginal positions within English law. The Admiralty was to all intents and purposes emasculated in the early seventeenth century, and it is hard to trace any significant civilian influences flowing from it into the later mercantile law; and while the ecclesiastical courts remained more vital until the nineteenth century they drifted further and further away from their civil law roots, so that again it is not easy to identify any lasting effect of their civilian heritage.

Finally, there were occasional pulses of explicitly civil law-based reasoning filtering into Common law practice. Lawyers of the twelfth century exploring the problems of protecting occupiers of land are, or become, happy with the Roman differentiation between *dominium* and *possessio*, even if their successors moved away from all such terminology[14]. The emergence of the action of covenant, and the early framing of contractual ideas, in the thirteenth century probably owes more than a little to the infiltration of the civilians' distinction between liability *ex delicto* and *ex contractu*. The settling down of the action of detinue - and hence the foundation of the law of moveable property - in the fourteenth century seems to have been influenced by the division between rights *in rem* and rights *in personam*, between property and obligation[15]. It is impossible not to suspect a Roman law influence when in the seventeenth and eighteenth centuries the emergent law of unjust enrichment is described in terms of quasi-contract (all the more so when the language is found in the mouth of the Scottish Lord

---

12 R. H. Helmholz, 'Records and Reports: the English Ecclesiastical Courts' in A. Wijffels, ed., *Case Law in the Making* (Berlin, 1997)

13 A. Wijffels, 'Sir Julius Caesar's Notes on Admiralty Cases' in C. Stebbings (ed.), *Law Reporting in Britain* (London, 1995), 89, 90-93.

14 F. Pollock and F. W. Maitland, *History of English Law*, 2.29-80, especially at 31-32; D. J. Seipp, 'The Concept of Property in the Early Common Law' (1994) 12 *Law and History Review* 29.

15 Donahue, '*Ius Commune*, Canon Law, and Common Law in England' (1992) 66 *Tulane Law Review* 1745, 1760-1764.

Mansfield)[16]. It is not difficult to discern the influence of the natural law school in the early eighteenth century in such matters as the formalisation of the standard of care demanded of bailees or, more generally and less explicitly, in the articulation of fault as the principal criterion for the imposition of delictal responsibility[17]. Similarly, in the early nineteenth century, it is well known that Pothier's analysis of contracts served to give shape to the emergent classical contract doctrine, supplemented by citations culled directly from the *Corpus Iuris Civilis*[18]. These pulses of civilian influence were in themselves fairly short-lived, but their consequences were long-lasting.

The amalgam of these factors ensured that English law was repeatedly, if not constantly, enriched by ideas drawn from the civilian tradition, so that the caricature of the Common law developing in total isolation from the Civil law has to be seen as an over-crude generalisation. Nonetheless, we must beware of going too far in the opposite direction in characterising English law as just another emanation of the Western European legal tradition based on the *ius commune*. Accepting that the 'reception' of Roman law operated differently in different areas of continental Europe, there are still very significant differences between the English experience and that of continental Europe.

The most fundamental, and most visible, way in which such reception of Roman law as occurred in England differed from that in the mainstream of continental Europe is that in England any rules based on Roman law or the later *ius commune* were immediately cut off from their roots. This has serious implications for the differential nature of English and continental legal cultures. English law undoubtedly received some, perhaps many, injections of Roman law; but these were immediately assimilated into the specifically English framework and given a life outside their original context. Unlike in continental Europe, the new law which resulted did not remain in dialogue with the old law from which it was derived. Even where a proposition of English law could be traced back to a Roman source, it was no argument in a subsequent case that a proper interpretation of Roman law would have

16 P. Birks, 'English and Roman Learning in *Moses* v. *McFerlan*' (1984) 37 *Current Legal Problems* 1.

17 Bailment: *Coggs* v. *Bernard*, (1703) 2 Ld Raym 909; W. Jones, *Essay on the Law of Bailments* (1781). Negligence: F. Buller, *An Institute of the Law relative to Trials at Nisi Prius* (1758), 35, compared with D.9.2.31 and S. Pufendorf, *The Law of Nature*, III.1.6.

18 A. W. B. Simpson, 'Innovation in Nineteenth Century Contract Law' (1975) 91 *LQR* 247.

led to a different result. Hence, even where the borrowing from Roman law had been explicit (as in some aspects of contract law in the nineteenth century, to take the best example) once the Roman injection had taken effect that was the end of the matter. There is nothing comparable to the pre-codification continental practice of repeatedly citing the *Corpus Iuris*, of continually rooting and re-rooting the modern law in Roman soil. In, say, France, Holland, or Germany, the adoption of a version of a Roman rule did not involve ripping it out of its context; it remained a rule of Roman law, logically connected to other rules of Roman law, which happened to apply in France, Holland or Germany. It would be misguided to regard these injections of Roman law as examples of the English assimilation of a Roman legal culture (or an English assimilation into a Roman legal culture): once the borrowings are cut off from their roots they cease to be part of the same culture.

The repeated citation of sources from the *Corpus Iuris* found in mainstream continental legal systems, and the absence of such repeated citations in the English tradition, therefore represents something rather more substantial than a surface variance between the acceptable forms of legal argument in different systems. The continental systems, in admittedly different ways, are knitted together in a common legal culture in a way in which the English system is not. Nor is it merely that judges in one culture cite Roman law and judges in the other do not. Continental judges of the seventeenth century, for example, frequently cite decisions from continental jurisdictions other than their own; so far as I am aware, they never cite decisions of the English courts. We see, for example, citations of the French Jean le Coq and Guy Pape in de Grysperre's reports from Malines, of the French Jehan Papon in Neostadius' notes from the Dutch Hoge Raad, of Guy Pape in Meichsner's *Decisiones* from the German Reichskammergericht, or of the Neapolitan Matteo d'Afflitto in Siena; *a fortiori* this was the case with the decisions of the Roman Rota, for these had pretensions to general applicability found in the decisions of no other court[19]. There is no parallel to this trans-nationalism in the English common-law courts; judges repeatedly cite English common-law decisions, but it is almost unthinkable for them to cite any continental case-law[20].

Behind this disparity between English practice and that found in the mainstream of continental Europe lies a fundamental theoretical difference. For the continental lawyer of the seventeenth or eighteenth

19 See generally, A. Wijffels, ed., *Case Law in the Making* (Berlin, 1997).

20 The only example known to the present writer is in Rolle's *Abridgement*, 2.139, tit. *Nusans, Privat* (F) 2, referring to Jean Papon's *Recueil d'Arrests Notables*.

century a central place was reserved for 'doctrine' (in the modern French sense of '*la doctrine*'), a densely textured mass of learning which could be found in books and taught in universities. Where this doctrine, particularly insofar as it was based on the learned laws, was recognised as a principal source of law there was comparatively little scope for arguments based on the practice of the courts. By contrast, in England there was no real equivalent to the civilians' doctrine, with the result that there was a far greater stress on the courts' past practice as the source of legal rules. While the continental lawyers' reliance on doctrine presupposed that the law had a coherent structure into which courts' decisions could be fitted, no such assumption can be discerned behind English law. These different assumptions are reflected in the different ways in which cases are reported. Much of the printed *decisiones* literature of the early modern continental systems explicitly structures case reports by reference to the Roman law categories to which they relate; the contrast with the printed law reports of early modern England, arranged chronologically and never related to any abstract structure, is violent.

The contrast between the practical leaning found in England and the theoretical leaning found in continental Europe is reflected in the different relations existing between the universities and legal practice. In England, connections between the universities and the judges or advocates were for all practical purposes non-existent until the nineteenth century. There was, it is true, nothing unusual in studying for a university degree before entering into legal practice; but it would have been very unusual to have studied law. Even those few Common lawyers who had obtained a degree in law (that is, in Roman Law) made no active use of whatever learning they had gleaned once they had moved into practice in the courts; it was not a part of English legal culture. We may contrast the position in France, where judges in the Parlement de Paris were required (though not necessarily expected) to be proficient in the (Roman) law, or in Germany, where half of the *assessores* in the Reichskammergericht were required to be learned in the (Roman) law[21]. Nor would a professor of (Roman) law at Oxford or Cambridge expect to have any influence over decision-making in the Common law courts; insofar as the continental practice of law faculties or individual professors of law giving *consilia* was found in England, it

21 F. Aubert, *Histoire du Parlement de Paris* (Paris, 1894), 1.77-78; M. Rousselet, *Histoire de la Magistrature Française* (Paris, 1957), 1.240-243; P. Ourliac and J.-L. Gazzaniga, *Histoire du Droit Privé Français* (Paris, 1985), 131-132. F. Wieacker, *A History of Private Law in Europe* (trans. T. Weir, Oxford, 1995), 132-133.

was limited to those courts in which civil law was practised, the admiralty and ecclesiastical courts. Modern legal historiography brings out this distinction. In John Baker's *Introduction to English Legal History* the universities merit no more than an apologetically belated mention of their awakening concern with the Common law between 1750 and 1850; in Manlio Bellomo's *L'Europa del Diritto Comune* they occupy the central chapter of the book[22].

While it would be absurdly simplistic and inaccurate to portray the reception of Roman law in continental Europe in terms of the wholesale supersession of customary legal rules by the rules of Roman law, it will hardly be doubted that (at different times and to different extents) there was a very substantial recasting of customary rules in the language of the civil law as well as a significant grafting of Roman rules on to the existing local law; lawyers wrote in Latin, using the divisions of the Roman law as well as its conceptual framework; it made sense for the seventeenth century Dutch lawyer Groenewegen to detail those parts of Roman law which did not apply in his own country[23], not those parts which did. This process had the effect of radically transforming European private law. No such recasting of English law in civilian terms occurred. It follows that if the *ius commune* did play such a leading part in establishing a genuinely (continental) European framework for private law - and few of us will dissent from Professor Zimmermann's view that it did - then English law was not integrated into this framework.

At this point, sceptics may be inclined to conclude that the whole enterprise of identifying a common culture of European private law is pointless, and that attempts to discover a historical framework for this common culture are at best absurdly misguided. If the enterprise necessarily involved the tracing of modern legal systems back to the *ius commune* it would be difficult to disagree with them; but there is no need for any such assumption. On the contrary, there is no difficulty in seeing the *ius commune* as one (extremely important) element in the formulation of the ideas of private law in many modern European legal systems at the same time as recognising that it was itself no more than one emanation of a wider and deeper European legal culture. Paradoxically, it may be the centrality of the *ius commune* in the history of much of continental Europe which blinds us to the common legal

---

22 5th edition (Rome, 1991), 125-138.

23 S. Groenewegen, *Tractatus de Legibus Abrogatis et Inusitatis in Hollandia* (1648).

culture which does indeed underpin the private law of the European nations.

Professor Zimmermann points forcibly towards the need to recognise a common legal vocabulary, not at some wished-for idealised past in which there was a European private law which generated identical answers to legal problems from nation to nation. The Common lawyer need have no difficulty with this; moreover, in that it gives full weight to 'customary' law as well as to the 'learned' law of the universities it is truer to Savigny's enterprise than would be an approach which placed the learned law at the root of everything. Such stress on a common vocabulary of concepts and ideas also enables legal scientists to comprehend not simply the main stream of European legal developments, but also the peculiarities of some of the more gothic features found in different systems. It is here that the insights of the legal historian can be the most valuable. Professor Zimmermann, for example, points to the abstraction and artificiality of Friedrich Mommsen's analysis of supervening impossibility which has been adopted into the German law of breach of contract, noting that the same logical framework had been found in the older writers of the *ius commune* in the far more specific context of the obligation *certam rem dare*[24]. Exactly the same mode of analysis characterised the development of the English law of breach of contract in the fourteenth and fifteenth centuries, largely because at this time the English law of contract was almost exclusively concerned with obligations to pay fixed sums of money, the classic case of the civilians' obligations *certam rem dare*. In England, as happened almost half a millennium later in Germany, this stress on supervening impossibility overlaid and superseded an earlier analysis of breach of contract formulated in terms of fault ('*culpa*'); we can observe the interplay between the two modes of analysis in the decades around 1400[25]. Moreover, the almost exclusive stress on contractual obligations to pay money meant that there would hardly ever be a situation in which subsequent impossibility of performance would ever arise; it was this fact (it seems) which led English law to adopt its theory of the absolute nature of contractual liability in the middle years of the seventeenth century. English law has slowly moved back in the direction of liability based on fault, though without disembarrassing itself of the language of absolute liability, thereby moving back towards the position taken in legal systems more

---

24 cf Zimmermann, *The Law of Obligations*, 806-810.

25 Ibbetson, 'Absolute Liability in Contract: the Antecedents of *Paradine* v. *Jayne*' in F. D. Rose (ed.), *Consensus ad Idem* (London, 1996), 1.

explicitly influenced by Roman law and the *ius commune*[26]. The detailed working out of individual rules in individual systems is not in itself of great moment; what is important is that, looked at from this historical point of view, the very different rules found in modern English, German and French law can be shown to have been built up from the same building blocks; and what is more important is that they can be explained in terms which are (or should be) comprehensible to legal scientists accustomed to working with their own national legal systems.

The same observation can be made of other features to which Professor Zimmermann draws attention. Contemporary English law's 'abracadabra of conditions, warranties and intermediate terms' wins no prizes for clarity or comprehensibility; yet from a historical perspective a 'condition' can be analysed straightforwardly as a condition precedent to the existence of legal liability (so that its failure, in civilian terms, would operate both as a defence to an action on the contract and as the basis for a *condictio indebiti*), while warranties are not in any significant respect different from the *dicta promissave* of the Roman law of sale and the *ius commune* (giving rise to a claim for damages either by an *actio quanti minoris* or an *actio empti*). What is interesting is English law's traditional formulation of the action for breach of warranty as a delictal action of trespass on the case rather than a transparently contractual remedy, which in its turn led to the separation within English law of actions for breach of contract and actions for breach of a term of a contract. The problem with the modern law is not that the ideas lying at its base are in themselves difficult, but that they have been shifted out of a remedial matrix into a substantive one, and that they have in the process become encrusted with a coating of progressively more arcane legal distinctions. The same point can be made about the modern law of restitutionary obligations. Continental legal systems have generally moved away from the fragmentary *condictiones* known to Roman law in favour of a general remedy for unjustified enrichment, building largely on Savigny's analysis of the centrality of the *condictio sine causa*[27]. Although the same building blocks as were known to the continental lawyers can be discerned in the shaping of English law, it has been a much later developer; so much so that it is still perhaps an open question whether there is any general principle behind the specific examples of

---

26 G. H. Treitel, 'Fault in the Common Law of Contract' in M. Bos and I. Brownlie (eds.), *Liber Amicorum for Lord Wilberforce* (Oxford, 1987), 185.

27 Zimmermann, *The Law of Obligations*, 872-873.

recognised liability[28]. It is, however, worth noting that without the centralising role of the *condictio sine causa*, English law has tended to analyse liability in terms of specific situations of 'unjust' (rather than 'unjustified') enrichment. A historical approach can again elucidate the different lines of development in different systems[29], and by doing so bring out the ways in which there is a common conceptual (if not linguistic) vocabulary in use even where the specifics of individual systems have either diverged or failed to converge. Nonetheless, we must beware of *faux amis*: though English lawyers for the better part of two or three centuries were happy to talk of restitutionary liability as 'quasi-contractual', and though as a matter of legal form the restitutionary actions were based on implied promises, this was the limit of any explicit parallel with the civil law; we cannot assume from the language that there was any wholesale importation of civilian doctrine.

The modern doctrine of consideration is another peculiarity of the English system; although it reaches roughly the same results as French law manages to reach with its doctrine of *cause*, it does so by a very different route[30]. Again, the legal historian may be able to cast some light on the reasons for these differences. The idea of *causa* elaborated by the glossators and the later writers of the *ius commune* had its base in the Romans' *causa stipulationis*, that is to say in terms of contracts whose actionability depended on the form in which they were couched[31]. It followed that it was not so much that the presence of *causa* made an agreement actionable, but that its absence undermined what would otherwise have been an actionable agreement; lack of *causa* was evidence of error[32]. As the requirement of form for the *stipulatio* became more and more attenuated in the *ius commune*, the theory of *causa* was transferred into the field of informal agreements, essentially duplicating the unsurprising requirement that an agreement must have been seriously intended in order to be actionable. Deprived of any

---

28 See the criticisms of *Westdeutsche Landesbank Girozentrale* v. *Islington London Borough Council* [1994] 4 All E R 890 (appealed on one specific point [1996] 2 All E R 961) by, for example, P. Birks, 'Restitution after Void Contracts' (1993) 23 *University of Western Australia Law Review* 195, and A. Burrows, 'Swaps and the Friction between Common Law and Equity' (1995) 2 *Restitution Law Review* 15, especially at 16 ('The Grounds for Restitution, i.e. the Unjust Factor').

29 See, for examples, the contributions to E. J. H. Schrage (ed.), *Unjust Enrichment* (Berlin, 1995).

30 B. Markesinis, 'Cause and Consideration: A Study in Parallel' [1978] *CLJ* 53.

31 Zimmermann, *The Law of Obligations*, 549-553

32 And as such would ground an *exceptio doli*. cf J. L. Barton, '*Causa Promissionis* Again' (1966) 34 *Tijdschrift voor Rechtsgeschiedenis* 41.

independent function, the doctrine disappeared from some systems (e.g., the German) but lived on in others (e.g., the French and the Italian). The English doctrine of consideration was from the start an emanation of the law relating to informal agreements[33]; its basic presupposition was that these were of no effect, but the law would give effect to them if they had a sufficiently strong element of reciprocity about them. In civilian terms, we can see it as the generalisation of the idea of reciprocity found in the consensual contracts (with the exclusion of mandate), a generalisation which had already been made by the post-classical lawyers in their category of innominate contracts. The increasing stress on the parties' will as the source of contractual obligation, reflected in the growth of an independent requirement of 'intention to create legal relations' and the formulation of rules relating to mistake, misrepresentation and the like (most explicitly in the nineteenth century, but with earlier roots[34]), reduced the importance of consideration; it has not been easy to grub out, though, for its underlying function - the exclusion of liability on gratuitous agreements - is not obviously duplicated by the requirement that the parties should have had a serious intention to be bound.

It is this final example which brings out most pointedly the real difficulties of comparative legal history. The description given of the early history of the doctrine of consideration is by no means uncontroversial; however much one historian might believe it to be true, other historians might favour wholly different analyses. In particular, there is a very strong line of argument to the effect that when the foundations of the modern doctrine of consideration were laid down in the sixteenth century the word 'consideration' meant little more than 'motive', and that the 'doctrine' of 'consideration' was more than functionally equivalent to the canon law theory of *causa*[35]. What should be the response of the scholar not personally expert in the niceties of English legal history? In an ideal world, of course, comparative legal historians, if they were to do their job properly, would gain expertise in the histories of the different legal systems about which they are writing and examine the primary sources for themselves; but the world may not be ideal. This, in its turn, carries the risk that the comparative legal

---

33 This is not to deny that there was a (distinct) doctrine of consideration applicable to *prima facie* effective juridical acts.

34 Simpson, 'Innovation in Nineteenth Century Contract Law' (1975) 91 *LQR* 247; the dangers of assuming (nineteenth-century) modernity in these developments are well brought out by J. L. Barton, 'Contractual Damages and the Rise of Industry' (1987) 7 *Oxford Journal of Legal Studies* 40.

35 The argument is put most strongly by A. W. B. Simpson, *The History of the Common Law of Contract* (Oxford, 1975), 316-488.

historian will succumb to the pressure to pick and choose those histories of foreign systems which either look most familiar or best fit a preconceived notion of the relationship between different systems. It is a pressure which has to be resisted, unless we are completely to subvert Savigny's enterprise.

There is a further problem, to which allusion has already been made in a different context. For most of the last millennium English law has been primarily concerned with procedure, with the way in which questions should be asked rather than the way in which they should be answered. Indeed, until the sixteenth century - and perhaps even as late as the eighteenth - judges seem almost pathologically concerned not to give answers to questions, preferring to leave them as far as possible to the determination of a jury of laymen[36]. In the middle of the last century Henry Maine observed that 'substantive law has at first the look of being gradually secreted in the interstices of procedure'[37], and the ensuing century or so has produced no reason to qualify this judgment. The same is not true of continental legal systems, at least not as soon as there had been sufficient reception of Roman ideas to bring in a coherent framework of substantive law. It is almost inevitable, therefore, that when English legal historians describe the history of English law their concern is with what are essentially procedural questions. What writ should be used in a particular case? What processes lie in order to get a defendant into court? To what extent can the defendant use delaying excuses in order to postpone the hearing of a case? How can defences to a particular claim be formulated? How should disputed points of fact (in the broadest terms) be resolved? How should a judgment be enforced? It is no less inevitable that the historian of continental law, blessed with the richness of discussion of substantive legal ideas in the writings of the glossators and after, should concentrate on questions of substance. The gap between these different approaches to law may be so wide as to be unbridgeable by the legal historian[38].

Professor Zimmermann argues that the construction of a European private law based on historical principles requires a different form of legal history from that which prevails today, an approach to legal history which looks not so much to the classical and post-classical Roman law as to the development of those rules in the Middle Ages and

---

36 Ibbetson, '*Juge et jury dans la common law*' in R. Jacob (ed.), *Le Juge et Le Jugement* (Paris, 1996), 89.

37 H. Maine, *Early Law and Custom* (London, 1883), 389.

38 The extent of the difference is easily visible in the various volumes of *Comparative Studies in Continental and Anglo-American Legal History* (Berlin, 1987-).

beyond. It is no less true that it demands an approach to English legal history different from that of the last century or more, an approach which concentrates not so much on the superficial form as on the substantive principles which underlay that form. This will not be easy to achieve, for it was only very rarely that any hint as to what these principles were pushes its way to the surface of legal debate. It may indeed be that it is impossible, for in a world in which only formal questions received detailed discussion there would have been room for a huge measure of variation in the way in which individual lawyers perceived the substantive issues; at some stage we have to recognise that this variation might have been so great as to preclude any meaningful consideration of what the substantive law actually was. There is no English equivalent of Professor Zimmermann's magisterial *Law of Obligations*; given the approach to law in pre-modern England it may be that such a book could never satisfactorily be written.

There is, therefore, good reason to desire the development of a European private law on historical principles, giving substance to Savigny's projected enterprise. On the other hand, if we are to hold true to Savigny, we must take realistic account of the genuine problems which stand in the way of such an enterprise. If Europe is to include England, we will have to look beyond the *ius commune* to the deeper principles which lie behind it, and also to come to terms with the English lawyer's historical concentration on matters of procedure at the expense of matters of substance. There is no reason why this should be impossible; but it will undoubtedly involve a serious re-thinking, both in England and in continental Europe, of the nature of the legal historical analysis which will allow the production of a truly European legal history.

BIBLIOGRAPHY

Abbott, G., Wingard, P. et al. eds. *The Teaching of English as an International Language*, (London, 1992).

Abraham, R., *R.F.D.A.* 1990, p.1058.

Administrative Law: Judicial Review and Statutory Appeals, Law Commission Consultation Paper No. 226.

Albrecht, H.-J., Heine, G., Meinberg, V., '*Umweltschutz durch Strafrecht?*' (1984) 96 *Zeitschrift für die Gesamte Strafrechtswissenschaft* pp. 943-998; 'Particular Difficulties in Enforcing the Law Arising out of Basic Conflicts between the Different Agencies regarding the best-suited Reactions upon Highly Sensitive Kinds of Crime', in: Council of Europe (Ed.): *Interactions Within the Criminal Justice System.* (Strasbourg 1987), pp. 45-90; *idem* and van Kalmthout, A. (Eds.): *Drug Policies in Western Europe*. (Freiburg 1989); '*Landesbericht Deutschland*'. in: Meyer, J. et al. (Eds.): *Gewinnaschöpfung bei Betäubungsmitteldelikten. Eine rechtsvergleichende und kriminologische Untersuchung.* (Wiesbaden 1989), pp. 25-84; '*Voraussetzungen und Konsequenzen einer Entkriminalisierung im Drogenbereich*'. in: *Institut für Konfliktforschung (Ed.): Entkriminalisierung im Drogenbereich?* (Köln 1991), pp.1-38.

Andenaes, J., *Punishment and Deterrence* (Ann Arbor, 1974).

Annual Report of the Attorney General of the United States 1992. U.S. Department of Justice 1993.

Ardagh, J., *France Today* (London 1990), in: Wright, V. *The Government and Politics of France* (3rd edn 1989).

Arrowsmith , S., *Government Procurement and Judicial Review* (London 1988).

Aubert, F., *Histoire du Parlement de Paris* (Paris, 1894).

Bacon, F., 'A Preparation toward the Union of the Laws of England and Scotland', in *The Works of Francis Bacon, Baron Verulam*, vol. IV (ed. London, 1824) pp.287.

Baker, J.H., *An Introduction to English Legal History* (3rd ed., London, 1990).

Barton, J. L. '*Causa Promissionis* Again' (1966) 34 *Tijdschrift voor Rechtsgeschiedenis* 41; 'Contractual Damages and the Rise of Industry' (1987) 7 *Oxford Journal of Legal Studies* 40; *Roman Law in England* (*Ius Romanum Medii Aevi*, V.13) (Milan, 1971).

Barton, J., (ed.), *Towards a General Law of Contract* (Berlin, 1990).

Beale, H., 'Privity of Contract: Judicial and Legislative Reform', (1995) 9 *Journal of Contract Law* 103 sqq.; 'Legislative Control of Fairness: The

Directive on Unfair Terms in Consumer Contracts', in: Jack Beatson, Daniel Friedman (eds.), *Good Faith and Fault in Contract Law* (Oxford, 1995), pp. 231 sqq.

Beatson, J., 'Reforming the Law of Contracts for the Benefit of Third Parties', (1992) 45 (2) *Current Legal Problems* 1 sqq.

Becker, G.S., *'Kriminalität und Strafe. Ein ökonomischer Ansatz'* in: Becker, G.S.(Ed.): *Der ökonomische Ansatz zur Erklärung menschlichen Verhaltens.* (Tübingen 1982), pp. 39-96.

Becker, H.J., *'Das Rheinische Recht und seine Bedeutung für die Rechtsentwicklung in Deutschland im 19.Jahrhundert'*, (1985) *Juristische Schulung* 338 sqq.

Bell, J., *French Constitutional Law* (Oxford 1992); 'English Law and French Law - Not so different?' [1995] CLP 63; (1995) 1 *European Public Law* 16 at pp 20-22.

Bellamy, R., Bufacchi, V., Castiglione, B., *Democracy and Constitutional Culture in the Union of Europe* (London 1995).

Bellomo, M., *The Common Legal Past of Europe 1000 - 1800* (Washington, D.C., 1995); *L'Europa del Diritto Comune*, 5th edition (Rome, 1991).

Berger, K.P., *'Die UNIDROIT-Prinzipien für Internationale Handelsverträge'*, (1995) 94 *Zeitschrift für Vergleichende Rechtswissenschaft* 217 sqq.

Bergfeld, C., *'Preußen und das Allgemeine Deutsche Handelsgesetzbuch'* (1987) 14 *Ius Commune* 101 sqq.

Berman, H. J., *Law and Revolution: The Formation of the Western Legal Mind* (Cambridge Mass., 1983); *idem* and Reid, C., *'Römisches Recht in Europa und das ius commune'*, (1995) 3 *Zeitschrift für Europäisches Privatrecht* 3 sqq.

Bernardi, A., *Comunitarizzazione del diritto e codificazione penale*; *'"Principi di diritto" e diritto penale europeo'*, *Annali Università di Ferrara* (1988).

Bettiol, G., *'Sull'unificazione del diritto penale europeo'*, in *Prospettive per un diritto penale europeo* (Padova, 1968) p.6.

Bingham, Sir Thomas (1992) 41 *International and Comparative Law Quarterly* 514.

Birks P., and G. McLeod, *Justinian's Institutes* (London, 1987).

Birks, P., (ed.) *'English and Roman Learning in* Moses v. Macferlan', (1984) 37 *Current Legal Problems* 11 sqq.; *An Introduction to the Law of Restitution* (Oxford, 1985, reprint 1989); *idem* and McLeod, G., 'The Implied Contract Theory of Quasi-Contract: Civilian Opinion in the Century Before Blackstone', (1986) 6 *Oxford Journal of Legal Studies* 46 sqq.; 'The English Recognition of Unjust Enrichment', (1991) *Lloyd's Maritime and Commercial Law Quarterly* 473 sqq.; *'Konkurrierende Strategien und Interessen: Das Irrtumserfordernis im Bereicherungsrecht des common law'*, (1993) 1 *Zeitschrift für Europäisches Privatrecht* 556 sq.; 'Restitution after Void Contracts' (1993) 23 *University of Western Australia Law Review* 195 'Adjudication and interpretation in the common law: a century of change', (1994) 14 *Legal Studies* 156 sqq.; *What are Law Schools for? Pressing Problems in the Law*, Vol.2 (1996).

Black, J., *Convergence or Divergence? Britain and the Continent* (London, 1994).

Blaurock, U., "Europäisches Privatrecht", (1994) *Juristenzeitung* 270 sqq.

Bloor, M., 'Council of Europe Syllabus Revisited: Lessons for the Future?', :in *Language in a Changing Europe,* eds. David Graddol and Stephen Thomas. (British Association for Applied Linguistics in association with Multilingual Matters Ltd., 1995).

Bolli, G.G. and Spiti, M.G., *Verifica del Grado di Conoscenza dell'Italiano in una Prospettiva di Certificazione,* (Università per Stranieri di Perugia, Guerra, 1992).

Bonavita, I.G., *Ricordi ossiano notizie de' fatti concernenti l'origine, il progresso e la terminazione della redazione delle Leggi Criminali promulgate per Malta nel 1854 e di alcune circostanze aventivi relazione che mi riguardano personalmente,* 1857.

Bonell, M.J., *Das UNIDROIT-Projekt für die Ausarbeitung von Regeln für Internationale Handelsverträge*, (1992) 56 RabelsZ 274 sqq.; *idem* and Garro, A.M., Veytia, H., Baptista, L.O. and Ferrari, F., in (1995) 69 Tulane Law Review 1121 sqq.

Bonesana, C., Beccaria, M., *An Essay on Crimes and Punishments* (II American ed., Philadelphia 1819, rep. Stanford 1953).

Bonichot, J-C, *R.F.D.A.* 1995, p. 166.

Braibant, *'Du simple au complexe quarante ans de droit administratif (1953-1993)' EDCE* 1994, 407.

Brand, P. *The Origins of the English Legal Profession* (Oxford, 1992).

Brauneder, W., *'Vernünftiges Recht als überregionales Recht: Die Rechtsvereinheitlichung der österreichischen Zivilrechtskodifikationen 1786-1797-1811'*, in: Reiner Schulze (ed.), *Europäische Rechts- und Verfassungsgeschichte* (1991), pp. 121 sqq.; *'Europäisches Privatrecht - aber was ist es?'*, (1993) 15 *Zeitschrift für Neuere Rechtsgeschichte* 225 sqq.

Brewer-Carias, A.R., *Judicial Review in Comparative Law* (Cambridge 1989).

Brown, L.N., 'New Judicial Architecture on the Kirchberg', in *Lecturers' News,* Sweet & Maxwell, Autumn 1994.

Brundage, J.A., *Medieval Canon Law* (London, 1995).

Bucher, E.,and Schmidlin, B. in: Bruno Schmidlin (ed.), *Vers un droit priv, Européen commun? - Skizzen zum gemeineuropäischen Privatrecht* 7 sqq., 33 sqq.

Buller, *An Institute of the Law relative to Trials at Nisi Prius* (1758), 35

Bürge, A., *Das französische Privatrecht im 19. Jahrhundert* (1991), pp. 150 sqq.

Burrows, A., *The Law of Restitution* (1993); 'Swaps and the Friction between Common Law and Equity' (1995) 2 *Restitution Law Review* 15.

Cabinet Office, *Service to the Public* (London 1988).

Cadoppi, A., ed., '*Colpevolezza e principi costituzionali: le recenti "coraggiose avventure" della Corte suprema canadese*', (1989) *Il Foro Italiano, IV, c.250;* 'Recent Developments in Italian Constitutional-Criminal Law', (1990) 28 *Alberta Law Rev.* pp.427 ff.; '*Dalla judge-made law al Criminal Code*', (1992) *Rivista italiana di diritto e procedura penale,* pp. 923 ff.; '*Colpevolezza e principi costituzionali: la Corte suprema canadese "colpisce ancora"*', (1992) *Il Foro Italiano, IV, c.456.;* '*Mens rea*', 7 *Digesto delle discipline penalistiche,* IV ed. (Torino, 1992) p.618.; *Omnis definitio in iure periculosa? Il problema delle definizioni legali nel diritto penale* (Padova, 1995); *idem* and McCall Smith, Prof. Alexander *Introduzione allo Studio del Diritto Penale Scozzese* (Padova, 1995); '*La genesi delle fattispecie penali. Una comparazione tra civil law e common law*', in G. Fiandaca, ed., *Diritto penale in transizione* (Padova, 1996).

Caenegem, R.C. van *Judges, Legislators and Professors* (London and Rio Grande, 1987); idem, *An Historical Introduction to Private Law* (Cambridge, 1988).

Cairns, J.W., 'The Influence of the German Historical School in Early Nineteenth Century Edinburgh', (1994) 20 *Syracuse Journal of International Law and Commerce* 191 sqq..

Campenhausen, A. v. *Staat und Kirche in Frankreich,* 1962; '*Vier neue Staatskirchenverträge in vier neuen Ländern*', [1995] *Neue Zeitschrift für Verwaltungsrecht* 757.

Cannata, C.A., '*Usus hodiernus pandectarum, common law, diritto romano olandese e diritto comune europeo*', (1991) 57 *Studia et documenta historiae et iuris* 383 sqq..

Cappelletti, M., *Judicial Review in Comparative Perspective* (Oxford 1989).

Card, Cross and Jones, *Criminal Law,* XIII ed. (London, Dublin, Edinburgh, 1995).

Caroni, P., '*Der Schiffbruch der Geschichtlichkeit - Anmerkungen zum Neo-Pandektismus*', 1994) 16 *Zeitschrift für Neuere Rechtsgeschichte,* p. 85; '*Die Schweizer Romanistik im 19. Jahrhundert*', (1994) 16 *Zeitschrift für Neuere Rechtsgeschichte* 243 sqq.

Carrington, P.D., 'Of Law and the River', (1984) 34 *Journal of Legal Education* 222 sqq.

Carsten, G., '*Europäische Integration und nordische Zusammenarbeit auf dem Gebiet des Zivilrechts*', (1993) 1 *Zeitschrift für Europäisches Privatrecht* 335 sqq.

Cassese, S. and Arabia A.G., *L'amministrazione e la Costituzione* (Bologna 1993).

Chabanol, D, '*Un printemps procedural pour la justice administrative?*' *A.J.D.A.* mai 1995, p. 398.

Chapus, *Droit Administratif Général,* Tome 1, 8ième ed.

Chiti, M., 'Are there Universal Principles of Good Governance?' (1995) 1 *European Public Law* 241.

Citizen's Charter, The. Second Report: 1994 (Cm 2540; 1994) p 2.

Coing, H., (ed.), *Handbuch der Quellen und Literatur der Neueren Europäischen Privatrechtsgeschichte, 1973-1988*; *idem* and Knut Wolfgang Nörr (eds.).*Comparative Studies in Continental and Anglo-American Legal History*; *'Rechtsvergleichung als Grundlage von Gesetzgebung im 19. Jahrhundert'*, (1978) 7 *Ius Commune* 168 sqq.; *'Das Recht als Element europäischer Kultur'*, (1984) 238 *Historische Zeitschrift*, p. 1; *Europäisches Privatrecht, Vol. 1: Alteres Gemeines Recht*, (Munich 1985), *Vol. 2: 19. Jahrhundert*, (Munich 1989); *Europäisches Privatrecht*, vol. I (1985); *Europäisches Privatrecht*, vol. II (1989); *'Europäisierung der Rechtswissenschaft'*, (1990) *Neue Juristische Wochenschrift*, p. 7.

Colvin, E., 'Chapter Seven - Interpretation of Criminal Legislation and Codes', in J.A. Riordan, gen. ed., *The Laws of Australia*; *Principles of Criminal Law*, II ed. (Canada 1991).

Commonwealth Secretariat: *Basic Documents on International Efforts to Combat Money Laundering*. (London 1991).

Comparative Studies in Continental and Anglo-American Legal History (Berlin, 1987-)

Conseil D'Etat 1992 Report.

Council of Europe Press, *Language Learning in Europe: the Challenge of Diversity,*. (Strasbourg, 1989).

Council of Europe, 'Consistency in Sentencing: Recommendation to Member States and Explanatory Memorandum', 4 (1993) *Criminal Law Forum* 355.

Council of Europe: *Explanatory Report on the Convention on Laundering, Search, Seizure and Confiscation of the Proceeds from Crime*. (Strasbourg 1991).

Craig, P., *Public Law and Democracy in the United Kingdom and the United States of America* (Oxford, 1990).

Cram, Ian., 'Public Authorities, Political Protest and Judicial Review' 1995 *SLT* 213

Criminal Code for England and Wales Law Comm. No. 177, (London, 1989).

Criminal Statistics. England and Wales 1991, Home Office.

Currie, D., *The Constitution of the Federal Republic of Germany* (Chicago, 1994).

Dölemeyer B., in: Helmut Coing (ed.), *Handbuch der Quellen und Literatur der neueren europäischen Privatrechtsgeschichte,* vol. III/2 (1982), pp. 1421 sqq..

Dahl, H. 'The Influence and Application of the Standard Penal Code for Latin America', (1990) 17 *Am. J. Crim. Law* 235 ff.

David, R., *International Encylopaedia of Comparative Law*, (Dordrecht, 1986) vol. 2, ch 5.

de Groot, G.R., 'European Legal Education in the 21st Century', in: Bruno Witte, Caroline Forder (eds.), *The Common Law of Europe and the Future of Legal Education* (Deventer 1992), 7 sqq.

de Roo, A.J., *Transfrontier Mobility of Law* (The Hague, 1995).

de Witte, B., Caroline Forder (ed.), *The common law of Europe and the future of legal education*, (Deventer 1992).

Department of the Environment Circular 11/94.

Dessecker, A., Smettan, R.: '*Gewinnabschöpfung bei Betäubungsmitteldelikten. Kriminologische Untersuchung*' in: Meyer, J. et al. (Eds.): *Gewinnabschöpfung bei Betäubungsmitteln*. (Wiesbaden 1989), pp.539-681.

Detzkies, J., '*Landesbericht Frankreich*', In: Meyer, J. et al.(Eds.): *Gewinnabschöpfung bei Betäubungsmitteldelikten*. (Wiesbaden 1989), pp. 103-156.

Dicey, *An Introduction to the Study of the Law of the Constitution* (10th edn. by E.C.S. Wade, London 1959).

Dilcher, G., '*Vom Beitrag der Rechtsgeschichte zu einer zeitgemäßen Zivilrechtswissenschaft*', (1984) 184 *Archiv für die civilistische Praxis*, p. 255 et seq. and 286 et seq; '*Die januskoöpfige Kodifikation - das preußische Allgemeine Landrecht (1794) und die europäische Rechtsgeschichte*', (1994) 2 *Zeitschrift für Europäisches Privatrecht*, 446 sqq.

Domat, J., *Les loix civiles dans leur ordre naturel* (1694).

Donahue, C. Jr., '*Ius Commune*, Canon Law, and Common Law in England' (1992) 66 *Tulane Law Review* 1745.

Dreher, Tröndle: *Strafgesetzbuch. Kommentar*. 46th Edition, (München 1993), §§43a, 73d.

Duyne, P. Van: '*Geldwäscherei. Umfangschätzung in Nebelschwaden*' *Kriminologisches Bulletin* 1995.

Eco, U., *Die Suche nach der vollkommenen Sprache* (1994).

Edward, D.A.O. and Lane, R.C., *European Community Law* (2nd ed., Edinburgh, 1995).

Edwards, H.T., 'The Growing Disjunction Between Legal Education and the Legal Profession', (1992) 91 *Michigan Law Review* 34 sqq.

Ek, J A van and J L M Trim *Threshold Level 1990,*. Council of Europe Press, Strasbourg, 1993; *Waystage 1990,* Council of Europe Press, Strasbourg, 1994.

Englehardt, H., '*Die Vereinbarungen des ungarischen Staates mit den Kirchen*', in; *Verantwortlichkeit und Freiheit. Festschrift für Willi Geiger* (1989), pp. 722 sqq.

Enschedé, C.J., *Een uniform Europees Strafrecht* (Arnhem,1990).

Erdö, P., in: 29 *Essener Gespräche zum Thema Staat und Kirche* (1995), p. 134 sqq.; *idem* and Schanda, B., *Egyház és vallás a mai magyar jogban*, (1993).

Ernst, W., *Rechtsmängelhaftung* (1995).

Esser, J., *Grundsatz und Norm in der richterlichen Fortbildung des Privatrechts* (2nd ed., 1964); idem, *Vorverständnis und Methodenwahl in der Rechtsfindung: Rationalitätsgarantien der richterlichen Entscheidungsfindung* (1970).

Evans-Jones, R., (ed.), *The Civil Law Tradition in Scotland* (Edinburgh, 1995).

Falk, U., *Ein Gelehrter wie Windscheid* (1989).

Farmer, L., '"The Genius of Our Law...": Criminal Law and the Scottish Legal Tradition', (1992) 55 *Modern Law Rev*. p.25.

Favoreu, L., and Jolowicz, J.A. (eds.), *Le contrôle juridictionnel des lois* (Paris 1986).

Feenstra, R., '*Die Klagbarkeit der pacta nuda*', in: Robert Feenstra, Reinhard Zimmermann (eds.), *Das römisch-holländische Recht: Fortschritte des Zivilrechts im 17. und 18. Jahrhundert* (1992), pp. 123 sqq.

Feenstra, Robert, Reinhard Zimmermann (eds.), *Das römisch-holländische Recht: Fortschritte des Zivilrechts im 17. und 18. Jahrhundert* (1992);

Fehervary, J.: '*Transnationale Kriminalität. Erkenntnisse aus Österreich*', August 1995.

Feinberg, *The Moral Limits of the Criminal Law,* in four volumes *Harm to Others* (New York-Oxford, 1984); *Offense to Others* (New York-Oxford, 1985); *Harm to Self* (New York-Oxford, 1986); *Harmless Wrongdoing* (New York-Oxford, 1988).

Ferguson, P.W., 'Jurisdiction and Criminal Law in Scotland and England', in R.F. Hunter, *Justice and Crime: Essays in Honour of Lord Emslie* (Edinburgh, 1993) pp 96 sqq.

Ferrari, F., '*Vom Abstraktionsprinzip und Konsensualprinzip zum Traditionsprinzip - Zu den Möglichkeiten der Rechtsangleichung im Mobiliarsachenrecht*', (1993) 1 *Zeitschrift für Europäisches Privatrecht* 52 sqq.

Fiandaca, G., *Problematica dell'osceno e tutela del buon costume* (Padova, 1984).

Fisse, B., *Howard's Criminal Law,* V ed. (Sydney 1990); *Criminal Law Principles*.

Flauss, J.F., *Les Petites Affiches*, 9.1.1995.

Flessner, A., '*Rechtsvereinheitlichung durch Rechtswissenschaft und Juristenausbildung*', (1992) 56 *RabelsZ*, p. 259 et seq.

Fortescue, Sir John, *De Laudibus Legum Anglie*.

Freedland, M., 'Government by Contract and Private Law'[1994] *PL* at 104.

Friedland, M.L., 'R.S. Wright's Model Criminal Code', (1981) 1 *Oxford Journ. Legal Studies* pp.307 ff..

Frowein, '*Die Bedeutung des die Gedanken -, Gewissen - und Religionsfreiheit garantierenden Artikels 0 der Europäischen Menschenrechtskonvention*', 27 *Essener Gespräche zum Thema Staat und Kirche* (1993), p. 46 sqq., at p. 50.

Frydman, P., *R.F.D.A*. mars-avril 1995, p. 361.

Fülbier, A., Aepfelbach, R.R.: *Das Geldwäschegesetz*. 3rd ed., (Köln 1993).

Gabel, P., Kennedy, D., 'Roll Over Beethoven', (1984) 36 *Stanford Law Review* 1.

Gaius, *Institutes*.

Galmot, Y., '*Réflexions sur le recours au droit comparé*' *R.F.D.A.* 1990, 255.

Ganado, A., 'The Historical Development of the Criminal Code', 2 *The Law Journal.(Malta)*, No.4, p.211; No.5, p.258; No.6, p.355.

Ganado, M., 'Sir Ignazio Gavino Bonavita', 1 *The Law Journal (Malta)*, No.5, p.19.

Genevoix, B., *'Le Conseil D'Etat et l'ordre juridique communautaire'*, *E.D.C.E.* 1979-1980.

Gerven, W. Van, 'Bridging the Gap between Community and National Laws: Towards a Principle of Homogeneity in the Field of Legal remedies?'[1995] 32 *CMLRev*. pp. 679-702 .

Giaro, T., *Europäische Privatrechtsgeschichte: Werkzeug der Rechtsvereinheitlichung und Produkt der Kategorienvermengung*, *Ius Commune*, Vol. XXI (1994).

Gilmore, W.C., 'International Efforts to Combat Money Laundering' (1992) *Commonwealth Law Bulletin*, pp. 1129-1142.

Glenn, P., *'Le trust et le jus commune'*, in: Pierre Legrand Jr. (ed.), *Common law d'un siècle l'autre,* pp. 87 sqq.

Godding, P., *Le droit privé dans les Pays-Bas méridionaux du 12e au 18e siècle* (1987).

Goff , Lord of Chieveley, Jones G., *The Law of Restitution* (4th ed., London, 1993); (1994) 58 RabelsZ 443 sqq.

Goode, M., 'Codification of the Australian Criminal Law', (1992) 16 *Criminal Law Journal* pp.5-19; (1993) 13 *Legal Studies* 3 sq.

Goode, R., 'The European law school', (1993) 13 *Legal Studies* 1.

Gordley, J., *The Philosophical Origins of Modern Contract Doctrine* (Oxford, 1991); (1992) 40 *American Journal of Comparative Law* 1002 sqq.; *'Common law und civil law: eine berholte Unterscheidung'*, (1993) 1 *Zeitschrift für Europäisches Privatrecht* 498 sqq.; 'Mere Brilliance: The Recruitment of Law Professors in the United States', (1993) 41 *American Journal of Comparative Law* 367 sqq.; 'Myths of the French Civil Code', (1994) 21 *American Journal of Comparative Law* 459 sqq; (1994) 21 *American Journal of Comparative Law* 459 sqq.; 'Can We Study Our Own Law in Isolation?', (1996) 44 *American Journal of Comparative Law.*

Grande, E., *Accordo criminoso e conspiracy* (Padova 1993); *'Dissociazione dei formanti e diritto penale: analisi di un chiasmo'*, in P. Cendon, ed., *Scritti in onore di Rodolfo Sacco*, vol. II (Milano, 1994), pp.593 ff.

Grasso, G., *Comunità europee e diritto penale* (Milano, 1989).

Green, P., *Drug Couriers. The Howard League for Penal Reform*, (London 1991).

Grief, N., 'The Domestic Impact of the European Convention on Human Rights as Mediated through Community Law' [1991] *Public Law* 555.

Griffith, S.W., *Explanatory Letter to the Honourable Attorney-General*, 29 Oct 1897, in Id., *Draft of a Code of Criminal law, Prepared for the Government of Quuensland* (Brisbane, 1897) (C.A. 89-1897).

Groáfeld B., *'Europäisches Recht und Rechtsstudium'*, (1993) *Juristische Schulung* 710 sqq.; idem and Karen Bilda, *'Europäische Rechtsangleichung'*, (1992) *Zeitschrift fiir Rechtsvergleichung*, p. 426 et seq.

Groenewegen, S. *Tractatus de Legibus Abrogatis et Inusitatis in Hollandia* (1648)

Grossi, P., *Quaderni Fiorentini per la storia del pensiero gluridico moderno*, Vol. 23 (1994).

Häberle, P., *'Europäische Rechtskultur'*, in: *idem*, *Europäische Rechtskultur* (1994), pp. 9 sqq.

Habermas, J., *Legitimation Crisis* (London 1975).

Hallstein, W., *'Angleichung des Privat- und Prozeigrechts in der Europäischen Wirtschaftsgemeinschaft'*, (1964) 28 *RabelsZ*, p. 211; *Angleichung des Privat- und Prozeßrechts in der Europäischen*.

Harden, I. and Lewis, N., *The Noble Lie* (London 1986); Harden, I.,'The Constitution and its Discontents' (1991) *British Journal of Political Science* 489.

Harding, R. ed., *The Criminal Laws* (ed. R. Harding) (Melbourne, 1993) .

Hart, H.L.A., *Law, Liberty and Morality* (Oxford-New York, 1963).

Hartkamp, A.S., Hesselink M.W., Hondius E.A., (ed.), *Towards a European Civil Code*, (Nijmwegen 1994).

Hattenhauer, H., (ed.), *Thibaut und Savigny: Ihre programmatischen Schriften* (1973); *Europäische Rechtsgeschichte* (Heidelberg, 1992) .

Hazeltine, H. D. General Preface, to Chrimes, S. B. *Sir John Fortescue* (Cambridge, 1942)

Heinrichs, H., in: Palandt, *Bürgerliches Gesetzbuch* (54th ed., 1995).

Helmholz, R.H., *Canon Law and the Law of England* (London and Rio Grande 1987); 'Continental Law and Common Law: Historical Strangers or Companions?', 1990 *Duke Law Journal* 1207 sqq.; *Roman Canon Law in Reformation England* (Cambridge 1990).; (ed.), *Canon Law in Protestant Lands* (Berlin, 1992); 'Records and Reports: the English Ecclesiastical Courts' in A. Wijffels, ed., *Case Law in the Making* (Berlin, 1997).

Herman, S., *'Schicksal und Zukunft der Kodifikationsidee in Amerika'*, in: Reinhard Zimmermann (ed.), *Amerikanische Rechtskultur und europäisches Privatrecht* (1995), pp. 52 sqq.

Hesse, J.J. ed., *Federalizing Europe?* (Oxford, 1995).

Hoeflich, M. H. 'John Austin and Joseph Story' (1985) 29 *American Journal of Legal History* 36.

Hogg, T.J., 'An Introductory Lecture on the Study of the Civil Law' (1831), as reprinted in Michael H. Hoeflich, *The Gladsome Light of Jurisprudence* (1988), pp. 96 sqq. (99 sq.).

Holdsworth, R. 'Directions to a Student in the University', in H. F. Fletcher, *The Intellectual Development of John Milton* (Illinois, 1961), 2.646.

Home Office: *Tackling Drug Abuse: A Summary of the Government's Strategy*. (London 1988)

Hommelhoff, P., *'Zivilrecht unter dem Einfluß europäischer Rechtsangleichung'*, (1992) 192 *Archiv für die civilistische Praxis* 71 sqq.

Honsell, H., '*Das rechtshistorische Argument in der modernen Zivilrechtsdogmatik*', in: Dieter Simon (ed.), *Akten des 26. Deutschen Rechtshistorikertages, Ius Commune Sonderheft* Vol. 30, (Frankfort-on-the-Main 1987), p. 299.

Howard, C., 'The Protection of Principle Under a Criminal Code', (1962) 25 *Modern Law Rev*. pp.189 ff.

Huber, U., '*Das Reichsgesetz über die Einführung einer allgemeinen Wechselordnung für Deutschland vom 26. November 1848*', (1978) *Juristenzeitung* 785 sqq.

Hübner, H., '*Sinn und Möglichkeit retrospektiver Rechtsvergleichung*', in: *Festschrift für Gerhard Kegel* (1987), pp. 235 sqq.

Hüffer, U., *Leistungsstörungen durch Gläubigerhandeln (1976),Institutional Reform,* Opinion of 21 April 1995, (Committee of the Regions May 1995).

Ibbetson, D.J. 'Absolute Liability in Contract: the Antecedents of *Paradine v. Jayne*' in F. D. Rose (ed.), *Consensus ad Idem* (London, 1996), 1; '*Juge et jury dans la common law*' in R. Jacob (ed.), *Le Juge et Le Jugement* (Paris, 1996), 89.

Ius Commune (vols. 1- 9 edited by Helmut Coing, vols. 10 -13 by Dieter Simon and Walter Wilhelm, and from vol. 14 (1987), as *Zeitschrift für Europäische Rechtsgeschichte* by Dieter Simon).

Jacobs, F.G., 'Preparing English Lawyers for Europe', (1992) 17 *E.L.Rev.* 232.

Jakobs, H.H., *Die Begründung der geschichtlichen Rechtswissenschaft* (1992).

Jeandidier, W., *Droit Pénal General.* (Paris 1988),.

Jessau & Huglo, *AJDA* 1988, at 129.

John, M., *Politics and Law in Late Nineteenth-Century Germany* (Oxford, 1989).

Johnson, A. M. Jr., 'The New Voice of Color', (1991) 100 *Yale Law Journal* 2007 sqq.

Johnson, B.D., Kaplan, M.A., Schmeidler, J., 'Days with Drug Distribution: Which Drugs? How many Transactions? With what Returns?' in: Weisheit, R.(Ed.): *Drugs, Crime and the Criminal Justice System.* (Nunn Hall, Cincinnati 1990).

Johnson, *The Laws and Canons of the Church of England* (Oxford 1850/51 (new ed.)).

Jones, W., *Essay on the Law of Bailments* (1781).

Junker, A., '*Rechtsvergleichung als Grundlagenfach*', (1994) *Juristenzeitung* 921 sqq.

Kaiser, G., '*Gewinnabschöpfung als kriminologisches Problem und kriminalpolitische Aufgabe*' in: Jescheck, H.-H., Vogler, T.(Eds.): *Festschrift für Herbert Tröndle zum 70. Geburtstag.* (Berlin 1989), pp.685-704.

Keyser-Ringnalda, F., 'European Integration with regard to the Confiscation of the Proceeds of Crime' (1992) 17 *European Law Review*, pp.499-515.

Kimminich , O., *Deutsche Verfassungsgeschichte* (2nd ed., 1987).

King, R., 'The Unwinnable War on Drugs. Why the ABA should pull out', (1992) *Criminal Justice*, pp.10-15, pp. 49-52.

Kirchhof, H.P., (1994) 2 *Zeitschrift für Europäisches Privatrecht* 352 sqq.

Kirchhof, P. in: *Handbuch des Staatskirchenrechts der Bundesrepublik Deutschland*, 2nd ed., Vol. 1.

Kleinheyer, G., Schröder, J., *Deutsche Juristen aus fünf Jahrhunderten* (3rd ed., 1989).

Klinck, D.R., '"This Other Eden": Lord Denning's Pastoral Vision', (1994) 14 *Oxford Journal of Legal Studies* 25 sqq.

Knütel, R., '*Rechtseinheit in Europa und römisches Recht*', (1994) 2 *Zeitschrift für Europäisches Privatrecht* 244 sqq.

Köhler, M., Beck, W.: '*Gerechte Geldstrafe statt konfiskatorischer Vermögenssanktionen*'. (1991) *JZ*.

Korf, D., de Kort, M., *Drugshandel en Drugsbestrijding*. (Amsterdam, Criminologisch Instituut Bonger 1990).

Koschaker, P., *Europa und das Römische Recht* (4th ed., 1966), pp. 341 sqq.

Kötz, H., '*Gemeineuropäisches Zivilrecht*', in: Herbert Bernstein, Ulrich Drobnlg, Hein Kötz *Festschrift für Konrad Zweigert*, (Tübingen 1981), p. 486 et seq.; '*Neue Aufgaben der Rechtsvergleichung*', (1982) 104 *Juristische; Rechtsvereinheitlichung Nutzen, Kosten, Methoden, Ziele*, (1986) 50 *RabelsZ*, p. 3.; '*Europäische Juristenausbildung*', (1992) *ZEUP*, p. 268; '*Was erwartet die Rechtsvergleichung von der Rechtsgeschichte?*', (1992) *JZ*, p. 20; 'Rights of Third Parties: Third Party Beneficiaries and Assignment', in: *International Encyclopedia of Comparative Law*, vol. VII, ch. 13 (1992), nn. 4 sqq.; '*Europäische Juristenausbildung*',(1993) 1 *Zeitschrift für Europäisches Privatrecht* 276 sq.; '*Die Ungültigkeit von Verträgen wegen Gesetz- und Sittenwidrigkeit*', (1994) 58 *RabelsZ* 209 sqq.; '*Vertragsauslegung: Eine rechtsvergleichende Skizze*', in: *Festschrift für Albrecht Zeuner* (1994), pp. 218 sqq.

Kramer, Ludwig *Focus on European Environmental Law* (London, 1992)

Krey, V., Dierlamm, A., '*Gewinnabschöpfung und Geldwäsche - Kritische Stellungnahme zu den matteriell-rechtlichen Vorschriften des Entwurfs eines Gesetzes zur Bekämpfung des illegalen Rauschgifthandels und anderer Erscheinungsformen der organisierten Kriminalität*' (1992) *JR*.

Kunkel, W., (1954) 71 *Zeitschrift der Savigny-Stiftung für Rechtsgeschichte (Romanistische Abteilung)* 511.

Ladrech, R., 'Europeanization of Domestic Politics and Institutions; The Case of France' (1994) 32 *Journal of Common Market Studies* 69.

LaFave, W.R. and Scott, A.W., *Handbook on Criminal Law* (St. Paul, Minn. 1972).

Lagebericht Rauschgift. Frankfurt am Main 1992, (Frankfurt 1993).

Laitinen, A., 'Finnish Drug Control: Change and Accommodation' in: Traver, H.H., Gaylord, M.S.(Eds.): *Drugs, Law and the State*. (New Brunswick, London 1992), pp.65-78.

Landau, P., *'Der Einfluß des kanonischen Rechts auf die europäische Rechtskultur'*, in: Reiner Schulze (ed.), *Europäische Rechts- und Verfassungsgeschichte: Ergebnisse und Perspektiven der Forschung* (1991), pp. 39 sqq.

Lando, O., *European Contract Law*, (1983) 31 *American JCL*, p. 653; 'Principles of European Contract Law', (1992) 56 *Rabels Zeitschrift für ausländisches und internationales Privatrecht*, p. 261, also published in (1992) 40 *American JCL*, p. 573; *idem* and Beale,H., (eds.), *Principles of European Contract Law*, Part I (1995).

Larzui, M., *Les Mutations des sources du Droit Administratif*, ed. L'Hermbs.

Law Commission Consultation Paper No. 121: *Privity of Contract: Contracts for the Benefit of Third Parties* (1991).

Layton, A., 'The Interpretation of the Brussels Convention by the European Court and the English Courts' (1992) 11 *Civil Justice Quarterly* 28.

Le basi del diritto amministrativo (Turin 1989).

'Le discordanze delle Corti di Cassazione in materia penale', (1889) 29 *Rivista penale*, pp.136 ff.

Legrand, P., 'Legal Traditions in Western Europe: the Limits of Commonality' in R. Jagtenberg, E. Örücü; 'Strange Power of Words: Codification Situated', (1994) 9 *Tulane European and Civil Law Forum* 1 sqq.

L'épreuve de l'intérdit général, January 1995.

Levack, B. P., 'The proposed union of English and Scots law in the seventeenth century', 1975 *Jurid.Rev.* 97.

Levi, M., 'Incriminating Disclosures: An Evaluation of Money Laundering Regulation in England and Wales' (1995) 3 *European Journal of Crime, Criminal Law and Criminal Justice*, pp. 202-217.

Levi, M., '*Pecunia non olet*: Cleansing the Money Launderers From the Temple', *Crime, Law and Social Change* (1991), pp. 217-302.

Levinson, S., 'Judge Edwards' Indictment of "Impractical" Scholars: The Need for a Bill of Particulars', (1993) 91 *Michigan Law Review* 2010 sqq.

Lewis, A. D. E. '"What Marcellus says is against you": Roman law and Common law' in Lewis and Ibbetson (eds.) *The Roman Law Tradition* (Cambridge, 1994), 199.

Lewis, N., Longley, D., 'Ethics and the Public Service'[1994] *PL* 596.

Lokin, J.H.A., *'Het NBW en de pandektistiek'*, in: *Historisch vooruitzicht, BW-Krant jaarboek 1994*, pp. 125 sqq.

Long, M., *R.F.D.A.* mai-juin 1995, p. 497.

Loughlin M., *Public Law and Political Theory* (Oxford 1992); 'The Importance of Elsewhere' (1993) 4 *Public Law Review* 44.

Lubbe, G.F., Murray, Farlam and Hathaway, *Contract: Cases, Materials and Commentary* (1988).

Luig, K., 'The institutes of national law in the seventeenth and eighteenth centuries', 1972 *Jurid. Rev.* 193, a revised version of *'Institutionenlehrbücher des nationalen Rechts im 17. und 18. Jahrhundert'*, (1970) 3 *Ius Commune* 64; *'Samuel Stryk (1640-1710) und der "usus modernus pandectarum"'*, in: *Die Bedeutung der Wörter:*

Festschrift für Sten Gagnér (1991), pp. 219 sqq.; *'Humanismus und Privatrecht'*, in: *Vestigia Iuris Romani: Festschrift für Gunter Wesener* (1992), pp. 285 sqq.; *'Dogmengeschichte des Privatrechts als rechtswissenschaftliche Grundlagenforschung'*, (1993) 20 *Ius Commune* 193 sqq.

Maine, H. *Early Law and Custom* (London, 1883).

Markesinis, B. 'Cause and Consideration: A Study in Parallel' [1978] *CLJ* 53; 'Judge, Jurist and the Study and Use of Foreign Law', (1993) 109 *Law Quarterly Review* 622 sqq; The Gradual Convergence: Foreign Ideas, Foreign Influences and English Law on the Eve of the 21st Century (1994).

Marshall, G., *Constitutional Conventions* (Oxford 1984).

Mazzoleni, M., and Pavesi, M., Università di Pavia, Milano, Franco Angeli eds. *'Il Certificato VHS/ICC: esperienze europea'*, in *Italiano Lingua Seconda: Modelli e Strategie per l'Insegnamento,* (1991).

McBryde, W.W., *The Law of Contract in Scotland* (Edinburgh, 1987).

McGregor, H., *Contract Code - Drawn up on behalf of the English Law Commission* (1993).

Mehren, A.T. van, 'The Formation of Contract', in: *International Encyclopedia of Comparative Law*, vol. VII, ch. 9 (1992), nn. 50 sqq.

Meier, S., *'Bereicherungsanspruch, Dreipersonenverhältnis und Wegfall der Bereicherung im englischen Recht'*, (1993) 1 *Zeitschrift für Europäisches Privatrecht* 365 sqq.

Mensuel d'Information du Ministere de la Justice, No. 27, Paris 1994, *Le Courrier de la Chancellerie.*

Meyer, J. et al.(Eds): *Gewinnabschöpfung bei Betäubungsmitteldelikten. Eine rechtsvergleichende und kriminologische Untersuchung.* (Wiesbaden 1989); *'Gewinnabschöpfung durch Vermögensstrafe?'*, (1990) 23 *Zeitschrift für Rechtspolitik* , pp. 85-89.

Ministry of the Exterior et. al: *Drugs Policy in the Netherlands. Continuity and Change.* (Rijswijk 1995).

Mommsen, F., *Die Unmöglichkeit der Leistung in ihrem Einfluß auf obligatorische Verhältnisse* (1853).

Moore, M.K., Buy and Bust. *The Effective Regulation of an Illicit Market in Heroin.* (Lexington, Toronto 1977).

Morris, H.F., 'A History of the Adoption of Codes of Criminal Law and Procedure in British Colonial Africa 1876-1935', (1974) *Journ. African Law*, p.15.

Müller, W., 'Political Traditions and the Role of the State' (1994) 17 *Western European Politics* 32.

Müller-Graff P.C., (ed.), *Gemeinsames Privatrecht in der Europäischen Gemeinschaft* (1993); *'Gemeinsames Privatrecht in der Europäischen Gemeinschaft: Ebenen und Gemeinschaftsprivatrechtliche Grundfragen'*, in: Jurgen F. Baur, Peter-Christian Müller-Graff, Manfred Zuleeg (ed.), *Europarecht Energierecht Wirtschaftsrecht,*

Festschrift für Bodo Börner, (Cologne 1992), p. 303 et seq.; '*Europäisches Gemeinschaftsrecht und Privatrecht*', (1993) *NJW*, p. 13.

Nanz, K.P., *Die Entstehung des allgemeinen Vertragsbegriffes im 16. Jahrhundert* (1985).

Nelken, D., 'A Legal Revolution? The Judges and *Tangentopoli*' in S. Grindle and S. Parker (edd.), *The New Italian Republic: From theFall of Communism to the Rise of Berlusconi* (London 1995).

Nicholas, B., *The French Law of Contract* (2nd ed., Oxford, 1992).

Nicholson, C.G.B., 'Codification of Scots Law: A Way Ahead, or a Blind Alley?', (1987) *Statute Law Rev*. pp.183ff.

Niekerk, J.P. van, 'Sources of Insurance Law', in: Robert Feenstra, Reinhard Zimmermann (eds.), *Das römisch-holländische Recht: Fortschritte des Zivilrechts im 17. und 18. Jahrhundert* (1992), pp. 305 sqq.

Nörr, D., *Savignys philosophische Lehrjahre: Ein Versuch* (1994).

Nuvolone, P., '*Problematica dell'unificazione del diritto penale dei paesi europei*', *Trent'anni di diritto e procedura penale*, vol. II (Padova, 1969) p.1518.

O'Dell, F., *English as a Foreign Language: Intermediate Examinations,* Longman Exam Guides, (London, 1986).

Odersky, W., '*Harmonisierende Auslegung und europäische Rechtskultur*', (1994) *ZEuP*, p. 1.

Office of the Attorney General: *1992 Annual Report of the Attorney General of the United States*. (Washington 1993).

Ogris, W., *Der Entwicklungsgang der österreichischen Privatrechtswissenschaft im 19. Jahrhundert* (1968); '*Zur Geschichte und Bedeutung des österreichischen Allgemeinen bürgerlichen Gesetzbuches (ABGB)*', in: *Liber Memorialis François Laurent* (1989), pp. 376 sqq.

ONCDP: *National Drug Control Strategy April 1995*. (Washington 1995).

Oppermann, T., *Europarecht* (1991), pp. 12 sqq.

Oppetit, B., '*Droit commun et droit européen*', in: *L'internationalisation du droit, Mélanges en I'honneur de Yvon Loussouarn*, (Paris 1994), p. 318.

O' Regan, R.S., 'Sir Samuel Griffith's Criminal Code', (1991) 7 *Australian Bar Rev.*; 'The Migration of the Griffith Code', in *idem*, *New Essays on the Australian* Colvin, E. Ch. 7 & 8, in J.A. Riordan, ed., *The Laws of Australia*, B. Fisse, ed., 9. *Criminal Law Principles*.

Ostendorf, H., '*Deutscher Anwaltsverein*', Anwaltsblatt 1990; '*Deutscher Richterbund*', in: Deutsche Richterzeitung 1990, p.106; *Der Entwicklungsgang der österreichischen Privatrechtswissenschaft im 19. Jahrhundert* (1968); '*Organisierte Kriminalität. Eine doppelte Herausforderung für die Justiz*'. *Kriminalistik* 1991, pp.509-514.

Ourliac P. and J.-L. Gazzaniga, *Histoire du Droit Privé Français* (Paris, 1985).

Pachmann, C., '*Gigantisches illegales und internationales Finanznetz*'. *Kriminalistik* 1985, pp. 182.

Pagliaro A., et al., *Schema di delega legislativa per l'emanazione di un nuovo codice penale, Documenti giustizia* (No.3, 1992).

Pagliaro, A., '*Limiti all'unificazione del diritto penale europeo*', (1993) *Rivista trimestrale di diritto penale dell'economia* p.204.

Palmer, Vernon V., *The Paths to Privity: The History of Third Party Beneficiary Contracts in English Law* (San Francisco, 1992).

Pannick, D., 'What is a Public Authority for the Purposes of Judicial Review?' in Jowell, J.L. and Oliver, D. (Eds.), *New Directions in Judicial Review* (London, 1988); 'An alien legal tradition', *The Times*, 8 Oct. 1992.

Passano, M. Da, '*La pena di morte nel Regno d'Italia (1859-1889)*', in S. Vinciguerra, ed., *Diritto penale dell'Ottocento. I codici preunitari e il codice Zanardelli* (Padova, 1993) pp.579-651.

Pieth, M., *Gewinnabschöpfung bei Betäubungsmitteldelikten. Strafverteidiger* (1990).

Plaschke, H., 'National Economic Cultures and Economic Integration', in S. Zetterholm, *National Cultures and European Integration* (Oxford & Providence, USA 1994).

Pollock, F., and F. W. Maitland, *History of English Law*, (Cambridge, 1895).

Posner, R.A., 'The Deprofessionalization of Legal Teaching and Scholarship', (1993) 91 *Michigan Law Review* 1923 sqq.

Pothier, R.J., *Traite des obligations.* (1761).

Pradel, J., *Droit pénal comparé* (Paris, 1995).

Pufendorf, S. *The Law of Nature; De Statu Imperii Germanici* (1667; most recent ed. by Horst Denzer, 1976).

Pugsley, D.F., 'The Advocate's Duty to the Court', in D. Lasok et al. (eds.) *Fundamental Duties* (1980) p.113; reprinted in D.F. Pugsley, *Lawyers and Precedents* (1989).

Ranieri, F., '*Eine Dogmengeschichte des europäischen Zivilrechts?*', in: Reiner Schulze (ed.), *Europäische Rechtsund Verfassungsgeschichte, Schriften zur Europäischen Rechts- und Verfassungsgeschichte*, Vol. 3, (Berlin 1991), p. 99 et seq.

Rapport du Sénateur Arthuis du 11.6.1992, Doc. Sénat No. 400.

Rapport Public du Conseil d'Etat, 1994, La Documentation Française.

Rawls, J., *A Theory of Justice* (Oxford 1992); *Political Liberalism* (New York 1993).

Reimann, M., 'Nineteenth Century German Legal Science', (1990) 13 *Boston College Law Review* 837 sqq; *Historische Schule und Common Law* (1993); *idem*, 'A Career in Itself - The German Professoriate as a Model for American Legal Academia', in: *idem*, *The Reception of Continental Ideas in the Common Law World 1820 - 1920* (1993), pp. 165 sqq.

Remien, O., '*AGB-Gesetz und Richtlinie über miáßbräuchliche verbraucherkreditverträge in ihrem europäischen Umfeld*' (1994) 2 *Zeitschrift für Europäisches Privatrecht* 34 sqq.

Report on the Drug Trafficking Offences Act 1986. The Home Office Working Group on Confiscation: (London 1991).

Report on the Proposed Code of Criminal Laws for the Island of Malta and its Dependencies (Government Press, Malta).

Reuter, P., 'Can The Borders Be Sealed?' in: Weishaupt, R.(Ed.): *Drugs, Crime and the Criminal Justice System.* (Nunn Hall, Cincinnati 1990).

Rheinstein Max, *Die Struktur des vertraglichen Schuldverhältnisses im anglo-amerikanischen Recht* (1932).

Rheinstein, M., *Einführung in die Rechtsvergleichung* (2nd ed., 1987).

Rittner, F., *'Das Gemeinschaftsprivatrecht und die europäische Integration'*, (1995) *Juristenzeitung* 849 sqq.

Robert, J.-H., *Droit Pénal General*. (Paris 1988).

Robinson, O. F., Fergus T.D. and Gordon, W..M. *European Legal History. Sources and Institutions*, 2nd edn (London, Dublin, Edinburgh, 1994).

Rodger A., 'Scottish Advocates in the Nineteenth Century: The German Connection', (1994) 110 *Law Quarterly Review* 563 sqq.

Rousselet, M. *Histoire de la Magistrature Française* (Paris, 1957).

Rückert J., *Savignys Konzeption von Jurisprudenz und Recht, ihre Folgen und ihre Bedeutung bis heute*, (1993) 61 *Tijdschrift voor rechtsgeschiedenis* 65 sqq.; *Idealismus, Jurisprudenz und Politik bei Friedrich Carl von Savigny* (1984);

Rüter, C.F., *'Die strafrechtliche Drogenbekämpfung in den Niederlanden'*,. (1988) 100 *Zeitschrift für die Gesamte Strafrechtswissenschaft*, pp. 385; *'Harmonie trotz Dissonanz. Gedanken zur Erhaltung eines funktionsfähigen Strafrechts im grenzenlosen Europa'*, (1993) *Zeitschrift für die Gesamte Strafrechtswissenschaft*, pp. 30-47.

Sacco, Prof.R., from B.L. Whorf, *Language Thought and Reality* (Cambridge Mass., 1956); *Introduzione al diritto comparato*, IV ed. (Torino, 1990).

Sagor, E.G., 'Innocent Owner and Other Defenses to Forfeiture Under the Drugs Laws, Money Laundering, and RICO', in: Lichtenberger, J.(Ed.): *Readings in White-Collar Crime*. (Westport, London 1991), pp. 35-51.

Samuel, G., *'System und Systemdenken - Zu den Unterschieden zwischen kontinentaleuropäischem Recht und Common Law'*, (1995) 3 *Zeitschrift für Europäisches Privatrecht* 375 sqq.

Savigny, F.C. von, *Das Recht des Besitzes* (The Law of Possession 1803) ; *'Ueber den Zweck dieser Zeitschrift'*, (1815) 1 *Zeitschrift für geschichtliche Rechtswissenschaft* 1 sqq ; (1815) 1 *Zeitschrift für geschichtliche Rechtswissenschaft* 3; *Geschichte des Römischen Rechts im Mittelalter* (History of Roman Law in the Middle Ages 1815 - 1831); *Sysyem des heutigen Römischen Rechts* (System of Contemporary Roman Law, 1840 - 1849); *Das Obligationenrecht* (The Law of Obligations, 1851 - 53).

Savona, E.U., 'The Organized Crime/Drug Connection: National and International Perspectives', in: Traver, H.H., Gaylord, M.S.(Eds.): *Drugs, Law and the State.* (New Brunswick, London 1992), pp.119-133.

Schäbel, H., *'Privatrecht und Europarecht in der Ersten Juristischen Staatsprüfung'*, (1995) 3 *Zeitschrift für Europäisches Privatrecht* 139 sqq. harmonisation in Europe, and on the concept of a Flessner, Axel *'Rechtsvereinheitlichung durch Rechtswissenschaft und Juristenausbildung'*, (1992) 56 *RabelsZ* 243 sqq.

Scheppele, K.L. *et al.* 'Symposium Legal Storytelling', (1989) 87 *Michigan Law Review* 2073 sqq.

Schlechtriem, P., *'Rechtsvereinheitlichung in Europa und Schuldrechtsreform in Deutschland'*, (1993) 1 *Zeitschrift für Europäisches Privatrecht* 217 sqq.

Schleswig-Holstein (Ed.), *Jahresbericht 1992 zur Rauschgiftkriminalität in Schleswig-Holstein.* (Kiel 1993).

Schmidlin, B., Préface, in: Bruno Schmidlin (ed.), *Vers un drolt privé européen commun? - Skizzen zum gemeineuropäischen Privatrecht,* (Basel 1994), p. 5.

Schmidt, K., *Das HGB und die Gegenwartsaufgaben des Handelsrechts* (1983); *Die Zukunft der Kodifikationsidee: Rechtsprechung, Wissenschaft und Gesetzgebung vor den Gesetzeswerken des geltenden Rechts* (1985).

Schrage, E.J.H. (ed.), *Unjust Enrichment: The Comparative Legal History of the Law of Restitution* (Berlin, 1995).

Schroeder, J.L. 'Chix Nix Bundle-O-Stix: A Feminist Critique of the Disaggregation of Property', (1994) 93 *Michigan Law Review* 239 sqq.

Schroeder, K.P., *'Der Dreißigjährige Krieg, das Alte Reich und Samuel von Pufendorf (1632 - 1694)'*, (1995) *Juristische Schulung* 959 sqq.

Schulze R. (ed.), *Deutsche Rechtswissenschaft und Staatslehre im Spiegel italienischer Rechtskultur während der zweiten Hälfte des 19. Jahrhunderts* (1990); *'Vom Ius Commune bis zum Gemeinschaftsrecht - das Forschungsfeld der Europäischen Rechtsgeschichte'*, in: Reiner Schulze (ed.), *Europäische Rechts- und Verfassungsgeschichte*, (Berlin 1991), p. 18 et seq., esp. at 20; 'European legal history - a new field of research in Germany', (1992) 13 *J. Leg. Hist.* 270; *'Gemeineuropäisches Privatrecht und Rechtsvergleichung'*, in: Peter-Christian Müller-Graff (ed.), *Gemeinsames Privatrecht in der Europäischen Gemeinschaft*, (Baden-Baden 1993), p. 83; *'Allgemeine Rechtsgrundsatze und europaisches Privatrecht'*, (1993) *Zeitschrift für Europäisches Privatrecht*, p. 454 et seq.; *Französisches Zivilrecht in Europa während des 19. Jahrhunderts* (1994).

Schwarze, J., *European Administrative Law* (1992);*Droit Administratif Européen*, (1994).

Schwennicke, A., *Die Entstehung der Einleitung des Preußischen Allgemeinen Landrechts von 1794* (1993).

Scott, A., Peterson, J. and D. Millar, 'Subsidiarity: A Europe of the Regions *v.* the British Constitution' (1994) 32 *Journal of Common Market Studies* 47.

Scott, G., 'A Model Criminal Code', (1992) 16 *Criminal Law Journal* pp.350-352.

Seiler, H.H. *'Die deliktische Gehilfenhaftung in historischer Sicht'*, (1967) *Juristenzeitung* 525 sqq.

Seipp, D. J. 'The Reception of Canon Law and Civil Law in the Common Law Courts before 1600' (1993) 13 *Oxford Journal of Legal Studies* 388;

'The Concept of Property in the Early Common Law' (1994) 12 *Law and History Review* 29..

Selb W., Hofmeister H.,(eds.), *Forschungsband Franz v. Zeiller (1751-1828)* (1980).

Seltenreich, R., '*Das römische Recht in Böhmen*', (1993) 110 *Zeitschrift der Savigny-Stiftung für Rechtsgeschichte (Germanistische Abteilung)* 496 sqq.

Sevenster, H.G. 'Criminal Law and EC Law', (1992) *Common Market Law Review* , pp.29-70.

Siems, H., *Handel und Wucher im Spiegel frühmittelalterlicher Rechtsquellen* (1992).

Simon D., (ed.), *Akten des 26. Deutschen Rechtshistorikertages* (1987).

Simpson, A. W. B. 'The Rule in *Wheeldon* v. *Burrows* and the Code Civile' (1967) 83 *Law Quarterly Review* 240; 'Innovation in Nineteenth Century Contract Law', (1975) 91 *Law Quarterly Review* 247 sqq; 'The Rise and Fall of the Legal Treatise: Legal Principles and the Form of Legal Literature', (1981) 48 *University of Chicago Law Review* 677 sqq.; *A History of the Common Law of Contract* (Oxford, 1975).

Slynn of Hadley, Rt. Hon. Lord, *Introducing a Legal Order* (1992) 'Looking at Community Texts' (1993) 14 *Statute Law Review* p.12.

Smith, T.B., '*Jus Quaesitum Tertio*: Remedies of the "Tertius" in Scottish Law', in: *idem*, *Studies Critical and Comparative* (Edinburgh, 1962), pp. 183 sqq.

Sossna, R.P., *Die Geschichte der Begrenzung von Vertragsstrafen* (1993).

Stahl, J-H and Chauvaux, D., *Maîtres des Requêtes at the Conseil d'Etat. A.D.J.A.*

Stein, Peter 'Legal Theory and the Reform of Legal Education in Mid-Nineteenth Century England', in: *idem, The Character and Influence of the Roman Civil Law* (London and Rio Grande, 1988), pp. 238 sqq.; *The Teaching of Roman Law in England around 1200* (Selden Society, Supplementary Series, vol.8) (London, 1990).

Steiner, J., 'Subsidiarity under Maastricht', in D. O'Keefe and P.M. Twomey, *Legal Issues of the Maastricht Treaty* (London 1994) 49.

Stephen, J.F., *A History of the Criminal Law of England*, vol. III (London, 1883).

Stirn, B., *Le Conseil d'Etat et le droit communautaire, de I'application à 1'élaboration*, A.D.J.A. 1993, p. 24.

Stolleis, M., '*Vom Monstrum lernen*' (Lessons from the monster), *Frankfurter Allgemeine Zeitung* of 24 Aug 1992.

Stolleis, M., *Geschichte des öffentlichen Rechts in Deutschland,* vol. I (1988), vol. II (1992).

Storbeck, J., *Internationale Dimension der Rauschgiftbekämpfung - Perspektiven. Bewährungshilfe* (1990).

Stortoni, L., ed., *Vivere: diritto o dovere?* (Trento, 1992).

Stryk, K.N.von *'Grenzen des Rechtszwangs: Zur Geschichte der Naturalvollstreckung'*, (1993) 193 *Archiv für die civilistische Praxis* 529 sqq.

Sundell, J.O., 'German Influence on Swedish Private Law Doctrine 1870-1914', 1991 *Scandinavian Studies in Law* 237 sqq

Temple Lang, J., in D. Curtin and D. O'Keefe (edd.), *Constitutional Adjudication in European Community and National Law* (Dublin 1992).

Thibaut, A.F.J., *Uber die Notwendigkeit eines allgemeinen bürgerlichen Rechts für Deutschland.*

Tilmann, W., *'Zur Entwicklung eines europäischen Zivilrechts'*, in: Walter Jagenburg, Georg Maier-Reimer, Thomas Verhoeven (ed.), *Festschrift für Walter Oppenhoff*, (Munich 1985), p. 495 et seq.; *'Zweiter Kodifikationsbeschluß des Europäischen Parlaments'*, (1995), 3 *Zeitschrift für Europäisches Privatrecht* p. 534; *`Eine Privatrechtskodifikation für die Europäischer Gemeinschaft'*, in: Peter-Christian Müller-Graff (ed.), *Gemeinsames Privatrecht in der Europäischen Gemeinschaft* 485 sqq.

Treitel, G. H. 'Fault in the Common Law of Contract' in M. Bos and I. Brownlie (eds.), *Liber Amicorum for Lord Wilberforce* (Oxford, 1987), 185; *Remedies for Breach of Contract: A Comparative Account* (1988), pp. 43 sqq; *Unmöglichkeit, 'Impracticability' und 'Frustration' im anglo-amerikanischen Recht* (1991).

Tullis, L., *Handbook of Research on the Illicit Drug Trade. Socioeconomic and Political Consequences*. (New York et al 1991).

Turner, R. V. *The English Judiciary in the Age of Glanvill and Bracton* Cambridge 1985).

Turpin, C. *Government Contracts* (London 1972);*Government Procurement and Contracts* (London 1989).

Udo, W., *Ius canonicum in iure civili* (1975).

Ulmer, P., *'Vom deutschen zum europäischen Privatrecht?'*, (1992) *Juristenzeitung* 1 sqq.

Unidroit, International Institute for the Unification of Private Law *Principles of International Commercial Contracts*, (1994).

Università di Pavia, Centro Stampa, *Le Lingue Straniere all'Università, Aspettative e organizzazione didattica.* 1992.

Usher, J., *Plender and Usher's Cases and Materials on the Law of the European Communities* (3rd ed., London, 1993).

Vallance, P.F., *Money Laundering: The Situation in the United Kingdom*. (The Money Laundering Conference, Strasbourg 28-30 Sept 1992).

Vallinder, T., 'The Swedish Jury System in Press Cases' (1987) 8 *Journal of Legal History* 190.

Vinciguerra, S. and Ricci Ascoli, A., *Introduzione allo studio del diritto penale inglese. I principi* (Padova, 1992); *'La giurisprudenza olandese in tema di eutanasia attiva'*, (1995) *Diritto penale e processo*, p.1012.

Visser, D.P., 'Responsibility to Return Lost Enrichment', (1992) *Acta Juridica* 175 sqq.

Waddams, S.M., *Law, Politics and the Church of England*, (Cambridge, 1992).

Wadle, E., *'Französisches Recht und deutsche Gesetzgebung im 19.Jahrhundert'*, in: Reiner Schulze (ed.), *Europäische Rechts- und Verfassungsgeschichte* (1991), pp. 201 sqq.

Wagstaff, A., Maynard, A.: *Economic Aspects of the Illicit Drug Market and Drug Enforcement* Smettan, J.: *Kriminelle Bereicherung in Abhängigkeit von Gewinnen, Risiken, Strafen und Moral. Financial Action Task Force on Money Laundering: Report.* (Paris, February 1990).

Walker, P., 'Irrationality and Proportionality', in Supperstone, M., Q.C. and Goudie, J., Q.C., *Judicial Review* (1992).

Warren, Earl, (1953) 1 *UCLA Law Review* 1.

Weatherill, S., Beaumont, P., *EC Law* (1993), pp. 1 sqq.

Weber, H., *'Der Wittenberger Vertrag - Ein Loccum für die neuen Bundesländer?'* in: *Festschrift Emst Gottfried Mahrenholz* (1994), p. 99 sqq.

Weir, T., *'Die Sprachen des europäischen Rechts: Eine skeptische Betrachtung'*, (1995) 3 *Zeitschrift für Europäisches Privatrecht* 368.

Wesenberg, G., *Neuere deutsche Privatrechtsgeschichte*, 4th edn by G. Wesener (Wien, Köln, Graz, 1985).

Westdeutsche Landesbank Girozentrale v *Islington London Borough Council* [1994] 4 All E R 890 (appealed on one specific point [1996] 2 All E R 961)

White, R.H.H., 'The Government Role - Negotiation, Legislation and Litigation', (1992) 11 *Civil Justice Quarterly* 52, pp.60-61.

Whitman, J.Q., *The Legacy of Roman Law in the German Romantic Era* (Princeton, 1990).

Wieacker F., *'Der gegenwärtige Stand der Disziplin der neueren Privatrechtsgeschichte'*, in: *Eranion Maridakis 1*, (Athens 1963), p. 339; *Privatrechtsgeschichte der Neuzeit* (Göttingen 1967); 'Foundations of European Legal Culture', (1990) 38 *American Journal of Comparative Law* 1 sqq.; *A History of Private Law in Europe,* transl. Tony Weir (Oxford, 1995).

Wiegand, W., *'Die privatrechtlichen Quellen des Usus modernus'*, in: Dieter Simon (ed.), *Akten des 26. Deutschen Rechtshistorikertages* (1987), pp. 237 sqq.

Wijffels, A. 'Sir Julius Caesar's Notes on Admiralty Cases' in C. Stebbings (ed.), *Law Reporting in Britain* (London, 1995); ed., *Case Law in the Making* (Berlin, 1997).

Wilhelm, W., *Zur juristischen Methodenlehre im 19. Jahrhundert* (1958).

Wilhelms, U., *'Politische und polizeiliche Dimensionen der organisierten Kriminalität'* (1993) *Der Kriminalist*, pp.233-236.

Willoweit, D., Großfeld, B., *'Juristen für Europa'*, (1990) *JZ*, p. 605.

Wilson, W.A., 'The Importance of Analysis', in: *Comparative and Historical Essays in Scots Law: A Tribute to Professor Sir Thomas Smith QC* (1992), p. 171.

Windscheid, B., *Lehrbuch des Pandektenrechts.* (9th ed., 1906).

Winter, H.J., *Die Bestimmung der Leistung durch den Vertragspartner oder Dritte (§ 315 bis 319 BGB) unter besonderer Berücksichtigung der Rechtsprechung und Lehre des 19. Jahrhunderts* (unpublished Dr. iur. thesis, Frankfurt, 1979).

Wisotsky, S.,Crackdown: 'The Emerging "Drug Exception" to the Bill of Rights' (1987) 38 *Hastings Law Journal*, pp. 889-926.

Witz, C., Gerhard W., *'Die Umsetzung der EG-Richtlinie über mißbräuchliche Klauseln in Verbraucherverträgen'*, (1995) 3 *Zeitschrift für Europäisches Privatrecht* 885 sqq.

Witz, W., *Der unbestimmte Kaufpreis* (1989).

Wollschläger C., *Die Entstehung der Unmöglichkeitslehre: Zur Dogmengeschichte des Rechts der Leistungsstörungen* (1970).

Wright, V., *The Government and Politics of France* (3rd edn , London, 1989).

Würthwein, S., *Zur Schadensersatzpflicht wegen Vertragsverletzungen im Gemeinen Recht des 19. Jahrhunderts: Grundsätze des Leistungsstörungsrechts im Gemeinen Recht in ihrer Bedeutung für das BGB* (1990).

Zachert, H.-L., *Erfahrungen mit der Geldwäsche in Deutschland. Bundeskriminalamt*, (Wiesbaden 1994).

Zander, M., *Confiscation and Forfeiture Law. English and American Comparisons*. (The Police Foundation. London 1989).

Zeldin, M.F., Moscowitz, J.W.: 'Innocent Third Parties In Federal Forfeiture Proceedings', (1993) 8 *Criminal Justice*, pp. 11-16,

Zetterholm, S., National Cultures and European Integration (Oxford & Providence, USA 1994).

Zimmermann, R., *The Law of Obligations: Roman Foundations of the Civilian Tradition* (Cape Town, 1990, reprint 1993); *'Das römisch-kanonische ius commune als Grundlage europäischer Rechtseinheit'*, (1992) *Juristenzeitung*, p. 8; 'Roman-Dutch Jurisprudence and its Contribution to European Private Law', (1992) 66 *Tulane Law Review* 1689 sqq; *'Der europäische Charakter des englischen Rechts: Historische Verbindungen zwischen civil law und common law'*, (1993) 1 *Zeitschrift für Europäisches Privatrecht* 4 sqq; '"Heard melodies are sweet, but those unheard are sweeter ...": *Conditio tacita, implied condition und die Fortbildung des europäischen Vertragsrechts*', (1993) 193 *Archiv fur die civilistische Praxis* 121 sqq; 'Extinctive Prescription in German Law', in: Erik Jayme (ed.), *German National Reports in Civil Law Matters for the XVIth Congress of Comparative Law* (1994), pp. 164 sqq.; 'Civil Code and Civil Law: The "Europeanization" of Private Law within the European Community and the Re-emergence of a European Legal Science', (1994/95) 1 *Columbia Journal of European Law* 82 sqq.; 'Roman and Comparative Law: The European Perspective', 'Roman Law and European Legal Unity', in: A.S. Hartkamp, M.W. Hesselink et al. (eds.), *Towards a European Civil Code* (1994), pp. 65 sqq.; (1995) 16 *Journal of Legal History* 21 sq; *'Konturen eines Europäischen Vertragsrechts'*, (1995) *Juristenzeitung* 477 sqq;

'Codification: history and present significance of an idea', (1995) 3 *European Review of Private Law* 95 sqq; 'Law Reviews - *Ein Streifzug durch eine fremde Welt*', in: *idem, Amerikanische Rechtskultur und europäisches Privatrecht* (1995), pp. 87 sqq; 'Unjustified Enrichment: The Modern Civilian Approach', (1995) 15 *Oxford Journal of Legal Studies* 403 sqq; *idem* and A. Dieckmann, '*Das schottische Privatrecht im Spiegel seiner Literatur*', (1995) 3 *Zeitschrift für Europäisches Privatrecht* 898 sqq; 'The Civil Law in European Codes' in: D.L. Carey Miller, Reinhard Zimmermann, 'An Introduction to German Legal Culture', in: Werner Ebke (ed.), *Introduction to German Law* (1996); *The Civilian Tradition and Scots Law: Essays on the occasion of the quincentenary of the teaching of law at the University of Aberdeen*, (forthcoming); *idem* and D.P. Visser (eds.), *Southern Cross: Civil Law and Common Law in South Africa* (Oxford, 1996).

Zlinszky, J., '*Das Recht, erhalten und neu belebt durch römisches Recht: Ungarns Verhältnis zum römischen Recht in der Vergangenheit und in der Gegenwart*', (1994) 62 *Tijdschrift voor rechtsgeschiedenis* 61 sqq.

Zweigert, K., '*Grundsatzfragen der Europäischen Rechtsvergleichung, ihre Schöpfung und Sicherung*', in: Ernst von Caemmerer, Arthur Nikisch, Konrad Zweigert (ed.), *Vom deutschen zum europäischen Recht. Festschrift für Hans Dölle, Vol. 2*, (Tübingen 1963), p. 411; *idem* and Kötz, H., *An Introduction to Comparative Law* (2nd ed., Oxford, reprint 1992, transl. Tony Weir).

INDEX OF PERSONS

GENERAL INDEX